Praise for *That Divine and Most Excellent Gift*

In this book, Mark P. Bangert's voice comes through so clearly. The fact that this volume was still in progress when he died allows the reader a window into his thinking while still at work. Here we see Mark's tenacity in exploring Luther as well as his familiarity with wide-ranging topics that provide new insights into Luther's intent and reveal intriguing possibilities for further research. In true Bangert form, the scholarship is well-founded, concise, and precise while also being set in a practical frame, always using Luther's question, "What does this mean?" Readers will find here a companion inviting them to explore more deeply how and why we preach, teach, and make music in the church, and what all this "*singen und sagen*" is about.

—Kathryn Pohlmann Duffy, Iowa Preachers Project and Department of Music, Grand View University

I knew Mark P. Bangert as a teacher dedicated to helping his students discover the particular beauty of Lutheran worship prepared faithfully, thoughtfully, and musically. Within that framework, Mark's guide and conversation partner was always Martin Luther. Mark's last book is a dialogue between two old friends and a gift to the rest of us.

—Donald P. Kreiss, bishop, Southeast Michigan Synod, ELCA

If church is an event and the gospel a spoken word, then we need to see that the event takes place in participatory music-making and that the word moves into our hearts in song. In an unfinished but brilliant and accessible essay, and in six eloquent supplementary articles, Mark P. Bangert gives us Luther on music, opening us to both event and song just as music can open us to the created world. Mark is too soon gone from us. But thanks to the gift of Kristi Bangert and the excellent editing of Martin A. Seltz, we hear him still in this book.

—Gordon W. Lathrop, Schieren Professor Emeritus of Liturgy, United Lutheran Seminary, and author of *The Assembly: A Spirituality* (Fortress, 2022)

In Luther's generation and the one that followed, a basic question was a preoccupation: What is music? In the small Latin treatises on music used in schools, it was often the first question asked: *Quid est musica?* The answer in German is not one we would expect: *Singekunst*, the art of singing, that human element that expresses the inexpressible. This illuminating collection of essays by the late Mark P. Bangert is an intriguing exploration of this basic question. It begins with Luther but reflects our own day by the use of striking metaphors. A stimulating read!

—Robin A. Leaver, author of *Luther's Liturgical Music: Principles and Implications* (Fortress, 2017) and editor of *A New Song We Now Begin: Celebrating the Half Millennium of Lutheran Hymnals, 1524–2024* (Fortress, 2024)

After a lifetime of teaching, preaching, and musicking, Mark P. Bangert has gifted the church with a revealing and thought-provoking collection that will engage clergy, musicians, and laypeople with a rich examination of Martin Luther's theology of music. Much more than the oft-repeated (and erroneous) Luther quotes about "drinking songs" and letting "the devil have all the good tunes," Bangert develops a meaningful Luther-theology of music that will serve the church with wisdom and fresh perspective as it continues to engage the ever-evolving questions about the nature of the church's song. With his characteristic wit and insight, Bangert beckons us to marvel along with Luther at God's divine and most excellent gift of music.

—Daniel E. Schwandt, cantor,
Mount Olive Lutheran Church,
Minneapolis

That Divine and Most Excellent Gift

That Divine and Most Excellent Gift

Martin Luther, Music, and the Arts

Mark P. Bangert

edited by Martin A. Seltz

FORTRESS PRESS
MINNEAPOLIS

THAT DIVINE AND MOST EXCELLENT GIFT
Martin Luther, Music, and the Arts

31 30 29 28 27 26 25 1 2 3 4 5 6 7 8 9

Images 1.1, 1.2, 2.4, and 10.1 are courtesy of International Music Score Library Project (IMSLP) / Petrucci Music Library.
Images 2.2, 3.1, and 8.1 are courtesy of the Richard C. Kessler Reformation Collection, Pitts Theological Library, Candler School of Theology, Emory University.

Library of Congress Control Number: 2025936398 (print)

Cover image: 16th Century Musicians 1 - from Chronicle / Alamy Stock Photo
Cover design: Kris E. Miller

Print ISBN: 978-1-5064-8669-7
eBook ISBN: 978-1-5064-8670-3

Contents

Editor's Preface

Among the wide-ranging activities in the lifetime of Mark P. Bangert—scholar, musicologist, teacher, mentor, preacher, conductor, oboist, pastor, confessor—one of the areas of interest he explored especially in the last decade of his life was the body of writing by Martin Luther about music. The fact that this decade included significant milestones in the history of the Reformation, such as the five-hundredth anniversary in 2017 of the posting of the Ninety-Five Theses, had something to do with that. But his thinking about this subject area predated the last decade, and he included it in his teaching already in the mid-1970s when he was a mentor to me and many others at the seminary level in matters of liturgy and music. About ten years ago, Mark shared with me some ideas about a book that was taking shape in his mind on Luther's insights regarding music, especially in the light of several trends in recent scholarship, and he continued work on this project in the intervening years.

In February 2023, Mark's death meant that this, his last work, was unfinished—although a substantial portion of the writing was in place. This volume, then, presents in part I the writing Mark did complete for the proposed six chapters of a book focusing on Luther's preface to the 1538 *Symphoniae iucundae*, a preface originally titled "Martin Luther to Students of Music," as uniquely representative of the Reformer's theological insights regarding music. Bangert's summary proposal for the book, which is included in the following introduction, provides his own framing of these chapters and the overall scope of the study.

To accompany the unfinished work, part II presents six additional writings by Bangert. Four of these selected writings offer substantive insights into themes that Mark's outline of the unfinished book chapters suggests he intended to address. The final two entries are broadly related to music and the arts, incorporating several of Mark's other scholarly interests and their implications for music in the life of the church.

Of the first four selected writings, the following three are dated from 2017, the year observed as the five-hundredth anniversary of the Reformation in many circles:

Pole-Vaulting the Word into the Heart: God, Luther, and Your Voice
What Do You Do with the "Braying of Donkeys"?: Luther on Re-Forming Worship
Hailing the New Creation: Singing as a Mark of the Church

These three writings, grouped as "Reformation Lectures" in this volume, were presented at a Reformation 500 Festival, "Reformation Roots, Fruitful Seeds: Singing Heritage, Sustaining Faith," October 27–28, 2017, sponsored by Grand View University in Des Moines, Iowa. There is some overlap of content between them and the book chapters, a testimony to the fact that Mark was working on the book at the same time he was preparing these lectures. The set of three, however, has a decidedly practical tone, intended for the audience of (primarily) church musicians and clergy he was addressing.

The title "Pole-Vaulting the Word" hints at Mark's penchant for expressing dense concepts with lively metaphors. The image encapsulates Luther's insistence that music is never a static concept or stationary entity. Music is always in motion—*im Schwang*. And when it comes to divine activity related to the human being, music is the instrument wielded by the wind of the Spirit to vault God's word, God's good news, into the believer's heart. Like the *Hüpfen* that begins many Reformation chorale tune phrases—the short-value pickup note that launches the singer into the phrase's rhythmic energy—music is a launching pad for the Spirit's energy to enliven the human spirit. Bangert begins to address this theme in his book's chapter 4; this essay is an earlier and more robust dive into the topic.

"Braying of Donkeys" is less directly about music, but it sets Luther's concerns about the need and use for music and the visual arts within the wider context of his thoughts and actions around the reform of worship. Intramural squabbles within the early 1520s Wittenberg community threatened the legitimate place of the arts in worship. Luther's intervention, especially as represented in revisions of the mass that appeared in 1523, offered a corrective that emphasized the participation of all the people in making music together.

In "Hailing the New Creation," Bangert explores another locus for Luther's insights about music besides the 1538 Preface. One year later, in 1539, his treatise *On the Councils and the Church* identifies public praise and thanksgiving to God expressed in the assembly's song as one of the seven marks of the church. From this theological vantage point, and with insights from musicologists Christopher Small and John Turino, Bangert addresses timely issues about "the point of singing" in an era when music has been commodified and performance-driven, often to the detriment of individual and group voices raised in song. Bangert's sketch for his book's chapter 6 suggests that these and further insights on this topic would have been represented there.

The occasion for the fourth of the additional writings, "That Was Glorious," is unknown, but it probably dates from about 2010. Here Bangert sets out Luther's convictions about music as a glorious gift of God in ways that are further developed in book chapters 1 and 2. The last section of this essay is notable for the attention Mark gives to the work of sociologist Christopher Small, whose groundbreaking work on music as a verb, *musicking*, aligns well with Luther's understanding of music *im Schwang*, always in motion and necessarily involving active participation to become fully realized. The connections Mark makes to the practice, the enacting, of church music are likely a first look at topics the book's chapters 5 and 6 would take up.

The last two entries highlight two areas of Mark's life and work in which he was deeply invested. "Johann Sebastian Bach and Martin Luther" is a brief encyclopedia entry published in 2017 that not only summarizes Luther's life and theology of music but also draws on Bangert's signal contributions—in both research and performance—related to Johann Sebastian Bach's music for the church. Finally, a lecture presented at Valparaiso University's 1989 Institute of Liturgical Studies, "With Countless Gifts of Love: Arts and the Liturgy" draws deeply on Mark's experiences with music makers in East Africa in 1988. It offers a glimpse of his extensive work on the relationship of music and culture, and it also reaches beyond music to address other arts employed in worship.

My deep gratitude as editor is due especially to Kristi Bangert, Mark's spouse and partner for nearly forty years. Kristi helped discern the future of Mark's manuscript, entrusted to me its development with the addition of related excerpts from his work, and provided assurance and guidance for the completion of the task. Kristi also assembled Mark's notes, books, and other related resources including other writings of his, without which assistance the project would not have been possible.

Above all, I give thanks to God for Mark Paul Bangert. Over a span of six decades, as mentor and model, Mark illuminated for me and many others how to hold in creative tension the ministries of word, sacrament, and music; how to pursue both excellence and practicality; how to inhabit the vocations of lively teacher and indefatigable scholar; how to be a gracious presence in presiding at the altar, the ambo, and the podium; and how to care for and collaborate with students, colleagues, singers, players, and more—all of these in the spirit of Christ and to the glory of God.

May the gifts of Mark, his person and work, continue to live—not only in this collection of his writings but also in all who have experienced those gifts—especially all the ones who shared with him "that divine and most excellent gift" of music to proclaim the gospel and praise God, music's Creator.

Martin A. Seltz
Minneapolis, Minnesota
Easter 2025

Acknowledgments

That Divine and Most Excellent Gift was made possible thanks to Laura Gifford, editor-in-chief, Fortress Press, who worked to keep the project alive after Mark's death and who suggested that Martin Seltz be invited to edit the volume. I am profoundly grateful to Martin for taking up that challenge and for so beautifully forging a whole out of many parts.

Mark was indebted to his many seminary and church music colleagues for their insights and comments as he developed this book. He was especially thankful to Kurt Hendel, Kathryn Duffy, Philip Hefner, and Victor Gebauer, who read and responded to early drafts; to Robin Leaver, Christopher Krentz, Timothy Wengert, and other scholars who challenged his thinking and inspired his work; and to treasured friends and colleagues Gordon Lathrop, Gail Ramshaw, and Daniel Schwandt, who provided unwavering support and encouragement during the writing process.

Kristi S. Bangert
Chicago, Illinois
Easter 2025

Biography of Mark P. Bangert

Mark Paul Bangert was the John H. Tietjen emeritus professor of pastoral theology, worship, and music at the Lutheran School of Theology at Chicago (LSTC), where he served as dean of the chapel; taught courses in worship, preaching, and church music; was codirector of the Chapel Music Series; and directed the Bach for the Sem LSTC benefit performances. In addition, he served as the Bach Choir artistic director and scholar in residence at Evangelical Lutheran Church of St. Luke, Chicago. Under his direction, the St. Luke Bach Choir from 1991 to 2012 presented 119 of the sacred cantatas; the Christmas Oratorio; the St. Mark, St. John, and St. Matthew Passions; and the Mass in B Minor.

An accomplished musician, Bangert studied oboe with Ray Still (Chicago Symphony), Grover Schiltz (Chicago Symphony), and C. Thomas Stacy (New York Philharmonic). He performed with the Indianapolis Philharmonic, the St. Louis-based Gateway Woodwind Quintet, and the St. Louis Symphony. Conducting studies were with Robert Bergt (American Kantorei and Musachino Institute, Tokyo) and Helmut Rilling of the Stuttgart Collegium. Pursuing an interest in multicultural church music, he researched local church music in Tanzania, Kenya, Zimbabwe, Taiwan, Bali, the Philippines, Thailand, and India.

Ordained to the ministry of word and sacrament in 1965, Bangert served congregations in Illinois (Grace Lutheran Church, Northbrook) and Missouri (Atonement Lutheran Church, Florissant, where he was choir director for twelve years). In St. Louis he taught at Concordia Seminary and Christ Seminary–Seminex before joining the LSTC faculty in 1983.

Bangert's scholarly and practical pursuits ranged widely across the landscape of church music. He served as a North American representative to the five-year Lutheran World Federation study on worship and culture. He was a member of and wrote chapters for publications of the Internationale

Arbeitsgemeinschaft für theologische Bachforschung (International Society for Theological Bach Research). He served on drafting committees for *Lutheran Book of Worship* (1978), notably contributing to its revival of assembly singing of the Psalter. Chairing the task force that developed *Occasional Services: A Companion to Lutheran Book of Worship* (1982), he also served as a theological and liturgical reviewer for *Evangelical Lutheran Worship* (2006).

Growing up in a musical family in Sheboygan, Wisconsin, a city with a highly regarded music education emphasis in its public and parochial schools, Bangert attended Concordia College, Milwaukee, Wisconsin, and received a bachelor of arts degree from Concordia Senior College, Fort Wayne, Indiana, with graduate study also at Indiana University. He graduated with master of divinity and master of sacred theology degrees from Concordia Seminary, St. Louis, Missouri, and with master of arts and doctor of philosophy degrees in musicology from the University of Minnesota.[1]

1 A video interview with Mark Bangert about his life and work was produced in August 2014 with Carl Schalk as interviewer. Posted as part of the Profiles in American Lutheran Church Music series by the Center for Church Music, Concordia University Chicago. YouTube, 53 min., 37 sec., https://youtu.be/pBaRG9HISC4.

List of Figures

PART I

“Martin Luther to Students of Music”

A Theology of Music

Introduction

Editor's note: Although the author did not write a formal introduction to his work, he included a description of its scope and intent in the following book proposal.

Music makers, be they singers, players, or active listeners, somewhere along the way tend to reflect on what it is they are experiencing in the musical event. Where did music come from? Why am I doing this? How come it's so much fun, although sometimes frustrating? What does it mean?

These questions and dozens more like them boil down to two inquiries that have driven philosophers (and theologians) for millennia: Just what is music? And what is its significance or importance? Attending to these questions is no mere heady exercise but rather a project that can yield practical implications surprisingly relevant and far-reaching.

In this book I plan to approach these questions by way of one historically significant theologian and thinker: Martin Luther (1483–1546), who is widely recognized as a major influence in the revitalization of participatory music in Christian worship. I propose to lay out some of Luther's most profound insights regarding music, hoping thereby to assist Christians as they are moved to make sense of their own diverse encounters with music, and to provide a framework in which those decisions that inevitably arise from the nature and practice of Christian assembly can be addressed with confidence and good faith.

To reach that goal, this study focuses on Luther's "Preface to the 1538 *Symphoniae iucundae*" (hereafter referred to as PSI), his introduction to a collection of motets designed especially for use in church schools. His essay flows from a rich history of treatises on music whose authors routinely began their documents by probing music's origins. PSI follows suit but clearly becomes more theological than its predecessors.

In this book the focus widens by shedding light on the document (1) with commentary and thoughts on music Luther offered in other writings, (2) with insights from largely inaccessible (to American readers) recent European scholarship on this subject, and (3) by dialoging with more recent critical studies that address the meaning and essence of music from a variety of disciplines, for example, the sociology of music, emotion and music, and the origins of music.

Yet the book chiefly aims to detect and explicate the theological themes in the Preface. There is some disagreement among current scholars as to whether one can find a real "theology of music" from the pen of Luther. Be that as it may, PSI, here presented in a recent translation, is the closest thing to a systematic theological valuation of music that Luther has left us. Looking at that document in context and perceiving its logical progression yields a better understanding of some of his more popular aphorisms regarding music, even as it demonstrates the consistency of his thinking, also with respect to music. The chapters of the book follow Luther's argument in PSI, providing an opportunity to closely follow his progression of thought, standing back now and then to hear contemporary echoes and raise questions. A final chapter primes the pump by suggesting some ways to implement Luther's theology in thought and practice today.

The purpose of this book, then, is to expand one's understanding of Luther's *theological* valuation of music, to assist one's own self-awareness concerning its presence in life, and to provide a framework for making decisions about its use, especially in Christian assemblies. The intended change triggered by this book has to do with thinking processes. Whether one can articulate it or not, everyone has some idea what music is and what it's for. This book intends to help people add some theological dimensions to their individual responses regarding the essence and purpose of music.

CHAPTER ONE

The Preface to *Symphoniae iucundae*

Origins and Text

WITTENBERG, EARLY 1500S

Because of its fame as the "cradle of the Reformation," today's Wittenberg enjoys a notoriety outsizing its population of some 50,000. It is a notoriety that Wittenberg enjoyed at least once before, when its population in the early 1500s amounted to no more than 2,500 people, living in a settlement that Martin Luther described as being on the edge of civilization.[1] Awareness of its stature at that time, and the reasons for it, provides a deeper comprehension of factors leading to the genesis of the "Preface to *Symphoniae iucundae*" (hereafter PSI) and other publications issued from the Wittenberg printer Georg Rhau.

Southwest of Berlin, both Wittenberg and its quasi-sister city, Torgau (about thirty miles still farther south), are in what was old Saxony. In 1180 Saxony became an electoral state,[2] meaning that its sovereign held the power to cast a vote for the emperor of the Holy Roman Empire. The elector chose Wittenberg as his seat in 1266, and the city enjoyed the prominence that decision yielded until 1419, when changes in ruling lineages led to a bisection of Saxony in 1485. Two brothers, Ernest and Albert, presided over the

1 Hans Schwarz, *True Faith in the True God: An Introduction to Luther's Life and Thought*, rev. ed. (Fortress Press, 2015), 15.

2 This historical sketch is based on Victor H. Mattfeld, *Georg Rhaw's Publications for Vespers* (Institute of Mediaeval Music, 1966), 19–22, and Robin A. Leaver, *The Whole Church Sings: Congregational Singing in Luther's Wittenberg* (Eerdmans, 2017), 36–39.

separated areas, with Ernest, being the elder, designated as elector. He chose to establish his seat in Torgau but shortly thereafter died, leaving the rule of the electorate in 1486 to his son, Frederick III, known as Frederick the Wise, the duke of Ernestine Saxony. Luther was then three years old.

Though keeping the seat in Torgau, Elector Frederick had a particular affection for Wittenberg as well. He liked relics. For one fond of relics, Wittenberg was the place to be. In 1353, Philip VI of France showed his respect for and gratitude to Saxony's Rudolph I by giving him a thorn from *the* crown of thorns. Moved by this gesture, Rudolph supervised the erection in Wittenberg of a Gothic chapel, consecrated to the Virgin Mary and All the Saints, with a side altar dedicated to St. Anne.[3] Rudolph's devotion to the thorn went beyond providing it a home. He established sizable endowments that guaranteed appropriate liturgical attention for this and other relics into perpetuity. By 1500 the foundation that supervised that activity, the *Allerheiligenstift* (All Saints Foundation),[4] accumulated substantial influence on affairs across the town, including administration of the city church, St. Mary's.[5] The widening reach of the relics' caretakers into matters ecclesiastical, liturgical, and musical reflects the growing prominence of the relics in all of Wittenberg life. Successors to Rudolph, including Frederick, expanded the collection and the personnel needed to surround it with a level of devotion fitting its importance. By 1520 the efforts of the elector and his predecessors resulted in a holy trove of 19,013 items, according to an official catalog. Shortly after becoming elector, Frederick initiated a thorough rebuild of the old, crumbling castle on the River Elbe, including the Castle Church, so that the collection might have a suitable home.

Frederick's dedication to the relics was vast and thorough. Luther's program and increasing popularity did not go well with the foundation. They were at cross purposes. At one point Luther even asked Frederick to disband the *Allerheiligenstift*, but the elector refused. One reason for the refusal is that the decision would not have been a simple one. Shortly after Rudolph's reception of the thorn, Pope Clemens VI declared the collection to be under

3 The two Wittenberg churches at the time have been identified in various ways. The chapel is sometimes referred to as All Saints or Castle Church or Foundation Church (*Stiftskirche*). St. Mary's is also known as the City Church (*Stadtkirche*) or the Church with a Pastor (*Pfarrkirche*).

4 Details regarding membership and responsibilities of the foundation may be accessed in Leaver, *The Whole Church Sings*, 37–39.

5 Mattfeld, *Georg Rhaw's Publications*, 22 and 22, n. 3.

his jurisdiction, leaving the local bishop in Meissen without any say in matters related to it. Later a papal decree conferred that jurisdiction on the canons of the Castle Church, and later still it came into the hands of the elector himself. Nevertheless, Frederick had to reckon with the source of his authority, so his hands were not entirely free.

Because he held the purse, however, the elector possessed a means of influence whereby he could impose his preferences on the workings of the foundation, allowing him to increase both the intensity and the splendor of the daily liturgical fare. By 1520 the clerical and lay personnel attached to the Castle Church totaled about ninety people. In one year, at least, they conducted 1,138 sung masses and 7,856 spoken masses, not to mention daily matins and vespers.[6] These endowed constituents of the foundation included clergy, chaplains, choristers, and other musicians including university students—a host of musicians who daily provided a rich sonic ambience via musical settings from some of the finest composers of the day.

How can the impressive ritual activity in the Castle Church during this time be imagined? A sense of what sounded there might be teased from an extant collection of music known as the Jena Choirbooks. This set of nineteen manuscript books, bearing the name of Jena, where they are currently housed, contains choral music used in Wittenberg during the first two decades of the sixteenth century. Many of the books display Frederick's coat of arms, suggesting that he was deeply involved with their inception. The collection contains the polyphonic repertoire used by the two choirs of the Castle Church,[7] with heavy representation from then current or recent court composers such as Pierre de la Rue, Heinrich Isaac, and Josquin des Prez.

Frederick was fond of his musicians and their music. In Wittenberg and Torgau, he fostered his court musicians in the early 1520s under the leadership of Conrad Rupsch, followed by Johann Walter. Frederick dispatched both to assist Luther during the time he was preparing the German Mass. The elector's musicians would often travel with him, as was the case for many of the enlightened nobility. While Frederick's devotion to his relic collection and its ritual dress was by every account honest and forthright, he may have had additional motivations behind his investments in the beautification, rebuilding, and expansion projects that supported the collection. As elector he was

6 Mattfeld, *Georg Rhaw's Publications*, 33.

7 Mattfeld, *Georg Rhaw's Publications*, 29. One choir led the liturgies of the main chapel, while a second, smaller group provided music for the services at the side altar.

keenly aware of the emperor's prestige and the imperial trappings coherent with the role. Kathryn Pohlmann Duffy posits that Frederick's nearly feverish attention to the relics was part of "a not-entirely-friendly competition between the two highest-ranking personages in the Empire," Emperor Maximilian I and Frederick the Wise.[8] Indeed, Frederick's founding of Wittenberg University in 1502 can be viewed as one more gesture by the elector in his grand plans for the city on the edge of civilization.

When Luther first came to Wittenberg in 1505, he entered a city whose inhabitants possessed growing pride in their community. He could not have avoided the rich and steady diet of liturgical and musical fare, not to mention the visual enhancements emanating from the studio of Lucas Cranach, the famous artist. The elector's musical forces may have been imperial-like, but the musical experiences were likely not new to Luther. Music was a part of his life from a very young age. His talent gained him, at the age of fifteen, a place among the choristers connected to St. George's school and church in Eisenach, where he soon also became a regular at the table of the musically astute Cotta family. Taking up university studies in Erfurt three years later introduced him to classic music treatises and gave him further exposure to music-making.[9] His sudden decision to become a monk in 1505 topped all of that with a daily rota of sung monastic prayer offices. That discipline wove the fibers that thereafter held together his spiritual life.

The key word here is *experience*. Contrary to a more typical late-medieval education in music that expounds on the science of music and its origins (*musica speculativa*)—some of which the Reformer had to digest as well—his reflections on music, increasingly theological, flowed from the experience of making music (*musica practica*) and the existential factors in such activity.[10] In the years that follow, this fundamental stance of his emerges as a kind of *cantus firmus*, the core melody that summons creativity of every sort.

---

8 Kathryn Ann Pohlmann Duffy, "The Jena Choirbooks as Imitation of Imperial Practices" (unpublished discussion paper for Faculty Colloquy of the Lutheran School of Theology at Chicago, November 10, 1991), 1, 17. See also Duffy's expanded work, "The Jena Choirbooks: Music and Liturgy at the Castle Church in Wittenberg Under Frederick the Wise, Elector of Saxony" (PhD diss., musicology, University of Chicago, 1995).

9 Robin A. Leaver, *Luther's Liturgical Music: Principles and Implications* (Fortress Press, 2017), 27.

10 Winfried Kurzschenkel, *Die theologische Bestimmung der Musik* (Paulinus, 1971), 165, and Carl Schalk, *Luther on Music: Paradigms of Praise* (Concordia, 1988), 18–19.

After his journey to Rome (1510), where he likely experienced still more musically rich liturgical gatherings, Luther returned to Wittenberg for good in 1511. There at the university he received his doctor's degree in 1512 and began his career as a professor in 1513, lecturing on the interpretation of the Psalms. He increasingly struggled with his own spiritual life, a struggle irritated by a growing adversarial relationship with the All Saints Foundation. Posting the Ninety-Five Theses a few years later in 1517 set him on an irreversible path. There was no clarity as to where it was leading. Political, ecclesiastical, and theological forces moved at different speeds and could offer no unclouded view of what should come next.

Luther found help and professional companionship in Philipp Melanchthon. Having joined the university faculty in 1518, Melanchthon provided Luther with another set of eyes to interpret unfolding events. Evolving theology mandated changes in liturgical activity. Capitalizing on his standing, Luther released two quite different orders for holy communion, his Latin form of the mass (*Formula missae et communionis*), in 1523 and the German form (*Deutsche Messe*) in 1526. Before this, however, he had to deal in 1522 with Andreas Karlstadt, who, in Luther's absence while taking refuge in the Wartburg castle, introduced radical changes to liturgy and music in the city churches. Wading into this swirling mass of diverse currents, clerical jockeying, and an expanding realization of what the new theological insights would mean, Johannes Bugenhagen arrived in Wittenberg to become pastor of St. Mary's in 1523.

Bugenhagen's arrival sealed what was apparent to most: Wittenberg was becoming the hub of the fledgling Reform movement. But it wasn't the only part of the apparatus. Spokes led to other locations where well-meaning leaders introduced ill-advised liturgical revisions or where those responsible were simply not equipped to imagine new ways of being the church.

Luther's two mass orders were meant to mitigate the increasingly chaotic situation, but his efforts at first yielded little change. By late 1526 there was so much confusion in Electoral Saxony that he asked the elector to form a group of visitors who, in the regions where the Reformation had taken hold, were to tease out a common will regarding matters of worship and church administration. The task required a handbook. Bugenhagen agreed to write it, and Luther wrote the preface. Once a visitation was completed, the process of writing a "church order" commenced, each region or city having its own version. One of the earliest church orders, Braunschweig (1528), came from the pen of Bugenhagen, who in subsequent years authored similar works for a wide variety of locations.

The church orders were attempts to address unanticipated liturgical needs brought about by an emerging church not fully aware of its birth and growing pains. Musically speaking, the awakening to opportunity and potential came slowly too. Nevertheless, out of his commitment to the experiential dimensions of music, especially congregational singing, Luther, like a tiny tugboat pushing mightily against an ocean liner, began to nudge the ship of the Reform movement in a direction that would lead to musical terrain hardly imaginable at that time.

The pace to an embrace of what might be called fully blossomed evangelical liturgy and music was slow, as Joseph Herl has so meticulously laid out. Popular lore has it, he writes, that "Luther opened the floodgates of song to the people, and suddenly churches were filled with eager singers belting out *A Mighty Fortress Is Our God*. . . . It's an inspiring picture, but even allowing for a bit of Hollywood excess, it isn't even close to reality."[11]

If the Latin Mass can serve as an example, anticipated musical participation from the people in this liturgy is minimal. There are several reasons for this, not the least of which was Luther's pastoral concern that the people should not be overwhelmed with change. The music for the Latin Mass rests with the choir, although Luther does provide for vernacular hymnody, especially during the distribution of the sacrament. He expresses the wish that "we had as many songs as possible in the vernacular which the people could sing during mass."[12]

Off the press three years later, the German Mass shows movement toward possibilities Luther perceived in his evolving articulation of evangelical worship. Together with musical leaders and composers Rupsch and Walter, he brought to life vernacular text tied to easily sung music. Even if it's not clear just who was to sing what,[13] this iteration of sung liturgy foreshadowed a time when all the people would sing. The expanded provision for vernacular hymns reflects his deep desire for all to join the musical activity, experience its joy, and be moved in deeper ways.

---

11 Joseph Herl, *Worship Wars in Early Lutheranism: Choir, Congregation, and Three Centuries of Conflict* (Oxford University Press, 2004), v.

12 An Order of Mass and Communion for the Church at Wittenberg, LW 53:36.

13 See a helpful summary in Herl, *Worship Wars in Early Lutheranism*, 34–35.

The musical dimensions connected to the emergence of reformed rites carried over from the ventures taking place in Wittenberg to the visitations that began in 1528. Indeed, it was widespread confusion about worship matters that prompted the visitations in the first place. While musical matters made a showing in the resultant church orders, the visitations had in their purview a host of nonliturgical items as well, such as the appointment of congregation officers, pay for leaders, practices regarding marriage, care of those who were poor, and especially schools and the education of the young. Visitors and congregation leaders recognized that these concerns needed to be addressed locally and regionally to have a well-operating church. But these operational details exposed another process taking place, and that was the recognition of uncharted territory that emerged with the decentralization of authority formerly vested in the hierarchy. In turn that recognition gave rise to still other needs—many, it was realized, that might be met by the relatively new medium of the printing press.

When Wittenberg underwent its visitation in the early 1530s, followed by a 1533 church order, the process yielded a kind of wish list for printed materials: (1) texts, pamphlets, and treatises that helped propagate the new theology; (2) collections of music for the *Kantoreien* (choirs); (3) pedagogical materials, including treatises on music, for the *Trivialschule*, the first major level of schooling.[14]

Who among the 2,500 citizens of Wittenberg would be able and willing to meet these resource needs, responding to this wish list with a deep sense of commitment?

GEORG RHAU

Wittenberg did have a resident printer during the early decades of the century. His name was Johann Rhau-Grunenberg, who had been recruited from Erfurt and moved into his workshop on university property in 1512. Andrew Pettegree notes Luther's "mixed feelings about Rhau-Grunenberg": He offered Luther "unwavering support" but was "notoriously slow," which hindered Luther in the rapid pamphlet exchanges that followed the indulgence

14 The *Trivialschule* derives its name from the trivium/quadrivium curriculum widely used across Europe for centuries. The trivium consisted of grammar, rhetoric, and logic. Concerning this wish list, see Mattfeld, *Georg Rhaw's Publications*, 137–155.

controversy.[15] It was not Johann who rose to the occasion but rather Georg Rhau (1488–1548, possibly Johann's nephew). Georg was born in Eisfeld on the Warre River, received a bachelor's degree from the University at Wittenberg in 1514, and worked in Johann's shop for four years, continuing his studies in Leipzig at the university there. In 1518 he began serving as a lecturer at Leipzig University and as the cantor at the *Thomaskirche* (St. Thomas Church), some two hundred years before J. S. Bach took that position. His time in Leipzig was short-lived since his allegiance to the Luther movement was not well received there. After several years of teaching in Eisleben and Hildburghausen, Rhau returned to Wittenberg, where he began his printing business in 1523. In short order Rhau became the official Wittenberg printer (*typographus Wittenbergensi*) and the go-to printer for the Wittenberg Reformers.[16]

His literary publications included books on rhetoric, grammar, and poetry; biblical commentaries; the first printing of Luther's Large Catechism; the Augsburg Confession; and other doctrinal treatises. Rhau had a passion for pedagogy. Between 1517 and 1520 his theoretical treatises *Enchiridion utriusque musicae practicae* and *Enchiridion musicae mensuralis* came into print. His own works enjoyed subsequent printings[17] even while he was publishing similar works by some of the most notable figures of the day, such as Sixtus Dietrich, Nicolaus Listenius, and Martin Agricola.[18]

Rhau's pedagogical inclinations put him in good company with Luther and Melanchthon. Text-based works in theology and pedagogy demanded his attention at first, but, sensing the dearth of printed music for use in schools and congregations, he deliberately changed his agenda in 1538 to include the publication of polyphonic music for choirs that were navigating new or altered worship practices. During the next ten years, his shop issued seventeen such publications amid a steady stream of texts, both musical and theological.

15 Andrew Pettegree, *Brand Luther* (Penguin, 2015), 42. Pettegree details the positive developments of the shift in printers, including also the influence of Lucas Cranach the Elder, who housed the new print shop, 153–163.

16 Carl Schalk, "Georg Rhau," in *The Canterbury Dictionary of Hymnology*, ed. J. R. Watson and Emma Hornby (Canterbury Press), https://hymnology.hymnsam.co.uk/.

17 Mattfeld, *Georg Rhaw's Publications*, 139–141.

18 Dietrich was a well-known composer and teacher who for a time lectured on music at Wittenberg University; Listenius, influenced by Melanchthon's pedagogical theories, authored a widely used textbook on music that probed the concept of musical poetics; Agricola was a teacher and cantor, publishing one of the first comprehensive, illustrated classifications of musical instruments.

The first of the collections was *Selectae harmoniae quatuor vocum de passione Domini*[19] (Select harmonizations in four parts concerning the passion of the Lord), 1538, a gathering of eighteen works including motets, a mass, and two settings of the Passion, by various composers. The preface to this volume is by Philipp Melanchthon. Later in the same year, Rhau released *Symphoniae iucundae arque adeo breves quatuor vocum*[20] (Symphonies, delightful as well as short, in four voices) with a preface by Martin Luther. This volume contained fifty-two motets for four to five voices (contrary to the title) by a variety of composers, national and international, including weighty names such as Josquin, Brumel, de Sermisy, Fevin, Forster, la Rue, Mouton, Senfl, Verdelot, and Walter. All the works are in Latin and feature texts popular at the time, even "Ave Maria gratia plena" ("Hail, Mary, Full of Grace") and "Tu es Petrus" ("You Are Peter").

Given the situation in Wittenberg and elsewhere, the Melanchthon and Luther prefaces ought to be regarded as more than a parade of imprimaturs. More importantly, these prefaces affirm and make public the causes all three Reformers were seeking to foster: the provision of suitable repertoires for both pedagogical and liturgical purposes, the production of musical materials that would please young singers, and a solid articulation of and support for the musical dimensions related to the Reform movement. Six years after PSI, in 1544, Rhau expanded his stable of influential preface writers by asking Johannes Bugenhagen to contribute an introduction to a collection of responsories, *Responsorium numero octoginta* (Eighty responsories),[21] composed by Balthasar Resinarius. Rhau commissioned these pieces, asking Resinarius to submit compositions for the entire church year and for a sizable number of saints' days.

The four Wittenbergers involved with these publications were not always of the same mind. Even though Resinarius dedicated his collection to Bugenhagen, the latter complained in his preface that some of the texts of the

19 Rhau issued this title in the format of partbooks, that is, one book each for discantus, altus, tenor, and bassus. The tenor partbook contains the preface by Melanchthon, pages 202–203 of the download at https://imslp.org/wiki/Selectae_Harmoniae_quatvor_vocum,_de_passione_Domini_(Rhau,_Georg).

20 The collection may be viewed here: https://imslp.org/wiki/Symphoniae_iucundae_arque_adeo_breves_quatuor_vocum_(Various).

21 Additional information on this collection can be found at https://imslp.org/wiki/Responsorium_numero_octoginta_de_tempore_et_festis_iuxta_seriem_totius_anni_(Resinarius,_Balthasar).

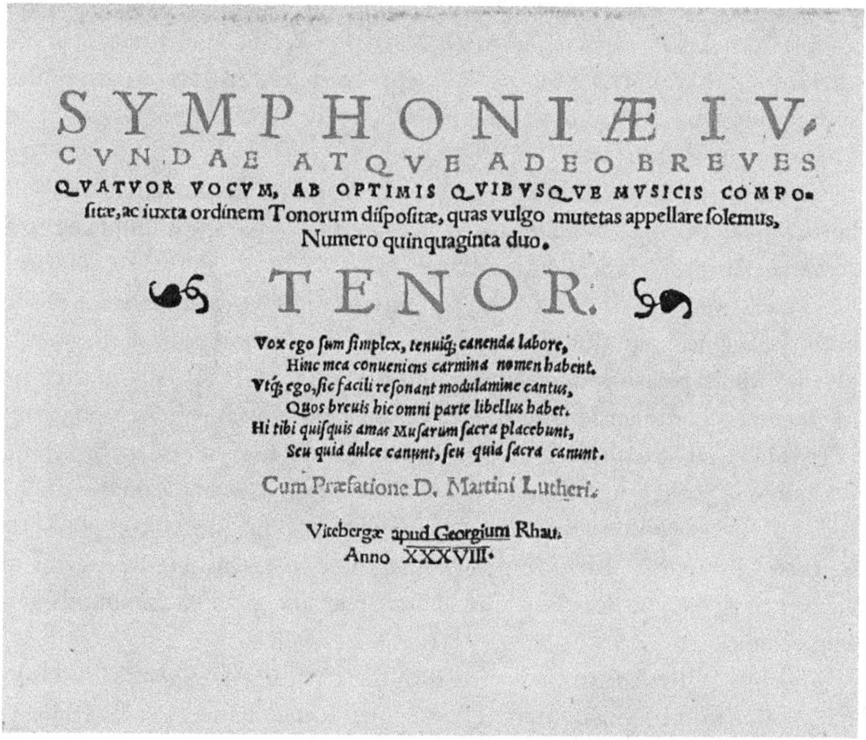

SYMPHONIÆ IV-
CVNDAE ATQVE ADEO BREVES
QVATVOR VOCVM, AB OPTIMIS QVIBVSQVE MVSICIS COMPO-
ſitæ, ac iuxta ordinem Tonorum diſpoſitæ, quas vulgo mutetas appellare ſolemus,
Numero quinquaginta duo.

TENOR.

Vox ego ſum ſimplex, tenuiq; canenda labore,
Hinc mea conueniens carmina nomen habent.
Vtq; ego, ſic facili reſonant modulamine cantus,
Quos breuis hic omni parte libellus habet.
Hi tibi quiſquis amas Muſarum ſacra placebunt,
Seu quia dulce canunt, ſeu quia ſacra canunt.

Cum Præfatione D. Martini Lutheri.

Vitebergæ apud Georgium Rhau.
Anno XXXVIII.

Figure 1.1. Title page of tenor partbook, *Symphoniae iucundae*, 1538

responsories, particularly those for saints' days, were not scriptural. He was aware that the composer had tried to fix matters, as did an "unknown typographer"[22] (Rhau), but he nevertheless still had scruples about the result. In an introduction to one of his own publications two years earlier, Rhau made the solemn declaration that "with pious men he too condemns all dogmas that deviate from Scripture."[23] Apparently, gaining shared clarity about which materials would be useful and healthy for the reformed assemblies did not come easily. Detaching themselves from favorite texts, from cherished contexts, and from the language that for many bore the corpus of faith turned out to be a slower process than imagined. Indeed, Rhau did not issue his first major collection of motets in the vernacular (123 items), *Neue deutsche geistliche Gesänge* (New German spiritual songs), until 1544.

If matters of text, context, and language presented obstacles, style factors seem not to have been an issue. Traditional chant held its place alongside vernacular hymns, together with motets in the *Tenorlied* style (predominant in the Latin editions of Rhau).[24] In this style, the tenor line combines an unornamented melody with text, while other voices weave new or derived lines around it. Elsewhere on the continent and contemporaneously, composers (including Josquin, Luther's favorite) began to favor newer techniques that moved the main tune from the tenor range to the highest-sounding voice, especially in nonliturgical choral music. Were the Reformers a bit behind the times? Rather than reading into this scenario a measure of ignorance or a resistance to what was new, Leo Schrade reckons, convincingly, that "Luther himself with his deep musical understanding declared the Netherlands polyphony without differentiation of style to be the accepted form of art in the young church."[25]

---

22 See my chapter "Rehabilitating the Vocation of Cantor with the Help of the Early Church and Johannes Bugenhagen," in *Subject to None, Servant of All: Essays in Christian Scholarship in Honor of Kurt Karl Hendel*, ed. Peter Vethanayagamony and Kenneth Sawyer (Lutheran University Press, 2016), 85–86.

23 Leo Schrade, "The Editorial Practice of Georg Rhau," in *The Musical Heritage of the Church*, vol. 4, ed. Theodore Hoelty-Nickel (Concordia, 1954), 37.

24 *Tenorlied* style is the German iteration of the so-called Franco-Flemish motet style popular across the continent from about 1450 to 1540. Friedrich Blume has shown statistically that during the late 1540s Lutheran composers increasingly placed the melody in the highest voice, setting the stage for a transition to congregational singing. Friedrich Blume and Ludwig Finscher, "Der Zeitalter der Reformation," in *Geschichte der evangelischen Kirchenmusik*, 2nd ed., ed. Friedrich Blume (Bärenreiter, 1965), 44. Chapter translated as "The Period of the Reformation," in *Protestant Church Music: A History*, ed. Friedrich Blume (Norton, 1974), 1–124.

25 Schrade, "Editorial Practice of Georg Rhau," 37.

THE PREFACE

One can imagine how important the prefaces by Melanchthon, Luther, and Bugenhagen were to cantors and those developing musical materials. Here three giants gave some of their best thoughts on music. The resulting products served as clarion calls amid manifold uncertainties. A sense of urgency underlies Luther's PSI, a characteristic that sheds light on its lasting significance.

"Martin Luther to students of music," PSI begins, a clear indication that this Rhau-sourced essay reflected the purposes of the collection in which it appeared. There are three variants of PSI, also sometimes called *Encomion musices* (A tribute to music, also Musical companion), and until recently their histories have been variously understood and presented. Widely accepted now is that Luther wrote the first draft in German, perhaps a few years before Rhau's 1538 publication; it was later published as a preface to a 1575 musical collection by Wolfgang Figulus. Luther then edited and translated his first draft into a Latin version for *Symphoniae iucundae.* In 1564 Johann Walter in turn translated the Latin version back into German.[26] Luther's edits for the Latin version show a quest for clarity, even-keeled rhetoric, and emphasis but do not substantively alter his core points.

It is worth noting that Luther prepared PSI about eight years before his death. One might assume that his thoughts about music had matured. In any event, the years surrounding Rhau's 1538 publication yielded some of Luther's most profound and seasoned writings, such as the *Smalcald Articles* (1537), a compendium of core Lutheran accents on Christian teachings, and *On the Councils and the Church* (1539), the latter containing his proposals for identifying the marks of the church, one of which—no surprise—is singing.

The versions related to the complicated and often misunderstood history of PSI have teased into existence several English translations. That by Ulrich Leupold stands out because it is based on the Latin version from the Weimar edition (WA) of Luther's works.[27] Others are of less substantive interest since they offer either Luther's first draft or translations of translations. For those

26 A full account of the versions and the subsequent confusion they generated is in Leaver, *Luther's Liturgical Music*, 11–12.

27 Leupold's translation is "Martin Luther to the Devotees of Music," LW 53:321–324. The Latin text is "Martinus Luther musicae studiosis," WA 50:368–374.

interested in looking at the differences in detail, Robin Leaver has placed pertinent passages in translation side by side for comparison.[28]

One drawback of Leupold's translation is that it follows the formatting scheme used by Luther and reproduced in the WA. The outcome offers the current reader long, oversize paragraphs that blur the flow of presentation and bundle together otherwise distinct subjects. Recently Leofranc Holford-Strevens of Oxford University prepared a translation for J. Andreas Loewe, Australian Anglican bishop and Reformation scholar, a translation that seeks to overcome presentational obstructions by arranging the material in a kind of chapter/verse pattern. That translation appears below with my own additional paragraphing to make evident the progression of thought. Here and there, in the notes, are a few of my own translations, offered as assistance for gaining clarity regarding the sense and context of the Latin.

The "chapters" unfold in this way:

1) The music of nature and of living beings
2) The wonders of the human voice
3) The moving of human passions as music's intended use
4) The unique human ability to join music and text
5) The wonders of composed part-music
6) The character of music as creature and its potential abuse

The logic behind this presentation is transparent. Perhaps the progression of thought was also meant to be a demonstration on his part to let the young students who were studying logic and rhetoric in *Trivialschule* know that he could still think his way from A to Z. A further nod in their direction resides in the translation from German to Latin, a way to enforce their growing skills at languages.

The following chapters of this book coincide with the outline identified above, with one exception. Since Luther's final words address the matter of the creature's (music's) abuse, they represent the flip side of the coin that he begins to describe in the opening sections. In chapter 2, then, both the concluding material and the opening sections will be considered together.

Contemporary readers will benefit now from placing themselves in the shoes of the "students of music" Luther addresses by encountering the complete preface in translation.

---

28 Leaver, *Luther's Liturgical Music*, 313–319.

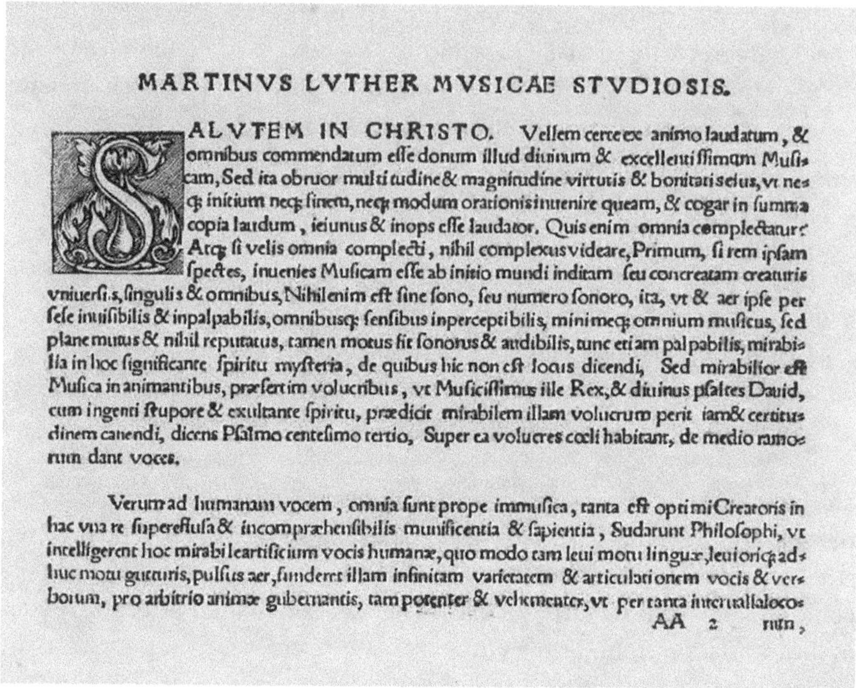

MARTINVS LVTHER MVSICAE STVDIOSIS.

SALVTEM IN CHRISTO. Vellem certe ex animo laudatum, & omnibus commendatum esse donum illud diuinum & excellentissimum Musicam, Sed ita obruor multitudine & magnitudine virtutis & bonitatis eius, vt neq; initium neq; finem, neq; modum orationis inuenire queam, & cogar in summa copia laudum, ieiunus & inops esse laudator. Quis enim omnia complectatur? Atq; si velis omnia complecti, nihil complexus videare, Primum, si rem ipsam spectes, inuenies Musicam esse ab initio mundi inditam seu concreatam creaturis vniuersis, singulis & omnibus, Nihil enim est sine sono, seu numero sonoro, ita, vt & aer ipse per sese inuisibilis & inpalpabilis, omnibusq; sensibus inperceptibilis, minimeq; omnium musicus, sed plane mutus & nihil reputatus, tamen motus fit sonorus & audibilis, tunc etiam palpabilis, mirabilia in hoc significante spiritu mysteria, de quibus hic non est locus dicendi, Sed mirabilior est Musica in animantibus, praesertim volucribus, vt Musicissimus ille Rex, & diuinus psaltes David, cum ingenti stupore & exultante spiritu, praedicit mirabilem illam volucrum peritiam & certitudinem canendi, dicens Psalmo centesimo tertio, Super ea volucres coeli habitant, de medio ramorum dant voces.

Verum ad humanam vocem, omnia sunt prope immusica, tanta est optimi Creatoris in hac vna re superefusa & incomprahensibilis munificentia & sapientia, Sudarunt Philosophi, vt intelligerent hoc mirabile artificium vocis humanae, quo modo tam leui motu linguae, leuiorique adhuc motu gutturis, pulsus aer, funderet illam infinitam varietatem & articulationem vocis & verborum, pro arbitrio animae gubernantis, tam potenter & vehementer, vt per tanta interualla loco-

AA 2 rum,

Figure 1.2. Preface to *Symphoniae iucundae*, 1538, page 1

MARTIN LUTHER TO STUDENTS OF MUSIC[29]

1

1 Greetings in Christ. 2 I should heartily wish that divine and most excellent gift [*donum*] of music to be praised and commended to all. 3 But I am so much overwhelmed by the abundance and magnitude of its virtue and goodness that I cannot discover how to begin or end or limit my words, and am compelled, amidst such a multitude of things to praise, to be faint and inadequate in my praises.

4 For who could cover everything? 5 And if you wished to cover everything, you would seem to have covered nothing.

6 First of all, if you examine the thing itself [*rem ipsam*], you will find that music was impressed on or created with every single creature, one and all. 7 For nothing is without sound, or sounding number, so that the very air, which on itself is invisible and impalpable, and imperceptible to all the senses, and least musical of all things, but utterly mute and of no account, yet in motion sounds and can be heard[30] and even touched; in this the Spirit signifies marvelous mysteries of which this is not the place to speak.

8 But more marvelous is music in living beings, especially birds, as that most musical king and divine harpist David, with great amazement and exultant spirit proclaims that wondrous skill and assurance birds have in singing, saying in Ps. 103 [104:12]: By them shall the fowls of the heaven have their habitation, which sing among the branches.[31]

---

29 This translation is from J. Andreas Loewe, "'Musica est optimum': Martin Luther's Theory of Music," *Music and Letters* 94, no. 4 (November 2013): 573–605. At key places I have inserted the Latin word or words in brackets for purposes of clarification. (Editor's note: Loewe's article, updated, and Holford-Strevens's translation have subsequently been republished in J. Andreas Loewe and Katherine Firth, *Martin Luther and the Arts: Music, Images, and Drama to Promote the Reformation* [Brill, 2023].)

30 In the first (German) draft, Luther writes that the air "makes a sound when a stick is struck through it." Leaver, *Luther's Liturgical Music*, 314.

31 Luther is quoting the Latin Vulgate version of the psalm; this cited verse by itself is puzzling. The Hebrew reads "by them the fowls," *them* referring to "springs" that gush forth in the valleys, v. 10. The NRSVue reads, "By the streams the birds of the air have their habitation; they sing among the branches."

2

1 But beside the human voice all things are almost unmusical, so great are the excellent Creator's [*Creatoris*] superabundant and incomprehensible munificence and wisdom in this one matter.

2 Philosophers have labored to understand this miraculous artifice of the human voice:[32] how the air, struck with so slight a motion of the tongue and an even slighter motion of the throat, pours forth that infinite variety and articulation of voice and words at the will of the governing soul, so powerfully and vigorously that through such great distances of the area all around it can not only be heard distinctly by all, but understood.[33]

3 But they merely labor, never find, and end up in wonderment and amazement. 4 Indeed, none have yet been found who could determine and establish the nature of that hiss [*sibilus*] and as it were alphabet or prime matter of the human voice, namely laughter (of weeping I will say nothing).[34] They wonder, but do not comprehend.

5 But let us leave these speculations on God's infinite wisdom in this one creature [*creatura*] to better men with more time on their hands; we hardly touch even on a taste of the question.

3

1 I ought to speak now on the use of something so great; 2 but that too in its infinite variety and utility far surpasses the most eloquent eloquence of the most eloquent.

3 This one thing I can contribute for the moment, 4 that experience bears witness to music's being the one thing that, after God's Word, deserves and

32 Or "this miraculous handiwork of the human voice."

33 Or "voice and words; or, at the will of the governing soul, how the human voice can sound so powerfully and vigorously that through such great distances of the area all around, it can not only be heard distinctly by all, but understood."

34 Or "laughter—to say nothing of weeping." The first German draft reads, "Truly they have come no further than establishing the 'abc' of music, namely, that of all known creatures only humans can use it to express the joy of their hearts in laughter and their afflictions in weeping." Leaver, *Luther's Liturgical Music*, 316.

ought to be celebrated, which rules and governs the human passions[35] (at the moment I must say nothing of beasts) by which men themselves are governed as if by their masters and quite often carried away. 5 Than this praise of music none greater can be imagined, at least by us.

6 For whether you wish to cheer the miserable, or deter the cheerful, encourage the despairing, break the proud, calm the lovers, soothe the haters—and who shall count all those masters of the human heart, the affections and impulses or spirits that drive all virtues or vices?—7 what could you find more efficacious than music herself?[36]

8 Even the Holy Spirit honors her as the instrument of his own function, bearing witness in Holy Scripture, that his gifts are instilled into the prophets through music, as may be seen in the case of Elisha [2 Kings 3:15], and again that she drives out Satan, that is the instigator of all vices, as is shown in the case of Saul king of Israel [1 Sam. 16:23].

4

1 It was therefore not in vain that the fathers and prophets chose nothing to be more closely linked to God's Word than music.

2 That was the cause of all those canticles and psalms, in which words and song [*sermo et vox*, literally "word and voice"] act together on the listener's mind,[37] whereas in the case of other living beings and bodies music expresses itself alone without words.

3 Then again man alone apart from the rest was given the gift of words combined with song,[38] so that he should know that he ought to praise

---

35 The Latin *affectuum* may also be translated as *affection*.

36 The first (German) draft reads, "What could be better than to use this lofty, beloved, and noble art?" Leaver, *Luther's Liturgical Music*, 317.

37 The Latin word is *animo*, which can be translated as *mind* or *soul* but, as Miikka Anttila suggests, is perhaps best translated as *heart* because for Luther the love of God touches one's heart first of all and then eventually one's mind. Further, Anttila holds that for Luther, "heart" includes also the mind, will, and emotion. Finally, the context supports this more expansive understanding of *animo*. See Miikka Anttila, *Luther's Theology of Music: Spiritual Beauty and Pleasure* (de Gruyter, 2013), 109.

38 The Latin may also be translated as "words joined together with song."

God, that is with loud preaching and words combined with sweet melody.[39]

4 And if you compare human beings themselves you will see how manifold and varied the glorious Creator [*Creator*] is in distributing the gifts of music, how much they differ from each other in song and speech, so that one marvelously excels another, for they say that no two persons can be found alike in all respects of song and speech, even though some are often seen to imitate others as if they were their apes.

5

1 But when in time there are added the study and technical knowledge of music to correct, enhance, and develop natural ability,[40] then at last we may relish[41] with amazement (but not understand) God's absolute and perfect wisdom in his astonishing work of music;

2 in which field the greatest excellence is that, while one and the same voice continues in its course, several voices[42] play, exult, and adorn it with the most delightful gestures all round it in wondrous ways and, so to speak, lead a kind of divine dance, so that those who are even moderately affected by it think there is nothing more wonderful in the world.[43]

3 But those who are not affected by it are truly without the Muses, and worthy to listen to some shit-poet or the music of pigs.

6

1 But music is too great a thing[44] for its benefits to be described in this brief compass.

---

39 Or "praise God with words and song, namely with sounded proclamation and with words joined to sweet melody."

40 Or "But when at last there is added to all of this both learning and the artful skill of composing music that reorders, enhances, and develops the natural thing itself."

41 The Latin word, *gustare*, also means *taste*.

42 Or "while one and the same voice continues to sing the tenor [melody], at the same time several voices play."

43 Or "those who are at least a little bit musical know nothing more wonderful in this world."

44 Or "But the thing [*res*—that is, music] is too great a subject."

2 May you, excellent young man, accept the commendation of this noble, salutary, and happy creature [*creaturam*], to be on occasion medicine for your passions against shameful lusts and evil company.[45]

3 Then may you become accustomed in this creature [*creatura*] both to recognize and to praise the Creator [*Creatorem*].

4 With the greatest care shun and avoid the depraved minds who abuse this most beautiful thing, both art and nature, like indecent poets, for their own mad loves, certain that the devil seizes them against nature, so that she who wishes and ought by this gift to praise only God its author, is developed by those bastard sons, the raiders of God's gift,[46] as an enemy of God and an adversary of this most delightful nature and art.

5 Farewell in the Lord.

45 Or "passions, combatting shameful lusts and evil company."

46 Or "indecent poets committed to their own erotic rantings. Rest assured that the devil goads them on against nature so that these bastards, who with this gift could and should praise only God its author, having plundered this gift [*dono*] of God, cultivate it for the enemy of God and an adversary of this most delightful nature and art."

CHAPTER TWO

The Thing Itself

Noble, Salutary, and Happy Creature

"First of all," Martin Luther writes in PSI, his mini treatise on music, you want to examine the "thing itself" (1:6). Lest we imagine him a crusader for reckoning music as an object—a distinct no-no for many contemporary commentators—it is best recalled that the Latin word *res* can also mean *subject matter* or simply *matter*. Moreover, he was clearly writing from an Aristotelian platform, according to which any matter gets examined by asking four questions: First, from where does the matter come? Then, of what does it consist? Then, as what does it exist? And finally, toward what does it aim?[1]

With this nod to the students and the philosophical world in which nearly all learning occurred, Luther steers his discussion of music to the second question, saving his final word on the first question until the very end of the entire essay (6:2–3). There he declares music to be a noble, salutary, and happy creature. Consistency on this matter doesn't at first glance seem to be a salient feature of his, for in the very first paragraph, he refers to it as a gift (1:2). We seek some resolution to that conundrum below.

But to reach that goal, we begin in this chapter with an exploration of the context from which Luther by habit declared music to be a gift, determine what the "matter" of music was in his mind, and then, on the basis of his own theology of creation, make a case that for him music is ultimately a *creature*—a

1 According to Wayne D. Bowman, there are two basic questions that drive most, if not all, philosophical inquiries into music: (1) What is it? (2) What is its significance? See his *Philosophical Perspectives on Music* (Oxford University Press, 1998), 2.

creature of God; a noble, salutary, and happy one, to be sure—and that as creature it is also gift.

THE THING ITSELF—ORIGINS CONSIDERED

Christian forebears from the second to the fourth centuries had plenty to say about music, most of which addressed suspicions over its use in liturgical gatherings, the low esteem in which music makers were held, fears regarding syncretism via musical adaptation, distrust of its beguiling powers—all mixed in with expressions of approbation and a friendly embrace as long as music served to help one better understand the scriptures.[2] Alongside the earnest experience-centered evaluations and practical advice coming from church leaders, however, another body of literature existed, which had roots in the time before Christ yet gained favor and interest among Christians as the church began to settle into an environment of public recognition in the fourth century. Representative authors considered questions of how music works, what makes "harmony," and, importantly, what music's origins were. Resultant treatises followed a common pattern, and the whole enterprise came to be known as *musica speculativa*, or speculations about music. The tradition captivated such legendary thinkers as Plato and Aristotle and eventually anyone who claimed to be knowledgeable.

Theologians from the middle of the first millennium forward, increasingly conversant with philosophical trends, also joined in the debate. Augustine of Hippo (354–430) famously personally struggled with music and penned a sizable treatise on music, while Anicius Manlius Severinus Boethius (ca. 480–525/526) set a model for subsequent generations by leaving behind a compilation/summary of the accepted theory passed down to him, nevertheless with a clear Christian perspective.

With the rise of universities in the fourteenth and fifteenth centuries, compilations such as that of Boethius, but now also bearing the tropes of those who handed on the collected wisdom, found a central place in the established curricula. As Robin Leaver has pointed out, Luther himself, while at Erfurt University, more than likely read the treatises of three prominent theorists from his own generation or the centuries immediately preceding him: John

2 See James McKinnon, ed., *Music in Early Christian Literature* (Cambridge University Press, 1987), 1–11.

of Murs (ca. 1290–ca. 1347), John Tinctoris (ca. 1435–1511), and Adam of Fulda (ca. 1445–1505).[3]

The Erfurt University curriculum prescribed that students set aside a month to read *Musica speculativa secundum Boetium* (1323) by John of Murs. The treatise addressed a wide variety of subjects. When John turned to musical intervals, he invited his readers to consider the origins of the three "perfect harmonies" or "consonances" (intervals such as the octave, fifth, and fourth) and then observed, "The author of nature, God, of course, made the miraculous consonances—a thing implanted, not of human origin. For consonances existed before humans discovered them. To whom did they first manifest themselves? Pythagoras was the first. Experience teaches us, moreover, that they are not less than three. But if there are more nature wishes to reveal, God will make something new."[4]

The legend of Pythagoras (sixth century BCE) was something of an empowering touchstone for speculative writers. Mention of it, in whatever context, served to legitimize the substance of what followed because Pythagoras was esteemed for having discovered the basic laws of music. According to the hallowed tradition, he listened to the pitches of a blacksmith's four hammers and related the pitches to their comparable weights.[5] John of Murs demonstrated an expected obeisance to Pythagoras but also urged attention to God as the author of the discovered ratios.

More than a century after John of Murs, Adam of Fulda, a German composer and theorist, completed his encyclopedic four-part treatise titled *De musica* (1490). Not only was it expansive in content, but it also encompassed a sampling of wide-ranging views on the origins of music. The first section, "Musica, pars prima," concludes with a chapter discussing music in general. He wishes to pass on what others have written, he explains, and so presents an

3 Robin A. Leaver, *Luther's Liturgical Music: Principles and Implications* (Fortress Press, 2017), 27–32. The curriculum specified a monthlong reading of John of Murs; Adam taught at Wittenberg University during the first decade of the sixteenth century.

4 Latin: "*Auctor naturae, scilicet deus, mirabiles consonantias fecit rebus insitas et non homo. Praeerant enim consonantiae, antequam hominibus apparerent. Cui autem se primo ostendere voluerunt, Pythagoras primus fuit. Quod autem non sint pauciores tribus, experientia docuit. Sed si sunt plures, quas natura voluit revelare, Deus novit.*" John of Murs, *Musica speculativa* (Propositio 3), "Iam tres harmonias perfectas esse sonantes," in Christoph Falkenroth, *Die Musica speculativa des Johannes de Muris* (Steiner, 1992), 108. Translation by the author.

5 Editor's note: For additional detail on the Pythagoras legend, see ch. 10 in this volume.

impressive list of authorities, including Aristotle, Marcus Aurelius, Boethius, Guido of Arezzo (ca. 991/992–ca. 1033), Isidore of Seville (ca. 560–636), and John of Murs, to mention only a few, who have made their marks on the accepted narrative.

Aurelius (121–181) is the first authority Adam chooses for comment: "Aurelius reports that music in the beginning is from God, as noted also by everyone; this is a reminder of the great thing God has yielded to mortals."[6] "Everyone" may note music's author as God, but Adam knows there are other options competing for this honor. With a generous heart and apparently wanting all voices to be heard, he then relates how he, too, in step with John of Murs, has "read that" the Greeks have long held Pythagoras to be the first to discover and manipulate musical intervals.

A few lines later he notes that others have named Jubal to be the inventor of music. Genesis 4 mentions Cain's family, which includes Lamech, who with wife Adah had a son named Jubal, the "ancestor of all those who play the lyre and pipe" (4:21). The Jubal proposal gained traction in Christian thought even though it eliminated God's direct initiative in the matter.

John of Murs and Adam of Fulda approached the received tradition differently. Although John acknowledged Pythagoras as the one to whom the mysterious consonances were manifested, he names God as the maker of them; Adam, on the other hand, makes room for a variety of possible, if not conflicting, origins.

Luther steered clear of the thickets of trying to make sense out of these competing views of music's origins. As Robin Leaver has described in detail, Luther knew the Pythagoras legend well enough to cite it but ignored it when addressing music's origins.[7] Likewise, his commentary on Genesis gave little space to the Jubal theory as definitive for music's origins.[8]

Tracing the origins of music to God is a recurring theme in treatises on music Luther might have encountered. In fact, God's authorship of music persists in one way or another well into the eighteenth century. The famous Hamburg theorist Johann Mattheson, a contemporary of J. S. Bach, favorably

---

6 Latin: "*Musicam a Deo fore, omnibus notum est, hanc admonitionem rei magnae concessam mortalibus a Deo, Aurelius refert.*" Adam of Fulda, "Musica, pars prima," from *De musica*, in *Scriptores ecclesiastici de musica sacra potissimum*, ed. Martin Gerbert (Typis San-Blasianis, 1784; facsimile ed. [Olms, 1963]), 3:340. Online at Thesaurus Musicarum Latinarum, siglum FULMUS1. Translation by the author.

7 Leaver, *Luther's Liturgical Music*, 68.

8 Leaver, *Luther's Liturgical Music*, 69.

cited Parisian M. Rollin when laying out first principles in his 1739 book about the qualities of an accomplished leader of music. Rollin lauded music as a gift of God, an observation Mattheson then turned to support his own opinion that before the fall, Adam heard the music of angels and later attempted to replicate what he remembered.[9]

Yet even though PSI looks like a brief treatise of the same sort he had earlier read, Luther dealt with the matter of origins (the thing itself) by dragging music into the theological file dedicated to creation. Despite a brief detour at the beginning of PSI where he raves about this "most excellent gift," with building energy and verbal effervescence he finally arrives at what one might consider the coda of PSI, there hoping that the young students will find music to be a "happy creature" (6.2), a creature that delivers a relationship with its Creator (6.3). With God as music's "author" (6.4), then, Luther delivers what can be taken as his final thought on the matter: The "thing itself" is a *creature.* Insofar that music is a part of creation, it falls within theological parameters. Hence, one can accurately speak of Luther's theology of music.

The full impact of encountering music as creature follows below. Following Luther's own progression in PSI, let us turn attention to what he understands music to be—apart from its metaphysical and theological valuations.

EXPERIENCING THE THING ITSELF

Considering music theologically didn't prevent Luther from trying to help the young scholars better understand the essence of the "thing itself." In doing so, he was not haphazard. Music considered as creature according to PSI is at its core simply created sound. By laying out a kind of hierarchy of examples, he shows how sound is present in all of creation. He writes, "Nothing is without number or sounding number" (1.7). His mention of "sounding number" (a phrase incidentally not in the original German draft) can be explained by his desire to acknowledge the tradition he had learned as a young scholar himself. He echoes John of Murs, handing on the received tradition, who affirmed that the consonances were manifested to Pythagoras, and those consonances or intervals encapsulated numerical relationships. But that's about as much as

9 Johann Mattheson, *Der vollkommene Capellmeister* (1739), ed. Frederike Ramm (Bärenreiter, 1999), 12.

Pythagoras factors into this discussion: a single mention to support Luther's basic premise that sound is everywhere.

Sound is embedded in the air, he notes, because if some object moves through it fast enough, there is sound.[10] The air is created together with (1:6) sound, identified here as creature (*creatura*). As a scientific explanation of sound, Luther's observation obviously pales. What he managed to do was identify a relationship for which explanations continued to evolve. For the moment he is amazed by what he has named. Veering off course, even the Reformer stops in his tracks to muse on the mysteries of the Spirit (1:7), perhaps thinking of Pentecost and the sound of a mighty rushing wind. He quickly moves on.

Sound is even more marvelous when it shows up in "living beings" (1.8). We would love to ask: Does he include the nocturnal barking of a dog? The roar of a lion? The squawks of a hundred seagulls? Whether he even thought about sounds most people consider unpleasant didn't fit his purpose of training his young scholars to hear the marvelous creature—*sound*—in living beings. To drive the point home, he turns to his beloved birds, especially songbirds.

Listen to the Birds

Just when Luther developed a fondness for songbirds is unclear, but the months spent at the Wartburg castle translating the New Testament (1521–1522) surely provided a time of intensifying affection for songbirds. They occupy a special place in his thinking about the good news of God's grace. In a sermon he preached on September 5, 1529, based on the appointed reading for the fifteenth Sunday after Trinity (Matt. 6:24–34), he centered his message in the words of verse 24b, "You cannot serve God and mammon." A subtitle indicates his intentions for the sermon: "Mammon and God—Heathen and Christians." We get to the birds this way:

> Two examples are so beneficial and pointed that one is shamed to death before such good news; at which, even with ears half-open, we will be startled. Many a farmer, or citizen, going through fields and seeing

10 In the German draft published by Figulus in 1575, the text reads, "The air, which is invisible and imperceptible, makes sound when a stick is struck through it." See Leaver, *Luther's Liturgical Music*, 313–314.

the flowers and birds, is terrified. Another will dismiss the experience or be shocked. Every little flower and bird has the gospel written on their throats, and they provide this instruction: how you are a simple idolater who serves mammon.

Any flower or bird is more pious than you, because they serve the gospel, for them completely written on their wings, for you in your mouth, on your skin, and in your heart, among other things. What do I produce? Nothing. Not much more. Take the word to heart and consider whether with joy you can contemplate this in your heart; but your head hangs down if you look closely at the bird.

That bird sings "Te Deum" in the morning, "We praise you, O God." Ah, dear birds, wherefore then is your prey, your berries, your food cellar? The bird answers: "No need to labor." But [the bird says] "I have provisions, a Cook whose name is heavenly Father." Thus, the bird is worthy of more praise than any Caesar or king. Contrarily, the whole world is mammonistic while a single bird is much richer; there is no comparison because they are all richer.

For what of all treasure is comparable to God? Thus the bird sings: "You are foolish, a rogue; shame on you for your god and works. You get up and don't sing; you rest and work—and at night you don't sleep because of all your concerns. I sing."[11]

---

11 WA 29:550–551. Translation by the author. The sermon was recorded by two different scribes; the version here is by Georg Rörer in its original Latin/German mashup:

Dat duas similitudines, die sind so benichsch und spitzig, das sich einer zu tod schemen vor diesem Euangelio, das wir die oren nur halb auff theten, so wird wir erschrecken. Mancher bauer vel civis pertransit agrum videns so viel flosculos und voglein, terretur. Alias, so wird er sich entsetzen. All blumlein und voglein haben das Euangelium am hals geschrieben et illa docent: wie ein abgottischer tropff bistu qui servis Mammonae.

Omnis flos et avis ist fromer den du, quia illae serviunt Euangelio et illis tantum in pennas scriptum, tibi in os, cutem, cor scriptum, noch u. Quid facio? "Non" u. "Quanto magis." Nimb die wort zu hertzen et considera, an gaudio possis intueri in cor, sed caput tuum demitteres, si inspiceres avem.

Avicula illa canit "Te deum laudamus," metten. Ey, liebs voglein, quare tam ictus, ubi cocus, keller? Dicet avis: "Non laboro" u. "Sed habeo ein vorrad, Koch, der heist himmlischer vater." Sic gloriari potest avis ea quae nullus Caesar, rex. Econtra totus mundus ist Mammonisten et una avicula so viel reicher, ut nulla comparatio sit, quando omnes reicher.

Quid enim omnes thesauri in comparatione dei? Sic dic: Tu es nar, schelm, pfu dich mit deim Got und dienst. Tu surgis, non canis, die muhe und erbeit et nocte non dormis prae curis. Ego cano.

Luther clearly refers to birds in this sermon not as subject but as example to illustrate a concern. He wants to elicit carefree trust in God, the kind exhibited by birds that sing their way through the day without concern for stockpiling stuff. Consider the birds, for they know how to live, Luther declares: "Every little flower and bird has the gospel written on their throats."

For Luther, birds were more than examples; they provided delight and joy, especially the nightingale. Of all the birds and their songs, the nightingale was clearly his favorite, and that is not without significance. Building on what was then thought by many to be common knowledge about music and birds, fourth-century Augustine identified the "sweet song of the nightingale as the model for good singing,"[12] Luther's preferences were perhaps influenced by this mentor of his.

High praise and gratitude for the nightingale shine in a poem (attributed to Luther) titled "Frau Musica" ("Lady Music"), published in the same year as PSI to serve as an introduction to a much longer poem by Johann Walter.

> The best time of the year is mine
> when all the birds are singing fine.
> The heavens and the earth are filled
> with much good singing, clear, and skilled.
> Above all, the precious nightingale
> makes all now joyful overall
> with her delightful songs and lays
> for which she must be thanked always.
> But more so to God our maker,
> who carefully created her
> to be his own beloved songstress
> and of *musica* a mistress.[13]

Perhaps the nightingale earned its rave of "precious" because nightingales well populated the hills surrounding the Wartburg castle, where Luther was protectively confined for several months. He did think of the castle and its environs as the "region of the birds," and no doubt the local songbirds accompanied his translation project during those months. In any event, Hans

---

12 Leaver, *Luther's Liturgical Music*, 75.

13 Leaver, *Luther's Liturgical Music*, 78. Leaver provides much-needed help in sorting through the versions and the fortunes of both the poem and its translations.

Figure 2.1. *Fraw Musica*, Lucas Cranach the Younger, 1544

Sachs of Nürnberg (1494–1576), the most famous of the Meistersingers—a vocalists' guild that frequently met at the Wartburg—wrote a lengthy poem celebrating Luther's achievements, titling his 1523 salute *Die Wittembergisch Nachtigall / die man yetz höret uberall* ("The Wittenberg nightingale that one can hear now everywhere").[14]

Listen to the birds, the wise one urges, as it were, for they relentlessly sing sounds that come from God, bringing joy and delight. The experience of hearing an unannounced, impromptu, beautiful song from a bird struck many to also be the essence of the gospel. Songbirds are participatory heralds of proclamation. In his commentary on the Sermon on the Mount (referencing Matt. 6:26–27), following the lead of the evangelist, Luther again points to birds as examples of creatures who trust God: "Whenever you listen to a nightingale, therefore, you are listening to an excellent preacher. He exhorts you with this gospel, not with mere simple words but with a living deed and an example. He sings all night and practically screams his lungs out."[15] Screaming your lungs out joyfully is one aspect of acoustical birding, one might say. Luther is not reticent about his fondness for songbirds, yet this is not a music-loving ornithologist writing here, as if he were trying to convince the reader of the peculiar charm of these winged creatures. The entire world of sound fascinates him, and he can't help but also see God in this aspect of life, lauding God as the maker of this gift.

Songbirds had long inspired human imitation and solicited reflection on the mysteries of life and beauty. A survey demonstrates how pervasive interaction with songbirds has been.[16] Theological reflections, to begin with, reach back at least to the book of Psalms, as Luther advanced in PSI (1:8): "More marvelous is music in living beings, especially birds, as that most musical king and divine harpist David, with great amazement and exultant spirit proclaims that wondrous skill and assurance birds have in singing, saying in Ps. 103 [104:12]: 'By them shall the fowls of the heaven have their habitation, which sing among the branches.'" Because of its brevity, the depth of this

14 Leaver, *Luther's Liturgical Music*, 75.

15 LW 21:197.

16 See the author's article "Listen to the Birds: Luther on Music," *TEAR Online* [journal of the Centre de Recursos Litúrgicos de Faculdadas EST no Igreja Evangélica de Confissão Luterana no Brasil] 4, no. 1 (Summer 2015): 114–137, http://periodicos.est.edu.br/index.php/tear.

citation can be easily missed. Here is the pertinent selection (Ps. 103:10–13) in a recent translation:

> You make springs gush forth in the valleys;
>   they flow between the hills,
> giving drink to every wild animal;
>   the wild asses quench their thirst.
> By the streams the birds of the air have their habitation;
>   they sing among the branches.
> From your lofty abode you water the mountains;
>   the earth is satisfied with the fruit of your work.

The verses here clearly don't have birds as their subject but rather God. There is a reason the birds sing, Luther would say, for they recognize God as their caretaker. Calling out songbirds not only mirrors his personal love for them but also demonstrates the vastness of the world of sound and God's goodness in this "one creature" we call music (2:5).

His definitive dissection of music as creature peaks as he considers the human voice. Everything else so far pales in comparison and is "almost unmusical" (2:1). Experts have yet to sufficiently explain its capabilities, he notes. But in his estimation, the abilities of the human voice are nevertheless astounding. Specifically, he mentions the variety of what we might call vocal timbres.[17] In the same vein, he later (4:4) cites a saying that no two individuals are alike in matters of speech and song. He further marvels (2:2) at the many different sounds (articulations) humans can produce, probably referring to vowels and their variations as well as consonants, especially sibilants (2:4). Explanations for these human abilities, he writes, have heretofore been insufficient, just as no one has been able to account for the "primal matter" of the human voice, such as that showing up in laughter and weeping.

Nowadays, the linkage of laughter (or crying) with music appears a little fantastical. The commonality, of course, lies in sound, or in the "primal matter of the human voice" (2:4). It may be that Luther's real interest here is not in the physical aspects of such an expansive understanding of sound, as the

17 Luther's recognition of the variety of human voice qualities—and one might deduce also of worldwide musical systems—supports every reach into non-Western musical systems or idioms both to explore the vastness of the creature and to mobilize a recognized means for establishing cultural understanding.

Latin version of the preface seems to suggest, but rather in the purpose of laughter and weeping, more clearly brought out in the original German draft of the preface. There we read, "Truly they have come no further than establishing the 'abc' of music, namely, that of all known creatures only humans can use it to express the joy of their hearts in laughter and their afflictions in weeping."[18] Contrary to a sneeze, which also falls within the realm of sound, laughter and weeping are expressive and serve the well-being of the human.

This momentary reflective focus on marginal sounds comes with amazement on Luther's part, an amazement that would likely have been indulged, if not intensified, were he to have known studies like those of philosopher and anthropologist Helmuth Plessner, who has defined laughter and crying as emphatic interpretations of the predicament of human beings.[19] Plessner demystifies Luther's angle on these human sounds but does not thereby nullify his wonder over God's infinite wisdom in this one creature (2:3).

Human production of diverse sounds fascinates Luther, but that's not all. What impresses him even more is how "powerfully and vigorously" these sounds fill space all around, even at a distance. What we take for granted with our knowledge of sound waves and frequencies he does not yet know. Rather, he experiences in sound and music a dimension of space, an expansive acoustic that has sociological and liturgical implications. Word and song are proclaimed because they can be said/sung/heard by all and understood by all (2:2).

THE THING ITSELF—THEOLOGICALLY CONSIDERED

To consider the thing itself as *creature* may have come easily for Luther. Twenty-first-century readers of his short treatise will probably show some hesitation before signing on to this piece of ontology. So, just what *is* a "creature," they are likely to ask, or how does this identification fit into contemporary understandings regarding the origins of the universe?

Surely the Reformer's use of the word *creature* is not haphazard. His conception of God and of creation may not contribute to current quests for unifying all that we know about life, but it will certainly provide a perspective that

18 Translation from Leaver, *Luther's Liturgical Music*, 316.

19 J. M. Bernstein, "Toward a Philosophical Anthropology," foreword to Helmuth Plessner's 1941 *Laughing and Crying: A Study of the Limits of Human Behavior*, trans. J. S. Churchill and Marjorie Grene (Northwestern University Press, 1970), vii.

will allow people of faith, at least, to gain a more expansive view of what God is up to. How to read the book of Genesis, one might suggest, is foundational.

In his commentary on Genesis, Luther briefly considered a theory advanced by French theologian Nicolas de Lyra. Lyra, as he called him, wondered about the order of events presented in the first chapter of the book, but Luther dismisses the issue by reckoning that such matters "should not be viewed on the basis of our own judgment."[20] In other words, questions about how and when things came to be are of little consequence to him. Rather, he steers one's reading of these chapters toward matters that, in his mind, are of far more importance and urgency: "It is far better to meditate and wonder at this concern, care, generosity, and benevolence of God, both in this life and in the one to come, than it is to speculate about why God began to equip the earth on the third day."[21] Here the posture regarding creation bends not toward first things, matters of order, accuracy of narrative, or even length of process but rather toward the nature of this One who was enacting the things described. Such a focus places the inquiring individual into a relationship with God that will eventually be revelatory. And *that* did not turn out well for the first humans, creating a problem that God ever since goes about addressing. Luther scholar Oswald Bayer claims that for Luther, theological thoughts around creation run hand in hand with God's redeeming work in Jesus Christ. "Justification as Creation, Creation as Justification," he writes.[22] You can't have one without the other.

When Luther prepared his Small Catechism, he didn't wait until the second article of the Apostles' Creed to introduce this thought—even though that would be the logical place to do so. Linkage of creation and justification appears already in his explanation of the first article: "I believe that God has created me together with all that exists . . . daily and abundantly provides me . . . with all the necessities and nourishment for this body and life . . . protects me against all danger and shields and preserves me from all evil—*and all this is done out of pure, fatherly, and divine goodness and mercy, without any merit or worthiness of mine at all.*"[23] Considering music as creature in this kind of context yields a climate of engagement in which one can disconnect from earnest ponderings about

20 LW 1:39.

21 LW 1:39.

22 Oswald Bayer, *Martin Luther's Theology*, trans. Thomas H. Trapp (Eerdmans, 2008), 95.

23 BC 354. Emphasis mine.

first things and focus, more beneficially, on the experiential encounters God intends in and through the creatures.

With Luther as guide, then, we weigh music as creature brought into being from nothing (*ex nihilo*), the creature encountered in faith, the creature's problematic role in natural theology, and the creature and its abuse/misuse.

THE CREATURE FROM NOTHING

In Luther's thought, creation out of nothing is less an assertion about cosmological beginnings and more a call for people to embrace God as the sole and gracious source of all life: "*Creatio ex nihilo*, creation out of nothing, the formula that serves as the basis for Jewish and Christian teaching about creation, is to be understood in the sense that Luther uses it, as a term for the doctrine of justification. Every calculating *do ut des* (I give to you, so that you give to me) is annihilated."[24]

In Luther's mind, the perversity that leads one away from God centers in the persisting human desire to position oneself into the center of things, to construct a measure of reality with tools that are personally manageable with a goal of gaining control over one's own destiny. This Godless project will, however, land nowhere safely. Creation and its creatures did not bring themselves into existence, reckoned Luther. Conversely, there was nothing before God said, "Let there be" (Gen. 1:3),[25] and whatever comes to be is good (Gen. 1:4). While there is agency involved in this becoming, Luther is also quick to note that prior to such agency, there is word: "God said." This causes Bayer to describe creation as a "speech act,"[26] calling attention to its parallel in John 1:1 ("In the beginning was the Word"). "God said" in Genesis is a gracious word, it is a promise, and insofar as it continues into the present, it can be received as trustworthy, effecting what it proclaims.[27]

24 Bayer, *Martin Luther's Theology*, 96–97.

25 Luther scholar Johannes Schwanke also holds the *ex nihilo* principle to be central to Luther's theology of creation. He writes, "God's actions are all initial and initiating beginnings." Summary to "Martin Luther's Theology of Creation," *International Journal of Systematic Theology* 18, no. 4 (October 2016): 399–413.

26 Bayer, *Martin Luther's Theology*, 103.

27 Bayer, *Martin Luther's Theology*, 104. Even though matters regarding religion and science are tangential in this chapter, Bayer makes an observation worth repeating: "Luther identified the crucial issue when he understood creation as a gift and promise—creation

Nothing equals music as a means for grasping what Luther lays out here. Sound always comes out of silence, a factor probably better understood by Luther than by those of us who live in worlds of inescapable sound and noise. In this way sound echoes the profound silence from which proceeded both creation and the word of God. All of it comes from God's gracious hand. Therefore, both the creation and God's word are gifts.

Now it can be understood why Luther so easily alternated between creature and gift as he wrote and spoke about music. For him, music is *gift* because it is first of all *creature*. However, bringing music so deeply into God's creating and redeeming work makes it all the more vulnerable to the propensities of the human condition. Bayer writes, "The Biblical and reformational understanding of a generous God, who is continuously Giving, sharply contradicts the activism that is advocated in the present age, which wants nothing to be given as gift. But God is categorically the one who gives. . . . Creation and new creation are both *categorical gift*. The first Word to the human beings is a giving Word: 'You may freely eat of every tree!' (Gen. 2:16)—renewed in the gifting Word of the Lord's Supper: 'Take and eat. This is my body, given for you.'"[28]

Against the "activism" Bayer describes, God's speech act remains, so that for the faithful, at least, music as creature—despite human resistance—continues as gift meant to summon us to recognize the goodness and grace of its Creator. Like all of creation, music is a communication, a gesture of love intended to "establish and preserve" community.[29] Sullied and perverse as creatures turn out to be (humans *and* music too), such is God's purpose in the creation, music included. Humans especially are to understand themselves as the beneficiaries of God's grace and love and thereby to experience community as the assurance of God's boundless and unending love: "Lutheran theology interprets the reality of creation above all as the context for communication. God did not reveal himself for the first time in the redemption of the world, but already at its creation and in its preservation; he poured himself out, he gave of himself completely, his almighty nature is one that humbles itself.

as establishment and preservation of community—and thereby opened up perspectives that can be particularly instructive and fruitful for discussion and for an exchange of ideas in this day and age as we interact with the natural sciences and natural philosophy."

28 Bayer, *Martin Luther's Theology*, 98–99.

29 Bayer, *Martin Luther's Theology*, 101.

Creation thus understood is gift and promise—both as establishment and as preservation of community, and in this sense it is speech act."[30]

For those who customarily imagine God's residence as heaven, a place quite out of reach, Luther's lively grasp of creation as God's theater seems far-fetched, if not incomprehensible. Yet Luther asks us to see God's presenting presence in a "mature bug or even in the cesspool . . . no less than in heaven."[31] In the creature music, therefore, Luther urges one to "hear" God's communication, to find in it God's goodness, and to relish God's aim through it of establishing and maintaining community.

THE CREATURE ENCOUNTERED IN FAITH

Hearing and seeing God in creation is neither a natural ability nor a self-generated accomplishment. In Luther's mind, the human condition tends to override our ability to recognize God in the creature. Because of our own appetites, "God can no longer address us and call us through the natural world," Bayer writes.[32] Instead, creation has become something to be owned, used, and bartered so that people often give way to getting everything they can: "Hence humans cannot hear the Creator any longer from within the things of the world, because they no longer use them in a communicative way."[33] The gesture has been turned into object, torn from the creating communicator.

For that condition to change, some sort of conversion needs to take place. For Luther, such becomes a possibility only if God is the initiator. One cannot simply decide one morning to hear God in a songbird. God alone, who longs to be heard and to be close, restores creation's primal acoustic by generating the faith necessary for a new hearing.

In a sermon he preached on Mark 7:31–37 for the twelfth Sunday after Trinity (on September 8, 1538, the same year as the publication of PSI), Luther drew on the story of the healing of the deaf person by focusing on the words of Jesus, "Be opened." In the sermon, he deals with the tension that accompanies the experience of faith and unbelief: "The entire world is deaf . . . ! They

30 Bayer, *Martin Luther's Theology*, 104.
31 The Bondage of the Will, LW 33:45.
32 Bayer, *Martin Luther's Theology*, 111.
33 Bayer, *Martin Luther's Theology*, 111.

have ears but do not hear."[34] In a similar vein, he remarks that "we have such beautiful creatures, but no one notices them because they seem so common."[35] The way to hear or hear again comes straight from Mark's story—Jesus needs to speak to us, "Be opened."

Bayer continues, "The transitional point, the change in orientation from unbelief to faith, involves a conversion to the world, a turning toward the creature. It involves a conversion toward the world as conversion toward the Creator when one hears his 'voice,' which he allows to be heard through all his creatures, in which he addresses us through the creatures."[36]

It cannot be said enough in this context: An individual's stance of faith is God's doing. God's address to us is trustworthy and creates faith. This is true not only in the realm of preaching and the sacraments but also in teaching about creation.[37] Conversion in these circumstances brings with it a certain awakening, accompanied by an expectancy for the discovery of God's sheer goodness in God's grand gesture of the cosmos. In, with, and under the creatures, as it were, the believer encounters the loving, wise, and generous Creator.[38]

The light that birthed Eden began to fade with "Adam's fall" until it ended in the midday night that came over the land at Golgotha. In that apocalyptic climate were heard the final words, "It is finished." More words followed. With "He is risen," a new thing came into being, which Paul describes as the "new creation," restoring to creation its happiest task of communicating the goodness of its Creator. Holding to this broad scope of redemption means, of course, holding also to the difficulties posed by a (new) creation *in progress*. Sometimes it is barely possible to hear anything new. Yet for Luther, the restoration of communication in the creature still out-sounds the whimpers *and* roars of the old order.

Before moving on to a reflection on natural theology and what bearing it has on the musical encounter, it is important to ponder creedal theology in a way contrary to what some hear the Apostles' and Nicene Creeds affirming.

34 WA 46:495.

35 WA TR No. 5539, as qtd. in Bayer, *Martin Luther's Theology*, 107.

36 Bayer, *Martin Luther's Theology*, 107.

37 Bayer, *Martin Luther's Theology*, 101–102.

38 "Creatures are only the hands, channels, and means through which God bestows all blessings." Large Catechism, The First Commandment, BC 389.

Just because the articles of the creeds are arranged to move from creation through redemption to matters of faith, one is not compelled to adopt that progression as the platform for comprehending one's own spiritual history. Nor, in the Lutheran scheme of things, should the creeds be received as a step-by-step set of directions for fully and rightly embracing creation.

Although a uniform pattern does not guide every experience, coming to faith, according to Luther's catechetical reflections, routinely takes a route that begins with third-article matters and ends immersed in a first-article world. That becomes clear when encountering the Reformer's Small Catechism explanations in reverse order:

The Third Article: On Being Made Holy

> I believe that by my own understanding or strength I cannot believe in Jesus Christ my Lord or come to him, but instead the Holy Spirit has called me through the gospel, enlightened me with his gifts, made me holy, and kept me in the true faith.[39]

The Second Article: On Redemption

> I believe that Jesus Christ, true God, begotten of the Father in eternity, and also a true human being, born of the Virgin Mary, is my Lord.[40]

The First Article: On Creation

> I believe that God has created me together with all that exists. God has given me and still preserves my body and soul: eyes, ears, and all limbs and senses; reason and all mental faculties. In addition, God daily and abundantly provides . . . fields, livestock, and all property—along with all the necessities and nourishment for this body and life. . . . And all this is done out of pure, fatherly, and divine goodness and mercy, without any merit or worthiness of mine at all! For all of this I owe it to God to thank and praise, serve and obey him.[41]

39 BC 355.
40 BC 355.
41 BC 354.

Der Erste Artickel/
Von der Schöpffung.

Ich gleube an Gott den Vater Allmechtigen Schöpffer Himels vnd der Erden.

Was ist das? Antwort.

Ich gleube / das mich Gott geschaffen hat / sampt allen Creaturn / Mir Leib vñ Seel Augen / Ohren vnd alle Gelieder / Vernunfft / vnd alle Sinne gegeben hat / vnnd noch erhelt.

Dazu kleider vnd Schuch /

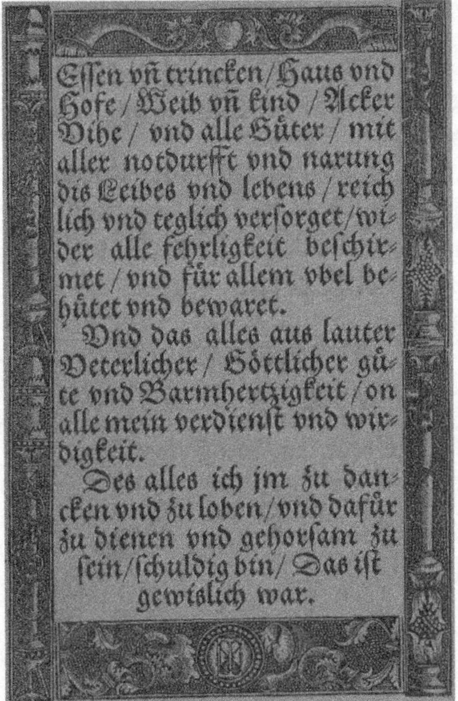

Essen vñ trincken / Haus vnd Hofe / Weib vñ kind / Acker Vihe / vnd alle Güter / mit aller notdurfft vnd narung dis Leibes vnd lebens / reichlich vnd teglich versorget / wider alle fehrligkeit beschirmet / vnd für allem vbel behütet vnd bewaret.

Vnd das alles aus lauter Veterlicher / Göttlicher güte vnd Barmhertzigkeit / on alle mein verdienst vnd wirdigkeit.

Des alles ich jm zu dancken vnd zu loben / vnd dafür zu dienen vnd gehorsam zu sein / schuldig bin / Das ist gewislich war.

Figure 2.2. First Article of the Creed, *Der kleine Catechismus* (Small Catechism), 1545

Reversing the well-worn catechetical presentation of the Apostles' Creed reveals a sequence of coming to faith that reflects the actual experiences of many and that more clearly demonstrates Luther's understandings regarding the ecology of faith. It also offers a dynamic habitude by which the person of faith is enabled to "hear" music as in its full primal acoustic, as communication from God, as animator of community, and as "place" where gratitude for God's goodness finds its home.[42]

THE CREATURE AND NATURAL THEOLOGY

For a book on music, the paragraphs immediately above may seem to be overloaded with fussy, irrelevant theological differentiation. Efforts to be precise, however, may be more germane than first impressions indicate. The point is that Luther has plainly led us into the thickets of what later philosophers and theologians called *natural theology*, a project ripe with possibilities for contention. It presses for recognition of creation as a positive factor in orienting people toward God. Is it possible, these theologians ask, to discover a gracious God in creation? Can a communal meal be sacramental? Does the thrush sing forgiveness? Luther seems to answer with a yes to all those questions, thereby sounding like a proponent of natural theology. After dinner, lauding the music of his favorite composer, Josquin, Luther reportedly and now famously blurted out, "*Sic Deus praedicavit evangelium etiam per musicam*" ("Thus God preaches the gospel even through music").[43] Some would eagerly agree; others get nervous.

Erlangen professor Werner Elert, for instance, maintained in the 1930s that some post-Reformation theologians (including Lutherans) misunderstood Luther by failing to grasp the Reformer's persistent assertion that without

42 Eighteenth-century writers on music imagined that with respect to this posture of faith they were on the same page as Luther, such as when Johann Heinrich Buttstett proposed that the "harmony of the heavenly bodies exerted real influence on earthly music," as Joyce Irwin observed in "So 'Faith Comes from What Is Heard': The Relationship Between Music and God's Word in the First Two Centuries of German Lutheranism," in *Resonant Witness: Conversations Between Music and Theology*, ed. Jeremy S. Begbie and Steven R. Guthrie (Eerdmans, 2011), 81. But that is "foreign to Luther's thought," Irwin concludes.

43 WA TR No. 1258.

faith humans remain under the wrath of God.[44] Elert would probably agree that they will not find relief by listening to pretty music. Such shortsightedness, Elert did write, not only laid the foundation for natural theology but also enabled it to quickly gain headway. A product of the Enlightenment, natural theology offered the attractive proposal that humans could discover a loving God in creation as a kind of warm-up to a full-scale encounter through word and sacrament.

Groundwork like that provided fertile soil for the Age of Romanticism. Early nineteenth-century literati, bolstered by German idealism and natural theology, saw in music the way to things divine.[45] Caught up in this effervescent view of music, Hegel, for instance, declared that the realm of romantic art is "that of divine truth."[46] One could argue that most of the nineteenth-century European music scene was driven by such persuasions and that they reigned well into the next century. On this side of the Atlantic, enthusiastic commentators such as Alfred Pike wrote, "I regard music as a means of penetration to the reality behind all appearance," also musing that "a transcendental conception [of music] elevates art to the exalted position of an intermedium between Man and his God."[47]

In one way or another, this version of natural theology shows its face whenever serious discussions arise regarding music's significance. Participants may not even be aware that it hovers in the background. Mid-twentieth-century Luther studies prompted a host of authors to reevaluate aspects of the Reformer's thought, including his understanding of music. In a well-received and oft-quoted work on Lutheran valuations of music, *Musik als Problem lutherischer Gottesdienstgestaltung* (Music as problem of Lutheran structuring of worship), Alfred Dedo Müller attempted to channel Luther by referring

---

44 Werner Elert, *The Structure of Lutheranism*, trans. Walter A. Hansen (Concordia, 1962), 50–51.

45 Jean Paul (1763–1825), an amateur musician, wrote about music without ever specifically writing about music. His writings heavily influenced musicians of all sorts; his contemporaries considered him to be the literary equivalent to Beethoven. In Paul's *Hesperus* (1795), he wrote, "O Music, thou who bringest past and future so near our wounds with their flying flames, art thou the evening breeze from this life or the morning air of the life to come? In truth thine accents are echoes, gathered by angels from the joyous sounds of a second world to bring to our mute hearts, to our deserted night, the faded spring song of the soaring heavens." In Oliver Strunk, *Source Readings in Music History: The Romantic Era* (Norton, 1965), 32–33.

46 Bowman, *Philosophical Perspectives on Music*, 101.

47 Alfred Pike, *A Theology of Music* (Gregorian Institute of America, 1953), x.

to music as a "kind of natural form of the gospel."[48] Apart from whether he accurately represented Luther, Dedo Müller's phrase elicited profuse and at times heated commentary from those interested in these things, including Lutherans Oskar Söhngen[49] and Walter Blankenburg,[50] even Roman Catholic Winfried Kurzschenkel, who both comprehensively traced the intellectual history of the phrase and identified the center of its contention as the "old issue" of natural theology.[51] Kurzschenkel responded irenically to the commotion. Christoph Krummacher, a next-generation colleague of Dedo Müller, found the whole fuss nothing but "irritating."[52]

What's not needed these days is policing the presence or absence of natural theology in heartfelt responses to musical experience. On the other hand, Luther's theology of creation does bring into question earnest, sometimes pious attributions of divine epiphanies in musical projects. Bayer writes:

> An aesthetically direct relationship to nature is no longer possible, "after the sun's light failed" and "darkness came over the whole land" (Luke 23:44-45). At the same time, when Jesus cried out on the cross, he tore asunder the difference between an aesthetic view of creation that is pious about natural things and that second naivete, by means of which he allows the lilies of the field and the birds under heaven to communicate the care and goodness of the heavenly Father—he, the Crucified One, who lives. Only through the mediation of the One, through his Word, can nature speak as creation; he is the mediator of creation.[53]

Taking music seriously as creature means that we ought to be wary of bypassing God's goodness on the way to experiencing the godly in music. To do

---

48 Alfred Dedo Müller, *Musik als Problem lutherischer Gottesdienstgestaltung* (Evangelische Verlagsanstalt, 1947), 10. Translation by the author.

49 Oskar Söhngen, "Theologische Grundlagen der Kirchenmusik," in *Die Musik des evangelischen Gottesdienstes,* vol. 4 of *Leiturgia: Handbuch des evangelischen Gottesdienstes,* ed. Karl Ferdinand Müller et al. (Stauda, 1961), 23, 66, passim.

50 Walter Blankenburg, "Luther und die Musik," in *Kirche und Musik: Gesammelte Aufsätze zur Geschichte der gottesdienstlichen Musik*, ed. Erich Hübner and Renate Steiger (Vandenhoeck & Ruprecht, 1979), 21–23.

51 Kurzschenkel, *Die theologische Bestimmung der Musik*, 183, 326–351.

52 Christoph Krummacher, *Musik als praxis pietatis: Zum Selbstverständnis evangelischer Kirchenmusik* (Vandenhoeck & Ruprecht, 1994), 19.

53 Bayer, *Martin Luther's Theology*, 115.

otherwise is to miss the communication creation offers to those who believe. Luther's positive grasp of the creature and of God's gesture of goodness included within it comprises in his view a universal component of faith. Luther offsets this bright outlook with the recognition that the creature and its users continue to be corrupted. To the abuse of music we now turn.

THE CREATURE AND ABUSE

The scolding at the conclusion of PSI reads like invective from a cranky old man suffering from digestive problems. He lets go a tirade against "depraved minds that abuse . . . both art and nature," "indecent poets" who write "erotic rantings," and then calls them "adversaries," "enemies of God," and "bastard sons, the raiders of God's gift" (6:4).

There is no hint as to the precise source of his displeasure, if there is one. Perhaps his mention of "indecent poets" signals a problem that has more to do with text than music. Indeed, ecclesiastical partisans of the time created an ample supply of edgy mockery designed to embarrass or shame their opponents. A favorite way to do that was to create new text from existing hymns so that snarky ridicule could be sung to well-known melodies. Members of all camps engaged in the practice. In a comprehensive study of Reformation propaganda music, Rebecca Wagner Oettinger cataloged several hundred of these songs, among which is this sixth and final stanza of a 1524 derision of Luther and his followers:

> How envy has blinded you,
> so that no saint in Heaven
> remains undefiled before you.
> It is a great wonder that God does not condemn
> this Luthery which has been in his sight so long.
> You will not carry on forever.[54]

Other such texts bear a tone that is much less reserved. Whether songs like this prompted Luther's ire cannot be known for sure. It is clear in PSI that

54 Rebecca Wagner Oettinger, *Music as Propaganda in the German Reformation* (Ashgate, 2001), 214. The poem's author "played on the German *Ketzerei* ('heresy') with his neologism *Luterei*" (Luthery).

he is irritated by texts that sully dearly held tunes simply by the linkage. The pleasant experience of song has been abused in his estimation. Apart from an occasional and rare disparagement of a musical experience, this scolding in PSI is unique.[55] One exception, as recorded in his 1530 sketch on music, might be his disapproval of the Lutheran dukes of Saxony, who love cannons and weapons but defund music institutions—unlike the Roman Catholic dukes of Bavaria, whose honor of music he says is "to be praised."[56]

But even that sounds more like an offhand opinion and not like the naming of spiritual corruption left dangling at the end of PSI. Luther has no fear of calling out the devil. His tirade emerges from a lively sense of the "already / not yet" of creation, the condition of faith that perceives the power of the new amid the corruption of the old.[57] The latter, though permanently overcome on the cross, is not going away and needs to be named and resisted.

ECHOES AND QUESTIONS

Much has been discovered, imagined, and written about music since the appearance of Luther's PSI. Positioning selected partners for conversation with Luther five hundred years later yields some surprising outcomes. With a focus on the "thing itself," this chapter concludes now with four points of intersection that give fuller perspective and expanded life to the Reformer's discourse. Music's origins receive attention, to begin with, because of recent proposals coming from the fledgling discipline of biomusicology. Then, the influence of songbirds on things musical over the years places Luther's embrace of songbirds into a broader context. Further, current enlightened views of deafness warrant a reevaluation of silence, as it has been treated here so far. Finally, we take a brief look at technology and its possibilities for unwelcomed sound that fans the fires of music's abuse.

---

55 Once, at table, in the context of a discussion on law and gospel, Luther is quoted as saying that a Zeitz-based organist by the name of Georg Planck played better when he played for himself because he was unbound by the expectations of others—a dynamic akin to the law, WA TR No. 5291. In his Latin Mass (1523), he included "organs and all the music" with a list of abuses that can be "tolerated until they can be completely removed," LW 53:22. The context, however, makes it clear that his real objection was the "priestly monopoly" of monetary accretions associated with the mass at the time.

56 See Leaver's translation and commentary, *Luther's Liturgical Music*, 86, 95–97.

57 See Bayer, *Martin Luther's Theology*, 118.

Origins of Music

In 1948 Curt Sachs, one of the first to develop what one might call an archaeology of music, declared that the old mythologies about music as a merciful gift of benevolent gods were dead.[58] His pronouncement didn't make it to the cover of *Time*—as did the God Is Dead movement a few years later—but it did in a way summarize attitudes of many who either didn't care about origins or would agree with Sachs for whatever reason. Near the end of the twentieth century, a small group of scholars took up the challenge implied by Sachs and began to pursue new pathways to music's origins.

Convinced that a key to music's origins lay in neurobiology, Nils L. Wallin undertook broad-based research that yielded a dissertation brimming with new vistas on age-old questions. In 1982 his work was made available as a book in Swedish, and in 1991 a revised and expanded version appeared in English with the title *Biomusicology*.[59] Wallin's groundbreaking study spawned a bevy of related studies, symposiums, a society, and a host of new avenues of research.

Findings from diverse but related pursuits poured in, resulting in four generally accepted theories for music's origins:

(1) a courtship device in the service of mate selection;
(2) an activity for promoting coordination, cohesion, and cooperation at the level of a social group;
(3) a means of improving parent-offspring communication;
(4) a partner with language in a unified mechanism for communication.[60]

The last of these has attracted much interest, and some scholars now talk about a kind of common root for language and music in what they call *musilanguage*. Drawing on research into the nature of phrase structure, for instance, Steven Brown has suggested that the referential character of musilanguage veered off

58 Steven Brown, Björn Merker, and Nils L. Wallin, "An Introduction to Evolutionary Musicology," in *The Origins of Music*, ed. Nils L. Wallin, Björn Merker, and Steven Brown (MIT Press, 2001), 20.

59 Nils L. Wallin, *Biomusicology: Neurophysiological, Neuropsychological, and Evolutionary Perspectives on the Origins and Purposes of Music* (Pendragon, 1991). It should be made clear that Wallin's work and that of his many colleagues have little to do with theories about the music of Mozart and children, for instance; evolutionary musicology is just that—the quest to find the origins of music.

60 Brown et al., "An Introduction to Evolutionary Musicology," 11.

to language itself, while the emotive aspects of musilanguage veered toward music, though neither exclusively.[61]

The homology of language and music proposed by Brown and others suggests that music originated as an answer to the need for a way to communicate. In one way or another, all four theories of origin resonate with such a conclusion. According to some scholars, communication in these early stages was of two sorts. At the local level, it attempted to be expressive. At the global level, it attempted to make sense of competing individual expressions by employing both language and music as "driving forces related to group function and social interaction capacities."[62] The precise way that music and language are engines for social interaction and social structure is a question for which there are still no definite answers.

It is true that the quests of biomusicology and the articulations of Luther are like apples and oranges. Yet there are intersecting interests. Both understand communication to be central to music, albeit for Luther the primary communication is from the Creator through the creature to the human. But because God's communication also creates and establishes community, the creature music serves also as the means of interaction with other humans. The social dimensions here are quite stunning and worth further attention. Finally, the musilanguage proposal serves to help comprehend the mating of text and music that Luther addresses further along in PSI, even though his take derives from a different perspective.

Songbirds

The term *songbird* conveys the reason lovers of music find a kinship with "singing birds": Certain birds emit sounds that simulate what humans know as song. Gulls and crows never show up in lists of songbirds. Of course, we know why; there are some birds whose calls are better described as noise rather than music. It should come as no surprise that the music-origins seekers described above have a deep interest in exploring birdsong. Their research has yielded remarkable observations.

More than half of the known species of birds, for instance, can be categorized as songbirds. Birds use song either to repel aggressors or to attract

61 Steven Brown, "The 'Musilanguage' Model of Music Evolution," in *Origins of Music*, ed. Nils L. Wallin, Björn Merker, and Steven Brown (MIT Press, 2001), 271.

62 Brown et al., "An Introduction to Evolutionary Musicology," 10.

mates. The syrinx structure of complex songbirds includes five or more pairs of muscles (as opposed to three in other birds) with two sets of membranes. This unique complexity enables these birds to produce two separate and harmonically unrelated sounds at the same time, a feat most associated with male birds during breeding season.[63] A song consists of a succession of smaller parts that come in a sequence, which can be altered as it progresses. It is estimated that the European nightingale has approximately two hundred such songs in its repertoire, all learned in a narrow timeframe of its developing life.[64]

The sounds that are shaped into songs in some instances number nearly a thousand remembered but also variegated "melodies" for purposes of mating, breeding, issuing warnings, and serenading.[65] Birds are among the most vocal of animals, and together with whales are among the few creatures that produce sounds that seem to be like music. Because birds in particular appear to shape these sounds into different combinations, they are of great interest to biomusicologists. Peter Marler explains, "The more accomplished songbirds create huge vocal repertoires, making extensive use of the same basic process of syntactical recombination or phonocoding that we use to create words."[66]

Yet ornithologist Heinz Tiessen cautions against reading too much into what ardent observers report about birdsong, simply because what the bird is experiencing cannot be known, at least for the time being. Nevertheless, the extraordinary features of songbirds, their extensive repertoires, their ability to recall and reuse, and their seeming purposefulness in delivery continue to impress the beneficiaries of their songs. These birds seem to be cousins on the continuum of creation, closer to humans than many of us are willing to concede—the relationship a matter of contention through the centuries.

Luther often refers to the (infinite, absolute) wisdom of God when considering music and sound (PSI 2:1, 2:5, and 5:2), even though he had no idea of the intricacies surrounding the song of his beloved nightingale. He recognized in that sound experience an echo of what he knew as song, even though contemporary researchers might demur from such a comparison. Nevertheless, he was not alone in finding a kinship with songbirds.

63 Peter J. B. Slater, "Birdsong Repertoires: Their Origins and Use," in *Origins of Music*, ed. Nils L. Wallin, Björn Merker, and Steven Brown (MIT Press, 2001), 50.

64 See Slater, "Birdsong Repertoires," 49–55.

65 Slater, "Birdsong Repertoires," 52, 54; Heinz Tiessen, *Musik der Natur: Über den Gesang der Vögel* (Atlantis, 1953), 84, 87; Tiessen, *Musik der Natur*, 21.

66 Peter Marler, "Origins of Music and Speech: Insights from Animals," in *Origins of Music*, ed. Nils L. Wallin, Björn Merker, and Steven Brown (MIT Press, 2001), 40.

Figure 2.3. Nightingale by duncan1890 / Digital Vision Vectors / Getty Images.

Indeed, it has been suggested that before the advent of scripted music, singers and players, responding to their acoustical surroundings, likely tried to imitate the sounds of birds. A thirteenth-century manuscript from Reading Abbey contains a six-part canon on the text "Sumer is icumen in," liberally sprinkled with references to the cuckoo. Its popularity shows up in the dozens of subsequent compositions the song inspired. Repertoires of French secular song from the fourteenth century hold a surprising number of *virelai* (a dance-based song with refrain and three stanzas), the texts for which explore interactions between the nightingale and the cuckoo, a subject with a long shelf life.[67] A hundred years later Clément Janequin (ca. 1485–1558) attempted to insert actual vocal imitations of birds in his *chansons* (songs generally in French). His contemporaries did likewise. The complexity of birdsong made it a perfect source for gestures of vocal virtuosity and pictorial representation. Contrasting the mellifluous strains of the nightingale with the naive wail of the cuckoo yielded desired laughter, but the cuckoo also served as subject matter all by itself, as demonstrated in the keyboard works of Antonio Frescobaldi (1583–1643), Johann Caspar Kerll (1627–1693), Bernardo Pasquini (1637–1710), and Louis-Claude Daquin (1694–1772).

The tradition continued. In the slow movement of his sixth symphony, the Pastoral, Beethoven (1770–1827) sought inspiration in the songs of the nightingale and cuckoo. Friedrich Delius (1862–1934) deployed his impressionistic style in the 1912 *On Hearing the First Cuckoo in Spring.* Ralph Vaughan Williams (1872–1958) followed two years later with *The Lark Ascending*, and Benjamin Britten (1913–1976) sought inspiration from birds in his 1949 *Spring Symphony.*

In nearly all these instances, a kind of musical translation functions, that is, composers in one way or another let the songbirds inspire whatever musical means were at hand. A different approach comes from Ottorino Respighi

67 Elizabeth Eva Leach, *Sung Birds: Music, Nature, and Poetry in the Later Middle Ages* (Cornell University Press, 2007), 127–137.

(1879–1936), who employed "concrete birdsong"[68] in his tone poem *Pines of Rome* (1924). Using the latest technology, Respighi directed that a specific recording of a nightingale be played toward the end of the third section of his four-part composition.

In recent memory the composer most notable for engagement with birds is Olivier Messiaen (1908–1992). Messiaen's career went through several distinct stages, each touched by his love for birds and birdsong. Steadying him along the way was also his attention to students, playing the organ, and being present for performances of his compositions.

From early in his life, he had been interested in nature, quoting birdsongs in some early works, though not with any systematic purpose in mind. He was, however, dedicated to transcribing the songs of birds from France, carefully noting terrain, time of day, and other circumstances. By the end of his life, he had filled nearly two hundred notebooks with these transcriptions.

During the years 1952–1959 Messiaen set himself to using his birdsong collections for specific musical ends. Rather than aiming to be truthful to nature, as he had done in earlier compositions, he now let his inner musician take the upper hand over the ornithologist,[69] creating three significant works that broke ground at the time and still significantly mark his composing life: *Reveil des oiseaux* (Waking of the birds), premiered 1953; *Oiseaux exotiques* (Exotic birds), premiered 1956; and *Catalogue d'oiseaux* (Catalog of birds), premiered in its entirety in 1959.

To assist in serving up the 1959 performance, Messiaen wrote an article in which he revealed his lifelong investment in birdsong:

> Nature, birdsong! There are my passions. They are also my refuge. In melancholy moments, when my uselessness is brutally revealed to me, when every musical language, whether classical, exotic ancient, modern or ultra-modern, seems to me reduced to being merely the praiseworthy result of patient research, without anything behind the notes to justify so much labor, what else is there to do except search

---

68 The term comes from Leach, *Sung Birds*, 293, in the comment, "The reproduction of a 'real' bird, but one introduced 'mechanically' and disembodied, throws into relief the eerie otherworldly sound of the performatively present, acoustic orchestra." Respighi also employed the sounds of birds in an imitative mode; he is famous also for *The Birds* (1927), an orchestral transcription of Jean-Philippe Rameau's (1683–1764) *Le rappel des oiseaux* (*The Call of the Birds*).

69 Peter Hill and Nigel Simeone, *Messiaen* (Yale University Press, 2005), 215.

> for the true face of Nature, forgotten somewhere in the forest, in the fields, in the mountains, on the seashore, among the birds!
>
> For me, it is here that music lives: music that is free, anonymous, improvised for pleasure to work off the excessive energy born of love and *joie de vivre*, to articulate time and space and join with your neighbors in constructing rich and improvised counterpoint.[70]

Just how thoroughly he let those sentiments permeate his compositions becomes clear in the way he used his early research. For the *Oiseaux exotiques*, the composer drew on the songs of forty-eight birds—a staggering number. Among them are the Baltimore oriole, American robin, South Asian *shama*, song sparrow, mockingbird, purple finch, and bobolink.[71]

Messiaen's devotion to birdsong parallels that of Luther, even though the latter directed his energies toward theological concerns without the assistance of technical information about the birds he loved. Messiaen had the benefit of his own research, but knowledge even more current than his additionally enriches one's grasp of songbirds.

Birds figure in the folk and popular song traditions as well. An internet search of "songs that refer to birds" will bring one to lists of more than fifty titles that refer to birds, coming from artists ranging from the Beatles to Jimi Hendrix to Lynyrd Skynyrd. To be sure, few of these works attempt to incorporate the actual sounds of birds, but these artists found the realm of birdsong to be a useful sonic envelope for trading their lyrical wares.

So it is elsewhere in the world. Ethnomusicologist Steven Feld discovered that among the Kaluli people of New Guinea, the *muni* bird (fruit dove) binds together the Kaluli culture in most profound ways. Not only does its song constitute generative material for the people's music-making; the bird itself is also thought to mysteriously embody the sinews of the culture as the people negotiate the past and future. On quoting one member of the Kaluli, "To you they are birds; to me they are voices in the forest," Feld reflects, "[This] meant that there are many ways to think about birds, depending on the context in which knowledge is activated and social needs are served. Birds are 'voices' because Kaluli recognize and acknowledge their existence primarily

70 Hill and Simeone, *Messiaen*, 226–227.

71 Hill and Simeone, *Messiaen*, 115–116. It should come as no surprise that in 1983, toward the end of his life, Messiaen premiered his only opera, *Saint Francois d'Assise*, a mammoth work based on the life of the saint who loved birds and other creatures.

through sound, and because they are the spirit reflections of deceased men and women."[72] It is hard to escape the observation that the Kaluli people respond to the call of the bird as if it has more to communicate than animal soundings that strike one as lovely. While the cuckoo may never be expected to prompt any profound thoughts, some birdsong experiences send their hearers into realms where the stuff of life is contemplated.

In one way or another, every example mentioned in this brief sketch demonstrates how people have found a way to respond to sounds of songbirds, jointly acknowledging with their imitations, inspirations, and collaborations a kinship with these unique creatures of earth. Luther would have enjoyed it all, urging the same for subsequent generations. At the same time, he boldly and courageously issues another invitation, and that is to hear in the song of birds a communicative address. The address is from God, and it is meant to woo people into God's infinite wisdom and abundant goodness.

Silence and Deafness

As noted earlier, Oswald Bayer underscores Luther's fondness for the notion of God always coming beforehand. When in God's word, God comes *for me,* that does not mean that God was absent until such an encounter but rather that God came beforehand in and for all creatures. The encounter is the momentous hearing of assurance for me. In part, Luther, with this phrase, is trying to steer clear of providing any opportunity for one to claim a role in coming to faith.

God is always there beforehand—also before creation. From nothingness (*ex nihilo*) came the word "Let there be." And there came forth sound (and music). If one were to explain nothingness as silence in this context, surely there would be an eruption of objections based on whether silence is nothing or something. Yet, because silence broken by sound is the closest analogous experience we have of nothingness turned to somethingness, it is tempting to imagine "in the beginning" as the breaking of silence.

Nothingness (in this case also silence) is crucial to Luther's understanding of good news. A hint of that shows up in PSI 4:3, where he pointedly modifies *proclamation* with the word *sounded.* The insistence that good news is at its core something sounded does not come as a new idea, of course. Behind

72 Steven Feld, *Sound and Sentiment: Birds, Weeping, Poetics, and Song in Kaluli Expression* (University of Pennsylvania Press, 1982), 45.

Luther's perception of good news lie these words from the apostle Paul: "How are they to believe in one of whom they have never heard? And how are they to hear without someone to proclaim him? . . . So faith comes from what is heard, and what is heard comes through the word of Christ."[73] The theological impact of the gospel and of music as creature both rely in one way or another on our experience of silence. But all that reaches a whole new level of complexity when deafness is factored in.

Did the Reformer ever address deafness? Little is known about his attitudes in this respect. There was a tradition within the church going back to Augustine that dealt with deafness as a wretched condition because deaf people could not hear the gospel. Some even took deafness to be a sign of the devil.[74] Was Luther more enlightened than his forebears?

The 1538 sermon he preached on Mark 7:31–37, cited above, provides some clues as to how he dealt with deafness. In that sermon Luther uses deafness as a metaphor for a universal condition: Humans tend not to listen to God. We have ears but fail to hear, he laments. He summons an example appropriate to this context: Pythagoras, he points out, taught that the stars in their courses sing a song, but nobody can hear it. Spiritual deafness prevents us from hearing the song.

The universal human condition that fails to hear the song needs the Lord God to draw near for healing, even as Jesus drew near to the deaf and mute person. To sense God's nearness amid our impaired hearing, Luther exhorts, one must intently listen to the creatures God has provided for this very purpose. The created world is speaking, but we all have such trouble listening. Reaching the apex of his proclamatory appeal, he turns to earthly sources of God's healing song: "Sheep, cows, trees when they bloom, say 'Ephphatha.'"[75] The Aramaic word means *be opened*, the word Jesus used in his healing.

Luther's handling of the text diverts attention away from the physical condition of deafness. His interpretation might be expected, and it summons people of every generation to "hear" in a different way. Although in our time we have rightly become more cautious and nuanced about using deafness as a

73 Rom. 10:14, 15, 17.

74 Christopher Krentz, *Writing Deafness: The Hearing Line in Nineteenth-Century American Literature* (University of North Carolina Press, 2007), 102.

75 German: "*Scheps, vaccae, arbores, wenn sie bluhen, sprechen: 'Hephethah.'*" WA 46: 495.

metaphor, we can appreciate Luther's interpretation of the human condition he finds in Mark's Gospel.

While Luther strongly affirms the *ex nihilo* aspect of creation, he does not posit silence as equivalent to nothingness. Such a suggestion must be evaluated in the context of its use, especially as it is perceived among those who are in fact deaf. In a perceptive and eye-opening study of American literature and deafness, Christopher Krentz, professor of English and American Sign Language at the University of Virginia, finds silence as a metaphor for deafness highly insufficient: "Silence does appear to resemble deafness in the way that it cannot be captured in words, and in the way that its significance depends on its opposite and its meanings are culturally produced, . . . metaphors of silence mistakenly make it appear that deaf people live in an utterly soundless world and are soundless themselves."[76] Luther, as far as we know, did not draw any kind of connection between deafness and silence. To think of deaf people as living in silence, against the background of imagining silence as the lack of sound, would be to relegate deaf people, following the suggestion above, to a state of *ex nihilo*—a despicable thought. Krentz offers an alternative way to think about deafness, a way by which one might embrace both Luther's high view of sound's value and a positive view of deafness. Considering ways to speak of deafness, he writes, "Metaphors of silence also fail to represent deaf experience because they focus only on the inability to hear or speak, *leaving out deaf people's community, language, and manner of being.*"[77]

Hearing a blossoming tree say "ephphatha" without sound is a different kind of hearing, but it is a hearing nonetheless. Moreover, Krentz's heightened mindfulness of deaf people's community calls for careful attention. Hearing people can only imagine what that community is like, though the energetic demeanor of a choir that *signs* its song provides a clue. The bottom line here may well be that communal activity—for some, signing; for others, making music; but for all, something done together—this communal activity is at the very core of what many think music's significance to be.

Even in light of Luther's privileging of sound when it comes to the dynamics of good news, his view of "hearing" makes it possible to encompass deafness as a unique way of experiencing and communicating God's grace and goodness.

---

76 Krentz, *Writing Deafness*, 76.

77 Krentz, *Writing Deafness*, 76. Emphasis mine.

Abuse of Sound

The remarkable sudden turn to a prickly scold at the conclusion of PSI raises a host of questions that cannot be solved with any certainty. It is safe to say that the behavior of the schoolboys in their dormitory rooms was legendary and that Luther was not alone in trying to address it. His friend and cohort Johannes Bugenhagen expressed similar concerns.[78] Luther may also have come to recognize at the end of PSI that his very positive presentation on music needed a shot of reality about its less salutary expressions. Whatever the motivation, his cautionary admonition seems to bear the marks of a long tradition of suspicion.

In his *Republic* (fourth century BCE), Plato famously rejected four of six available modes because of their effects on human behavior.[79] Early Christian forebears such as Clement of Alexandria, Arnobius of Sicca, and Isidore of Pelusium observed distasteful behaviors when music entered liturgical assemblies and strongly advised that it be eliminated.[80] Hundreds of years later, some Lutheran orthodox theologians, especially Theophil Grossgebauer (1627–1661), expressed their misgivings about music in worship and wrote at length about its abuse and misuse.[81] Papal pronouncements regarding music abound, especially those prompted by its perceived misuse in the liturgy. One of the most famous, *Annus qui hunc* (1749), came from the pen of Pope Benedict XIV, who with considerable detail cautioned against the use of instruments in the mass. He is far less diplomatic when he takes up what he calls music of the theater (e.g., late baroque Italian opera style), noting agreeably that numerous writers urged that "such abuse be banished from the churches."[82] In the nineteenth century, Englishman Robert Eastcott

78 "Indeed here in this school in Wittenberg we have (grateful to Christ) such great numbers of honest young men. . . . There are a few young men . . . [who] are all plainly Sybarites, in gestures, in their way of life, in drunkenness, lust, dress, gait, dance, nocturnal clamour, indecencies, and in life itself." Johannes Bugenhagen, preface to Balthasar Resinarius, *Responsorium numero octoginta de tempore* (1544), trans. Eyolf Østrem, in *Lutheran Music Culture: Ideals and Practices*, ed. Mattias Lundberg et al. (de Gruyter, 2021), 312.

79 Oliver Strunk, *Source Readings in Music History: Antiquity and the Middle Ages* (Norton, 1965), 4.

80 McKinnon, *Music in Early Christian Literature*, 18–74, passim.

81 Friedrich Kalb, *Theology of Worship in 17th-Century Lutheranism*, trans. Henry P. A. Hamann (Concordia, 1963), 138–149.

82 Robert F. Hayburn, ed., *Papal Legislation on Sacred Music 95 A.D. to 1977 A.D.* (Liturgical Press, 1979), 98.

(1740–1828) observed that it is a "lamentable truth, that the general manner of performing parochial music, is become an object of disgust."[83]

Except perhaps for Plato, each of these warnings and pleas could be dismissed as disagreements about appropriate style, quality of delivery, or behaviors accompanying the musical moment. Luther encountered those as well, but in PSI the stakes are higher. Consistent with his theology of creation, he unmasks the vulnerability of music to the powers of evil. In the last half of PSI 6, he cites the devil as perpetrator of such abuse and labels the "bastards" and "raiders" as the enemies of God. Their advances are directed toward music in all its manifestations, "both art and nature"—a clear reference to music as *musica artificialis* (composed music) and music in its most basic sense as sound, the *creatura.* Given his characteristic forthrightness about naming the forces of evil in daily life, his scolding (as we have called it) seems then not to be hyperbole but rather a frank theological recognition of the real world: Music can be abused to evil purpose.

Such an assessment could not be expected to find much resonance in more enlightened post-Reformation acoustical worlds, in which critiques of perceived musical abuse, even when earnestly identified, often seemed too intense for most. More recently, Tipper Gore's Parents Music Resource Center, founded in 1985, fostered a program of trying to corral lyrical tendencies in pop music but deferred from linking the campaign to theological impulses. Though voluntary labeling systems for commercial recordings are still present today, the movement lost any momentum it had, having faced intense pushback.[84]

In his captivating study of music as economic and social marker, Jacques Attali points to subtler forms of music's potential for abuse. He contends that life invariably unfolds in the presence of noise and that noise—actual and metaphoric—like other social forces, needs to be controlled to keep communities together. Music can serve as a controlling factor by counteracting noise or transforming it, but wherever there is music, there also is money, and where there is money, there is also power.[85] Therefore, "any organization of sounds

---

83 Elwyn A. Wienandt, ed., *Opinions on Church Music* (Baylor University Press, 1974), 97.

84 Mathieu Deflem, "Popular Music and Social Control: The Moral Panic on Music Labeling," *American Journal of Criminal Justice* 45 (2020): 2–24.

85 Jacques Attali, *Noise: The Political Economy of Music*, trans. Brian Massumi (University of Minnesota Press, 1985), 3.

is a tool for the creation or consolidation of a community, of a totality. It is what links a power center to its subjects, and thus, more generally, it is an attribute of power in all of its forms."[86]

Attali's overall purpose is to show how the organization and control of sounds have migrated from one musical clientele to another over the centuries. His insights should move even commentators on the church musical scene to perceive how power connected to music shapes music's use and value. In this context, however, Attali's work counts for something different. Throughout his study he recognizes that any part of the musical enterprise—be it publishing, recording, marketing, star power, or whatever—can get out of hand. It can revert to noise, become an unbridled force that is detrimental to the entire community, even though such "noise" might claim protection under the pretense of being music.

Here it's not necessary to measure the merits of the book as a text on economics or sociology. However, Attali's naming of the seemingly inseparable linkage of music, power, and money begs attention. Where there is power and money, there one inevitably finds corruption, suggesting that inherent to music is the likely possibility of behaviors that are hurtful and destructive to the community at large.

Some thirty years later, however, Luther's more unapologetic stance seems to have found an acoustic more welcoming to the echoes of his sharp critique. Alex Ross, music critic for the *New Yorker*, prompted by "a bleak stack of books on my desk," devoted a lengthy review article to "The Sound of Hate."[87] After describing aims and contents of the volumes, Ross concludes the column with these words: "What to do with these dire ruminations? Renouncing music is not an option—not even Quignard [Pascal Quignard, one of the authors] can bring himself to do that. Rather, we can renounce the fiction of music's innocence. To discard that illusion is not to diminish music's importance; rather, it lets us register the uncanny power of the medium. To admit that music can become an instrument of evil is to take it seriously as a form of human expression."[88]

Ross's recognition of "music as an instrument of evil" is stunning amid a long history of sugary measures of music's significance in society. Perhaps the most prominent reason such a view of music rings true today is

86 Attali, *Noise*, 6.

87 Alex Ross, "The Sound of Hate," *New Yorker*, July 4, 2016, 65–69.

88 Ross, "The Sound of Hate," 69.

the technological capacity now available to musicians and their resultant products. But it's not the only reason. The spectrum of abuse is extensive, as Ross's review makes clear, and even includes practices unmentioned in Ross's presentation. Four patterns of musical abuse unmask the ubiquity of the condition.

Several of the books Ross reviewed deal with the weaponization of sound. As early as 1944, the Nazis controlling the work forces at Auschwitz repeatedly played the "Rosamunde" polka (also known as the "Beer Barrel Polka") over loudspeakers to "welcome" the prisoners back to their bunkhouses. It was, as Ross writes, a "grotesque juxtaposition" of light music and the horrors of the place. Similarly, in 1989 the US armed forces set up speakers below Noriega's Panama City bedroom window and blasted out rock songs twenty-four hours a day, knowing that he was an ardent fan of classic opera.[89] Following the success of such employment of extreme sound, there are current attempts to develop "sound cannons" that from some distance can debilitate opposing troops.[90] The diabolical nature of such a prospect lies in the fact that sound is inescapable. Instances of sound coupled to violence have multiplied in past decades and sometimes emerge from disregard for employees, for instance, who are forced to work in noisy climes without protective gear. But then that, too, is abuse.

Akin to the weaponization of sound is the use of music to mask or temporarily render empathy inoperable. Even though the precise mechanisms behind music's seeming ability to stir human emotions remain somewhat of a mystery, common experience suggests some kind of causality. Hence, one of Ross's authors reported that soldiers in the Vietnam War used favorite songs to get themselves ready for lethal combat. Stirring up rage was the goal because "you've got to become inhuman to do inhuman things."[91]

Issues surrounding lyrics came up in a book by two pioneers of pop music study, Bruce Johnson and Martin Cloonan.[92] Many listeners, they say, prefer to see only the "positive side of pop,"[93] refusing to acknowledge songs that arouse or incite violence such as "Eminem's graphic fantasies of abuse and

89 Ross, "The Sound of Hate," 65.

90 Ross, "The Sound of Hate," 66.

91 Ross, "The Sound of Hate," 68.

92 Bruce Johnson and Martin Cloonan, *Dark Side of the Tune: Popular Music and Violence* (Ashgate, 2008).

93 As qtd. in Ross, "The Sound of Hate," 68.

murder."[94] While not moral crusaders, these two scholars refuse "to rule out links between violence in music—in terms both of lyrical content and of raw decibel impact—and violence in society."[95] Ross goes on to let readers know that for Johnson and Cloonan, such violence includes the debasement of women and a rape culture reflected in some popular songs.

Not mentioned in this column from the *New Yorker* is the twentieth- and twenty-first-century avant-garde movement known as Danger Music.[96] Proponents of this genre hold that musical performance should have elements of danger that impinge on both performers and listeners. With roots in the 1960s, this musical expression is viewed as a performance act that incorporates elements of theater and social protest. The danger often emerges from amplified sound at levels physically harmful but appears in other ways as well. One piece for a small ensemble ends with the musicians throwing tennis balls into the audience, some embedded with exposed razor blades. Some refer to this movement as "anti-music," a descriptor that strongly suggests its deviant purposes.[97]

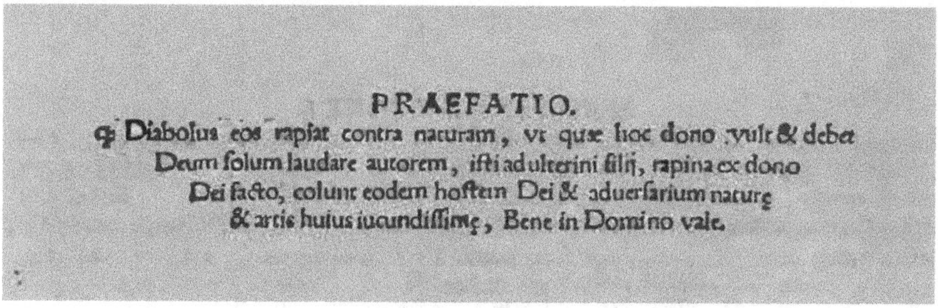

PRAEFATIO.

Diabolus eos rapiat contra naturam, vt quae hoc dono vult & debet Deum solum laudare autorem, isti adulterini filii, rapina ex dono Dei facto, colunt eodem hostem Dei & aduersarium naturę & artis huius iucundissimę, Bene in Domino vale.

Figure 2.4. Luther's "scold" concluding PSI, 1538

Some might wish that Luther would have ended his paean on music without the scold. Others may be put off by his lively sense of demons. Yet his naming of misuse and abuse is an essential reminder. In every generation, a deep love and appreciation for the creature music must proceed, as well as a

94 Ross, "The Sound of Hate," 68.

95 Ross, "The Sound of Hate," 68.

96 Not to be confused with [DJ] Danger, the stage name of Franck Rivoire, a French electronic musician.

97 David Cope, *New Directions in Music*, 7th ed. (Waveland, 2001).

profound desire to protect it and the joy it brings from senseless, self-serving purposes that mar the gift.

The accounts of music's abuse and Luther's stark assessment of the tendency are momentary detours in a trajectory he is developing in PSI, a trajectory that overwhelmingly values sound and music as indicators of God's love for the cosmos. If one signs on as a fellow traveler, then the next station at which Luther wants us to pause harbors the questions: If abuse is not the path, then what's the use? What is music for? Why, as creature, is it a gift?

CHAPTER THREE

What's the Use?

Music, the Anointed Governess of Human Hearts

LUTHER'S PERSPECTIVE

Framework: Enduring Questions

In the third section of PSI, having established that the "thing itself" is a creature of the Creator, Luther turned to a discussion of music's *use*. He explained, "I ought to speak now of the use of something so great" (3:1). This progression from thing to use is, I believe, more significant than the attention it has received. For one thing, use, as Luther treats it, is not what most contemporary readers would expect. We are more likely to anticipate at this point an effusive salute to music's partnership with the word of God. He addresses that, too, in PSI but not before he has settled the matter of *use*.

Moreover, the progression he chose flows in the ancient riverbeds of Aristotelian philosophy; that is, to understand something one must see how its distinctive nature relates to its ultimate purpose. Aristotle's influence was immense. For centuries, Wayne D. Bowman observes, philosophers have focused on two central questions when it comes to music: What is it? What is its significance or *use*?[1] These are enduring preoccupations, questions that students of music like those Luther addresses may raise as well.

In this chapter, we will first summon some other factors that help to assemble a perspective in which Luther delivers his views on the enduring

1 Wayne D. Bowman, *Philosophical Perspectives on Music* (Oxford University Press, 1998), 2.

use question. Then, to get to the meaning of use in his way of thinking, we examine his understanding of *affect*, the influence of medieval psychology, his stint as a monk, and the impact of the Psalter on all of that. Finally, as echoes of "on the use," the chapter concludes with a small excursus on John Calvin and a discussion of music and emotion.

Framework: Text Matters

To better understand some of the words and concepts addressed below, we briefly note some nuances of the Latin version of PSI that easily escape notice in translations. The opening sentence (3:1) literally reads, "I ought to address now the use of this great thing." The Latin word is again *res*, as in *res ipsam*, the "thing itself." That's not clear in the available translations. Vocabulary here suggests a tight connection between the "thing" and the thing's use.

The sentence at 3:4 contains so many subclauses that the main point gets lost during the linguistic journey. Clarity comes by eliminating various interjections to arrive at this: "Experience bears witness to music being the one thing that . . . rules and governs the human passions . . . by which [humans] themselves are governed as if by their masters and quite often carried away." The point is that human passions govern human behavior, sometimes "carried away" behavior, but those same passions are governed in turn by music. Of further note, the Latin syntax and vocabulary at the words "rules and governs" read, somewhat clumsily, "music being the one thing that, as a lady of the house and governess over human passions."[2] Gendering music this way was not unusual at the time, here perhaps even beneficially coloring his observations regarding music and the passions.

Finally, in 3:6 Luther again inserts tangential thoughts that blur his unfolding argument. The list of music's potential outcomes on human behavior sets him thinking more generally about all kinds of inner human workings that issue forth as virtues or vices. The workings he categorizes are affections, impulses, and spirits (*affectus*, *impetus*, and *spiritus*). The first of these is also the word he used at 3:4, translated in the version used here as *passion*. His case might be better served if the translation for *affectuum* in 3:4 were *affections* or *affects*, especially since the word is close to being a technical term for Luther and his generation. All three terms have their roots in medieval psychology.

2 Latin: "*domina et gubernatrix affectuum humanorum.*"

Framework: The Floor of Experience

In the opening chapter, I signaled Luther's extensive acquaintance with musical repertoires and exposure to musical performances as factors that shaped his outlook as he, the Reformer, faced decisions that would set the direction and shape of church life under new management. Experience emerged as a core metric for navigating the way from the old to the new. It is the floor on which he addressed music's use, both within and outside of the worshipping assembly. His PSI serves as a perfect example.

Resisting any move to summon as much wisdom from the past as he can (the "most eloquent eloquence from the most eloquent"), Luther, in making his case for use, instead appealed to common experience. Clearly, he argues (3:4), we all know that music governs the human passions,[3] and clearly, Luther seems to be saying, that is a good thing. Shared experience further brings us to recognize how music cheers those who are miserable, encourages those who are despairing, and so on (3:6).

In his study of Luther and music, Miikka Anttila has spotlighted the importance of experience in Luther's overall theological fabrication of the world.[4] Drawing on a bevy of contemporary Luther scholars such as Lennart Pinomaa, Gerhard Ebeling, and Oswald Bayer, all of whom in one way or another call attention to the Reformer's bend toward what's lived and felt, Anttila submits that Luther's theology can be thought of as centered in "affective faith," a particularly apt description in a musical context since the noun *affect* prominently figures in discussions of music over the centuries. As the last of a roll call of scholars, Anttila cites Birgit Stolt, who has called out Luther for the "intense emotional undercurrent" of his Bible translation.[5] Everywhere you look, Anttila marvels, Luther consistently built his convictions on experience and the array of emotions that attend it. Anttila then offers this: Referencing the all-so-familiar words that Luther used to expound the Ten Commandments, "We are to fear and love God," Anttila notes that "the most celebrated account of Lutheran theology is organized *emotionally*."[6] Luther's few words

3 Latin: "*affectuum*."

4 Miikka Anttila, *Luther's Theology of Music: Spiritual Beauty and Pleasure* (de Gruyter, 2013), 107–108.

5 Birgit Stolt, "Luther's Faith of 'the Heart': Experience, Emotion, and Reason," in *The Global Luther: A Theologian for Modern Times*, ed. Christine Helmer (Fortress Press, 2009), 141–147, as cited by Anttila, *Luther's Theology of Music*, 107.

6 Anttila, *Luther's Theology of Music*, 107. Emphasis mine.

in PSI on the use of music come from a posture firmly resting on the floor of experience. That is his characteristic perspective.

Framework: Pillars of Popular Opinion

Further, widespread experience of music, Luther boldly submitted, tells us that it affects human behavior in all kinds of ways. There follows in PSI a rather astonishing list of examples, as if he had given this more than passing thought: Music can "cheer the miserable, deter the cheerful, encourage the despairing, break the proud, calm lovers, and soothe haters" (3:6). A few of these examples may jolt, such as "deterring the cheerful" and "calming lovers."

The fact of the matter is that he had thought about these outcomes of music before. In his first lectures on the Psalms, originating sometime between 1513 and 1515, he wrote at Psalm 4:1, "It is the function of music to arouse the sad, sluggish, and dull spirit."[7] Again, in his short 1530 draft of a proposed study of music with the Greek title Περὶ τῆς μουσικῆς (Concerning music), he declared, "I love music / . . . For it creates joyful hearts / For it drives away the devil / . . . For it creates innocent delight, destroying wrath, unchastity, and other excesses."[8] In 1538 or perhaps a few years earlier, a similar sentiment shows up in the poem titled "Frau Musica" ("Lady Music"): When there is singing, there is "no grudge, hate, rage, or row; softened is all grief and sorrow."[9]

The ideas Luther expressed about the use of music in PSI are not new; they encapsulate thoughts he had harbored over many years. There's likely nothing original about his views on human passions and their subservience to music. Such certainties were popular among those educated, and they constituted basic pillars of shared beliefs about music and its use.

Robin Leaver has given us two examples of circulating material containing similar expressions, important because each may have been known to Luther. The first comes from cleric, composer, and theorist Johannes Tinctoris (ca. 1435–1511), who, several years before Luther was born, expounded on the glorious outcomes of music: "Music encourages souls to piety," he wrote, even as it "drives away sadness . . . creates rapture . . . delights humans . . . encourages

7 LW 10:43.

8 Robin A. Leaver, *Luther's Liturgical Music: Principles and Implications* (Fortress Press, 2017), 86.

9 Leaver, *Luther's Liturgical Music*, 74. Translation by Leaver.

love . . . increases the joy of conviviality . . . [and] makes spirits glad."[10] The second comes from Jean Charlier de Gerson (1363–1429), French theologian and author, who wrote a poem in praise of music that was subsequently cited by others, including Adam of Fulda. Luther may have known of it apart from his connection to Adam, however, since Gerson's writings were influential in his formation as a young student of theology. Among other celebrations of music, Gerson declares that it "refreshes the spirit [*cor*], drives away cares, and soothes ennui."[11]

Because Tinctoris and Gerson represent voices from Italy and France, respectively, and each wrote from postures well immersed in broader traditions, one gets the impression that thoughts about music's use expressed by Luther in PSI were rather widespread. No doubt it felt right for him to "speak about its use" at this point of PSI, and to do it in the way he decided, because such a choice would be the expected response to the topic at hand.

As Luther laid out what he held about music's use, he noted that he could think of no greater reason for praising it (3:5). That's quite an accolade, for it shows how strongly he valued the effects music had on him and others. Because he came to this understanding for reasons larger than fickle tendencies, we turn now to other significant factors that energized his views. An exploration of affect and medieval psychology is followed by a short interlude that briefly elaborates the fortunes of affect after Luther. A more probing look at the impact of his monastic experience brings us to a better-informed understanding of Luther's convictions about music's use.

THE PSALTER AND THE HEART: AFFECT AND MEDIEVAL PSYCHOLOGY

Perhaps Luther intended to stir up some chuckles from the students with the words "most eloquent eloquence of the most eloquent" (3:2).[12] Just what or whom he was referencing with the phrase are unanswerable questions. Since he was captivated by the ways music affects people, one might surmise he was referring to what has been broadly described as medieval psychology, a body of knowledge nurtured and promoted not by philosophers or practitioners

10 Leaver, *Luther's Liturgical Music*, 71.

11 Leaver, *Luther's Liturgical Music*, 72. Translation by Leofranc Holford-Strevens.

12 Latin: "*eloquentissimorum eloquentissimam eloquentiam.*"

of medicine but by theologians. The views of Tinctoris, Gerson, and Luther were founded on prevailing assumptions about human behavior. To those assumptions we now attend with the intent of better understanding what it was that Luther espoused for the students of music.

A place to start is his vocabulary. To make music's use plain, he chose the words *affect*, *impetus*, and *spirit*, the first by far receiving the most attention. These were words routinely used at the time to identify that elusive but universally experienced relationship between music and human response. *Affect* held an important place among then current accounts regarding human personality, moods, and their biological operating systems. Roots for this thinking were deep, going back to Hippocrates (460–370 BCE).

According to his theory, sometimes called *humorism*, Hippocrates proposed four fundamental personality types: sanguine, choleric, melancholy, and phlegmatic. These types are the result of a variable balance of four bodily fluids: blood, yellow bile, black bile, and phlegm. If the balance is disturbed for any reason, say, for example, too much black bile, then such a personality will veer toward being melancholy. Several centuries later, a physician named Galen of Pergamon (129–ca. 216 CE) developed this proposal into medical theory, the gist of which subsequent generations embraced as true to experience and therefore a usable foundation for developing diagnoses and treatments. In this later version of humorism, the key feature consisted of the balance of the humors, a condition that was subject to alteration via internal or external stimuli. That resulting alteration came to be known as an affect. One's experience of an affect could range from a pleasant sensation to a sense of serious disturbance, experiences later generations would recognize as emotional responses. Most understood music to be a major source of stimulation, though no one could quite explain why or how.

While some promoters of medieval psychology drew tangential cause/effect connections between affect and a variety of disorders, such as diet, mental capacity, and general moral attitudes, the most avid among them—the theologians—expropriated the system for purposes of identifying the causes and manifestations of what they thought was sinful behavior. Ironically, they were both fascinated by the nefarious power of emotions and fearful of welcoming emotions as positive factors for a life of faith. A measure of the prominence and draw of emotional theory among scholarly clerics resides in the *Treatise on Emotions* by Thomas Aquinas (ca. 1225–1274). Anttila reckons this work the most valuable and fully developed medieval theory of emotions.[13] In line with the early humorist explanations, Aquinas defined an emotion as an act "of the sensitive appetite, inasmuch as [it is] united to some bodily change."[14] His more contemporary self is revealed in the suspicion he held of emotions while promoting the Christian utility of (for him) the four principal "passions": joy, sorrow, hope, and fear.

Humorism had evolved with Aquinas. However, there existed the tendency to confuse the affect produced by the balance or imbalance of humors with its sensation, the emotion. This confusion may be why Luther perceived the "most eloquent" to be not eloquent enough and why he resorted to his own personal experience when it came to defining and evaluating affect.

By 1600, proponents of medieval psychology had extended their reach into musical matters by including various cosmological speculations. Some embraced notions of a symbiotic relationship between the harmonies heard and the harmony of the heavens (music of the spheres). Others found it easy to link such imaginative thinking to practices of the occult, identified as additional disclosures of the mysteries surrounding the workings of affect. At first these forays seemed to be privileged, esoteric wisdom reserved for those in the know. That changed when, in the interests of wider dissemination, Marsilio Ficino (1433–1499) published in 1489 *De vita coelitus comparanda*, the third of *De triplici vita* (Three books on life), a work that would come to be the classic text in subsequent centuries for discussions of music's effects.[15] Ficino linked together musical modes, bodily temperaments, and planetary harmonies. Alchemy and astrology came on board when Ficino espoused his theory of music and *spiritus*.[16] His German popularizer, Heinrich Cornelius Agrippa (1486–1535), proposed that music's harmony, deeply embedded in the structure of the universe, affected a person in such a way that could unify body and soul.[17]

It's a long way from Hippocrates to Ficino. Along the path, though, there is the ever-present specter of affect that both ties the journey together and

13 Anttila, *Luther's Theology of Music*, 64.

14 Anttila, *Luther's Theology of Music*, 64.

15 Penelope Gouk, "The Role of Harmonics in the Scientific Revolution," in *The Cambridge History of Western Music Theory*, ed. Thomas Christensen (Cambridge University Press, 2002), 226.

16 Gouk, "Role of Harmonics," 226.

17 Gouk, "Role of Harmonics," 226.

reveals how its dynamics pervaded every aspect of music-making. Attempts were made to parse it with greater precision, but its elusive nature at the outset contained a resistance to such efforts. For the present we might just as well consider its various stages to broadly signify music and emotion. With that in mind, we still pause to recognize that understandings of affect underwent notable shifts after Ficino—developments that impacted the creation and delivery of assembly music, particularly among those who were Luther's musical heirs. Within those shifts, however, affect in its various iterations keeps playing a role, even up to the present. To grasp the bigger picture is worth a brief excursus.

Interlude: Humanism, Affect, and Luther's Musical Heirs

After Ficino, further augmentation of medieval psychological theory occurred as Renaissance humanism (fourteenth to sixteenth centuries) gained a foothold across Europe. Proponents urged a return to the models of classical antiquity, with a major focus on Plato and Aristotle. New translations of their works elicited increasing interest in what these ancients thought about music. Among other things, humanists discovered hesitations from the two about endorsing all music within reach, especially when it came to employing it for educational purposes. Plato's misgivings had to do with certain modes, or scale patterns, particularly the Lydian and Mixolydian modes.[18] His student Aristotle disputed Plato for dismissing those two modes while accepting the Dorian and Phrygian modes.[19] They both agreed that more worrisome were the kinds of behavior the modes (in their minds) induced.

Humanism provided the ecclesial hierarchy with the kind of ammunition they were seeking to combat those freewheeling cantors who both permitted outrageous behavior from their singers during worship and themselves used nonecclesiastical tunes as musical building blocks for new compositions. Some music, it was reasoned, just cannot be trusted because it produces unacceptable behavior. Want proof? Just look at Plato and Aristotle. They even identified the modes that were culprits.

There was a problem with such argumentation. When Plato and Aristotle mentioned modes, they were referencing ancient Greek musical theory. That

18 Oliver Strunk, *Source Readings in Music History: Antiquity and the Middle Ages* (Norton, 1965), 4, n. 3 and n. 5.

19 Strunk, *Source Readings: Antiquity*, 23.

system recognized and identified specific scale patterns (modes) according to various successions of whole tones, half tones, and something like quarter tones. In some instances, people assigned ethnic names to a particular combination, such as Lydian or Dorian. Many years later, to categorize the many tunes used in ecclesiastical liturgies and in other music as well, some categorizers employed the ethnic naming system, even though the two systems were quite different. An anonymous theorist from about the year 1000 CE mistakenly assumed both systems were one and the same and proceeded to assign the ethnic names to the newly emerging church modes.[20] Hence, the use of the ancient polemic to address current behavioral issues was a clear misapplication, even as it gave a little new life to the persisting questions around music and human response.[21]

If the principal objective of music was to arouse the affections, as Luther had it toward the beginning of the sixteenth century, composers from the latter part of the century surmised there must be a way of helping achieve that goal via compositional techniques. Spurred on by the humanistic interest in classical languages, they asked: Why not think of music in terms of rhetoric? For the ends of linguistic rhetoric and musical endeavors are the same—to teach, to move the affect, and to delight.[22] Answering their own question, these same composer/theorists concocted an encompassing system of musical devices meant to achieve rhetorical purposes, complete with nomenclature (in Greek of course).

In Germany, this trend, known as *musical rhetoric*, found warm reception, especially among those devoted to the importance of sounded gospel. Throughout the period, Lutheran musicians[23] penned important treatises on the subject, all of which demonstrated growing interest in the second part

20 David E. Cohen, "Notes, Scales, and Modes in the Earlier Middle Ages," in *Cambridge History of Western Music Theory*, ed. Thomas Christensen (Cambridge University Press, 2002), 333–336.

21 A 1533 treatise by Stephano Vanneo (1493–ca. 1540) contains a complete chart of the eight church modes and their impacts on humans (e.g., "The eighth, the last of all modes, affects all who hear it with joy, pleasure, and sweetness"). See Cristle Collins Judd, "Renaissance Modal Theory: Theoretical, Compositional, and Editorial Perspectives," in *Cambridge History of Western Music Theory*, ed. Thomas Christensen (Cambridge University Press, 2002), 375.

22 See Patrick McCreless, "Music and Rhetoric," in *Cambridge History of Western Music Theory*, ed. Thomas Christensen (Cambridge University Press, 2002), 851–867.

23 Most prominent among them are Johannes Lippius (1585–1612), Joachim Burmeister (1564–1629), and Christoph Bernhard (1628–1692).

of the rhetorical trinity: how effectively music moves someone. Given that the treatises were being written while the baroque style had already gained a foothold across the continent, what began as an outgrowth of Renaissance humanism easily blossomed in the garden of baroque aesthetics. For, as Claude Palisca writes, "from the last decades of the sixteenth century the arousal of the affections was considered the principal objective of poetry and music."[24]

Later iterations of these psychological outlooks guided the careers of giants such as George Frederick Handel, Georg Philipp Telemann, and Johann Sebastian Bach. But during their lifetimes other changes occurred that, while not relevant to Luther's views, were seismic with respect to emerging views of emotion popular in the nineteenth century, still in currency today and therefore worthy of mention.

In the 1730s and 1740s, a Hamburg theorist by the name of Johann Mattheson (1681–1764), himself a church musician and well versed in musical rhetoric, sensed the changing musical tastes of his age. It was clear to him that pure instrumental music was being liberated from vocal hegemony and that the sensitive, elegant French *galant* style was replacing traditional heady Germanic counterpoint. Enlightenment ideals that were emerging supported the trends he noted. Though always respecting his own teachers and august musical contemporaries, Mattheson increasingly found himself at odds with them. In his mind the business of devising musical experiences to teach, move, and delight was simply old-fashioned. Instead, the essential goal is well-shaped melody. In terms of classical rhetoric, he was advocating, indeed waging war, for the primacy of invention over elocution, a move that put the focus on the individual originating the musical event rather than on the success of its ability to arouse the affects.

Mattheson, though not a lone voice, published widely and was very influential. In short order the trends he articulated evolved further into what one author describes as "the shift from a mimetic to an expressive aesthetic."[25] In plain words, by the end of the eighteenth century, people understood that the function of music was less about teaching, moving, and delighting and rather more about being an avenue for the expression of one's emotions. Such changes fueled Western music for the next two centuries.

24 Claude V. Palisca, *Baroque Music* (Prentice-Hall, 1968), 4.

25 Meyer H. Abrams, *The Mirror and the Lamp* (Oxford University Press, 1953), 33.

While it may seem that we have traveled a distance from Luther's understanding of the *use* of music, our current location is quite close to his deliberations. All along, the issue has been affect, and it has in one way or another permeated the past discourse. Continuing the trajectory, it is time to see how Luther theologically thought of affect.

Impact of the Monastic Detour

Over the centuries the word *affect* generated a host of nuances, though throughout, traces of those early psychological theories remained broadly foundational. Perhaps the diffuse understandings of the word prompted Luther to avoid any attempt at explaining it to his readers, or maybe he had other related interests. Regardless, he did use the word. Anttila's well-considered opinion is that the word *affect* for Luther had two fundamental meanings.

On the one hand, Luther thought of affects (plural) as, what we might call today, emotions. So, for instance, the list of moods in PSI (3:6), subject to alteration via music, Luther describes as "human passions [Latin: *affectus*] by which men themselves are governed" (3:4). Luther then supplemented this more traditional understanding with another meaning. Anttila observes that the Reformer used the word *affect* (singular) to describe a person's overall posture with respect to God. For him this affect was "either love/faith or hatred/unbelief."[26]

But, Anttila argues, the word *affect* just didn't serve Luther's purposes well; instead he moved away from it and chose to address matters of human emotion with the word *heart*. Psychology was made to step aside to give way to a biblical image. Anttila explains:

> A recurrent word considering affectivity is "heart." Luther states in the *Large Catechism* that trust and faith of the heart makes both God and an idol. Accordingly, he states in *Lectures on Hebrews*, the law must be written in the heart. Luther's theology could well be labeled as "theology of the heart." Yet, there are some preconditions for such an interpretation. First, "heart" today refers simply to "feelings." This kind of understanding immediately makes Luther's theology narrower and renders Christian faith as a mere emotive attitude with no cognitive

26 Anttila, *Luther's Theology of Music*, 113.

> content. Luther also uses the word "heart" differently. Commenting on Ps. 51:10, "Create in me a clean heart, O God," Luther explains that the German word *Herz* stands for a number of Latin terms: soul (*anima*), mind (*intellectus*), will (*voluntas*), and emotion (*affectus*). It is therefore necessary to bear in mind that for Luther, as in Christian theology in general, the heart (*cor, Herz*) is the innermost being of a person as well as the source of thoughts, volitions, and feelings.[27]

In Luther's mind, a person's relationship with God has both a cognitive side and an affective or emotional side. Intellect and heart, and their sometimes tensive interrelationships, are persistent themes throughout Luther's career. The gospel is preached not just to convey information but also that it might awaken new courage and joy within the believer, providing, as it were, a taste of the resurrection.[28] As rigorous as he was in thinking through his theology, so adamant was he regarding the human, fleshly response to God's address. It would be hard to contest that his high regard for the heart and its importance to faith came from his engagement with the Psalter.

When he became a monk at the Erfurt Augustinian monastery in 1505, he immediately came under the impress of the daily rota of the prayer hours. Among other practices, that meant he regularly joined the communal voicing of psalms eight times a day because each of the hours (matins, lauds, prime, vespers, and so on) contained a portion of the Psalter. Like other monastic orders, the Franciscan course of psalmody featured a system in which all 150 psalms were spread over a week's worth of communal prayer.

The impact of this routine on the Reformer was immense. Even though other biblical writings were also voiced in these gatherings, the Psalter stood out because of its weekly repetition. Every monk voiced every psalm about fifty-six times a year. The words, the phrases, the rhetoric, and the tunes embedded themselves, becoming vehicles for thought, piety, and meditation. It would not take long before most of the Psalter was known "by heart." Some scholars believe that Luther continued to engage the prayer hours for the remainder of his life.[29]

27 Anttila, *Luther's Theology of Music*, 109–110.

28 Anttila, *Luther's Theology of Music*, 109–110.

29 Johannes Block, *Verstehen durch Musik: Das gesungene Wort in der Theologie: Ein hermeneutischer Beitrag zur Hymnologie am Beispiel Martin Luthers* (Francke, 2002), 91–92.

We have described the mode of psalm usage as "voiced," to emphasize the sonic aspect of the experience. But, of course, the psalms were no doubt sung, employing one or another version of the widely used psalm tones. The significance of that comes clear in a short preface that Luther wrote for the 1513 published version of his lecture notes on the psalms. There he penned words that one would not expect as introduction to classroom Bible study: "'I will sing with the spirit and I will sing with the mind also' (1 Cor. 14:15). To sing with the spirit is to sing with spiritual devotion and emotion. This is said in opposition to those who sing only with the flesh."[30] His encounter with the Psalter was so inextricably musical, apparently, that any serious consideration of its content had to proceed from musical delivery. For one thing, the mind receives a big assist if it engages musically, Luther maintains in his commentary on Psalm 4.

Referencing all the "heroic songs and triumphal hymns of the poets" in general but having in mind the psalms, he wrote, "For in all these the listless mind is sharpened and kindled, so that it may be alert and vigorous as it proceeds to the task. But when these are at the same time sung to artistic music, they kindle the mind more intensely and sharply."[31]

Yet a bland salute to music because of its ability to set the mind on fire says way too little about Luther's engagement with the Psalter. In his estimation the psalms embody an expansive range of affects or emotions that serve to provide a spiritual parlance for the diverse delights and struggles of a believer. Johannes Block writes that for Luther, the Psalter is a "school of affect";[32] it trains one in useful ways of feeling by offering a vocabulary of affect. Luther himself lauded the Psalter as a "fine, bright, pure mirror that will show you what Christendom is."[33] By that he intended to urge people of faith to look to the psalms for ways of constructing life's encounters. Luther looked to the psalms for a vocabulary of faithful feelings. If you want to see "the holy Christian church painted in living color and shape," go to the Psalter.[34]

One might consider the Psalter as a book of pastoral care, bearing the wisdom and experience of the greatest strugglers with / lovers of God: "What is the greatest thing in the Psalter but this earnest speaking amid these storm

30 LW 10:3.

31 LW 10:43.

32 Block, *Verstehen durch Musik*, 138.

33 Preface to the Psalter (1545/1528), LW 35:257.

34 LW 35:256.

winds of every kind? Where does one find finer words of joy than in the psalms of praise and thanksgiving? There you look into the hearts of all the saints, as into fair and pleasant gardens, yes, as into heaven itself."[35] On one occasion a person might engage the Psalter as a fair and pleasant garden, but at another instant one might just as easily discover it to be a place of raging storms. The expansive range of affect accommodates and welcomes every human heart. That is the blessed essence of the Psalter.

The Psalter is the blueprint for the heart: "A human heart is like a ship on a wild sea, driven by the storm winds from the four corners of the world. Here it is struck with fear and worry about impending disaster; there comes grief and sadness because of present evil. Here breathes a breeze of hope and of anticipated happiness; there blows security and joy in present blessings. These storm winds teach us to speak with earnestness, to open the heart and pour out what lies at the bottom of it."[36] The mirror of Christendom schools by way of its hospitable embrace.

But that's not the end of it. In order for the believer to tap into its resources, to become one with its affects, the Psalter needs to be not just voiced but sung. The full experience of its "auditory/affective" impact[37] cannot happen without music. "The psalms and music have been designed to arouse devotion,"[38] Luther wrote, commenting on Psalm 4. David composed this psalm, he says, "as something inciting, stirring, and inflaming, so that he might have something to arouse him to stir up the devotion and inclination of his heart, and in order that this might be done more sharply, he did it with musical instruments."[39]

And we also need to consider this: Because the ears, nose, and throat are interconnected, the act of singing results in hearing oneself from within, but it is also true, and in this context more significant, that one hears oneself from without because the ears receive the sound waves generated externally. Johannes Block has seized on this common sensation, urging his readers to recognize in it a fundamental Reformation principle that God's word comes *nos extra nos* (to us from outside of ourselves).[40] This is even more pronounced when one sings in the company of others. In Block's analysis, the sung psalm,

35 LW 35:255.
36 LW 35:255; TAL 6:209.
37 Block, *Verstehen durch Musik*, 129.
38 LW 10:42.
39 LW 10:43.
40 Block, *Verstehen durch Musik*, 123–124.

Figure 3.1. Luther's translation of the Psalter, 1528, title page

therefore, is no longer an object with the singer as subject but is rather the subject to which the singer reacts as object. Hence, the psalm as musical event arouses affect/emotion or moves the heart (however one wants to reckon the action) and thereby accesses the innermost being of a person, simultaneously serving as a mechanism by which both intellect and heart encounter God in God's word.

Luther enthusiastically and beneficially plugged into the centuries-old monastic engagement with the Psalter. In the same way, he also opened himself to the wisdom of forebears in the faith with respect to the Psalter's interpretation. Block has noted the influence of Athanasius (ca. 296–373) on Luther's prefaces to both the lecture notes on the Psalter (1513) and his second version of German translations (1528).[41] In a "letter" to Marcellinus, bishop of Rome 296–304, Alexandrian Archbishop Athanasius encouraged his colleague to more intensely engage the Psalter. The communiqué is less a letter and more a lengthy introduction to the Psalter. In it, Athanasius extols the psalms as prophetic witnesses to the Messiah (a theme Luther takes up in his own psalm lectures) and as a mirror wherein one sees oneself and one's soul. Moreover, the "Lord himself has ordained that the psalms be sung and recited to chant." To do this beautifully is the heart's desire and joy, Athanasius revels.[42]

Luther's deep regard for the Psalter was not born from a fresh sweep of the scriptures through evangelical eyewear. It was a product of his monastic experience, when he learned and then continued to use those hallowed practices of prayer that served the faithful for generations. He took with him the discipline learned. He trusted and honored his own formation, so convinced of its value and usefulness that he tried to find ways to let the Psalter become a force among all the people. To do so would require translations from the Hebrew into German, a task, as mentioned, he accomplished to eventual great acclaim. There was more he could do.

Nearly a fifth of the hymns he wrote are what one could loosely call paraphrases of psalms. Typically, these hymns begin with a key phrase from its antecedent psalm and then expand into an exposition that considers current

41 Block, *Verstehen durch Musik*, 75–76.

42 "Letter of St. Athanasius . . . to Marcellinus, Concerning the Psalms," translator unidentified and pages unnumbered, https://www.fisheaters.com/psalmsathanasiusletter.html, passim. A less readable translation of portions of this letter appears in James McKinnon, ed., *Music in Early Christian Literature* (Cambridge University Press, 1987), 52–53.

affairs while offering comforting and encouraging assurances. Notably, most of these eight psalm-inspired hymns date to the first few years of his life as a Reformer, when the monastic experience was still fresh in his memory. Some, such as "A Mighty Fortress Is Our God" (based on Ps. 46), have found widespread favor across the centuries.[43]

This discussion of the Psalter may seem proportionately oversized in this study of PSI. However, the enormity of its impact on Luther calls for this attention. He found in the psalms a vocabulary and welcoming place for faith. Additionally, the musical delivery of the psalms affirmed his presumptions about the affective power of music. Together, the text and music of the Psalter, bolstered by its regulated usage, came to be for him a kind of prototype for embracing music in general.

WHAT, THEN, IS MUSIC'S USE?

When Luther decided "to speak about the use of something so great" (PSI 3:1), he was not just responding to an imaginary inquiry regarding ways people use music. The impetus behind his pointed consideration of music's use is more profound than that, for he was writing, even here, from a theological world in which *use* (*usus* in Latin) was a technical term referring to the innate, ordained function or purpose of a thing, activity, or concept.

For example, Melanchthon, Luther's friend and colleague, addressed the "use" of the Lord's Supper in the *Apology of the Augsburg Confession*. There he wrote, "The sacrament was instituted in order that, as the outward form meets the eyes, it might move the heart to believe. . . . Such *use* of the sacrament, in which faith gives life to terrified hearts, is the New Testament worship, because the New Testament involves spiritual impulses: being put to death and being made alive. Christ instituted the sacrament for this *use* when he commanded, 'Do this in remembrance of me.'"[44]

The word became a favorite for the generation of Lutheran theologians following Luther, especially when they sought to articulate their understanding of the function of the law. Such attempts became contentious when disagreement arose over the "third use of the law," which some saw as the

---

43 For several versions and translations of the hymn, see *Evangelical Lutheran Worship* (Augsburg Fortress, 2006), nos. 503–505.

44 BC 270–271. Emphasis mine.

rule or guide for the Christian life. Attempting to bring peace to the situation in the *Formula of Concord,* authors began their discussion of the topic with these telling words about purpose and use: "The law has been given to people for three reasons."[45] "What's the use?" was a ubiquitous question in this conversation.

While he was not a major voice in these deliberations, Luther was well acquainted with Melanchthon's presentation since Luther was intimately involved with the preparation of the text for the 1531 publication of the *Apology.* While he never chose the word *use* in his own contributions to the Lutheran confessional writings, the notion of use as advanced by Melanchthon permeated his thinking. In the Large Catechism he cites the "usefulness of the Creed"[46] and later in the same work declares, "What God institutes and commands cannot be useless."[47]

A word far more to Luther's liking, as he writes about function and purpose, is *office*. In his own handling of law in the Smalcald Articles, he avers that "the foremost office or power of the law is that it reveals inherited sin and its fruits."[48] *Office* signals province, function, or even duty and encompasses the acts and operations expected of a person or thing. So to ask Luther's question another way: What are the acts and operations expected of this thing, this creature, we call music?

Let's be clear: This question is asked from within an aura of theological conviction; it is asked with full awareness of Luther's certainty about music's creatureliness. In his mind, music bears an innate purpose, intended and anointed by its creator, in a way similar to the intended and anointed purpose of a sacrament. Its office, the expected acts or operations flowing from it, is to stir and arouse human hearts in ways that lead to beneficial and pleasant ends. Music's office is to be the governess of human hearts.

The Holy Spirit is the grand exclamation point that affirms his assertions. Following the lead of his predecessors, he notes that the Spirit eagerly enrolls music to achieve her purposes of calling, gathering, and enlightening the whole Christian church. Two classic examples follow. Elisha, momentarily stymied in his prophetic work, summoned a musician whose playing stirred

---

45 BC 502.
46 BC 431.
47 BC 457.
48 BC 312.

up the "power of the Lord" within his heart, thereby enabling him to again clearly speak the word of the Lord (2 Kings 3:15). In a second example, Luther recalled the touching story of David's faithful care of Saul: When an evil spirit came upon him, David would take "the lyre and play it with his hand, and Saul would be relieved and feel better, and the evil spirit would depart from him" (1 Sam. 16:23). Resonating here are Luther's words "cheer the miserable, encourage the despairing" (PSI 3:6).

ECHOES AND QUESTIONS

The musical matters Luther addressed in this section of PSI are neither time-bound nor irrelevant. Subsequent developments and ever-changing contexts gave and give place for reinterpretation of his practices and persuasions. Below we address three of these matters.

First, it's impossible to avoid the similarities shared by all the leaders of the Reform movement. Such is the case when one compares Luther's Psalter-bent hymnic output with the huge and significant repertoires of metric psalmody issuing from the followers of John Calvin.

Second, the connection between music and emotion has remained a lively area for birthing a host of opinions and theories, most of them battlegrounds for pitting hunch against hunch. More recently, researchers from various disciplines have tried to address that topic in a more organized fashion. Just how music and emotion relate continues to summon great interest, still sometimes heated, because the relationship is endemic to issues of taste, cohort identity, and behavior.

Finally, recognition of music's ability to affect the innermost beings of people has in one instance translated into the helpful practice of music therapy. Taught now as a discipline in many higher education contexts, music therapy has an impressive record of success and has provided affirmation of what Luther proposed about music and affect.

In the Company of Others: Calvin on Psalmody

Any consideration of Luther's psalm-based hymns necessarily leads to a comparison of those hymns to the metrical psalmody that issued from the Reform movements of John Calvin (1509–1564). Calvin and Luther had much in common in this regard. A year before PSI, Calvin let his opinions concerning music for the assembly be known in his *Articles* of 1537: "Furthermore it is a thing most expedient for the edification of the church to sing some Psalms in the form of public prayers to God or sing His praises so that the hearts of all may be aroused and stimulated to make similar prayers and to render similar praise and thanks to God with a common love."[49]

For his entire career Calvin regarded the Psalter as essential if there was to be singing at all. This was no fanciful preference on his part. The psalms were essential because for Calvin, forms of worship are derived from the "ordinances of our Lord,"[50] which is to say that the scriptures provide what is needed for public prayer, namely the psalms. But equally important to his developing schema for public worship was the inner disposition of those who worship. Like Luther, Calvin desires in a very pastoral way that public and private prayer come with the involvement of one's heart. The theme runs through nearly every stage of his reflection on these matters. Because some in the Reform movement fostered assemblies that were just shy of absolute silence, Calvin, according to Charles Garside, asserts that "speaking and singing in . . . prayer are thus permissible only if they are, quite literally, heartfelt; they must be confined to serving that fundamental emotion."[51]

To meet Calvin's goals, he and his followers deemed it necessary to create a vernacular psalter in such a form that enabled people's musical participation. While Calvin's base of operation was Geneva, the first complete metrical psalter (1562) was in French, published by a consortium of printers with strong connections to Paris.[52] As Calvinism spread to other parts of Europe, psalters in other languages soon followed, giving rise to a multilingual collection of psalmody that carried the worshipful prayer not only of Calvin's followers but, because of its charm and usefulness, also of Lutherans and Anglicans.

Like Luther, Calvin knew from experience that music affected the human heart. For that reason, he reckoned singing to be useful in the assembly, for it aroused and stimulated human hearts. But for these purposes not just any

49 Charles Garside Jr., *The Origins of Calvin's Theology of Music* (American Philosophical Society, 1979), 7–8.

50 Garside, *Origins of Calvin's Theology*, 31.

51 Garside, *Origins of Calvin's Theology*, 8.

52 For a fuller account, see Waldo Selden Pratt, *The Music of the French Psalter of 1562* (AMS Press, 1966 [reprint of 1939 edition]), 18–24. For a review, in French and English, of more recent literature, see *Le Psautier de Genève, 1562–1865: Images commentées et essai de bibliographie* (Bibliothèque Publique et Universitaire de Genève, 1986).

old music would do. He distinguished between the kind of music envisioned for the psalms and that used for other purposes: "And thus there is a great difference between the music which one makes to entertain men at table and in their homes, and the psalms which are sung in the Church in the presence of God and His angels."[53]

What kind of music *did* he have in mind? In a preface to *The Form of Prayers and Ecclesiastical Songs* (1542), an order of worship he prepared for his followers in Geneva, Calvin comes closest to describing what kind of music should uniquely and ideally carry the burgeoning collections of metrical psalms. He wrote, "In truth we know from experience that song has great force and vigor to arouse and inflame the hearts of men to invoke and praise God with a more vehement and ardent zeal. There must always be concern that the song be neither light nor frivolous, but have gravity and majesty, as Saint Augustine says."[54] Calvin must have had some idea what "gravity" and "majesty" sounded like, though in the long run these two descriptors may not be the most significant aspect of his commentary. *That* he specified stylistic characteristics of music for the assembly laid the groundwork for others to subsequently establish categories of music that differentiate between music used in the assembly (sacred) and music for other activities (secular).

Similarities shared by Luther and Calvin come also with divergences. Calvin promoted psalms because of their scriptural origins and the strong apostolic witness to their value for the assembly. Luther found the psalms to possess a vocabulary of affect or emotion that carried existential spiritual experience, a feature that was only intensified with the addition of music, creating an ideal event that profoundly embodied everything he knew the word of God to be.

Both Luther and Calvin labored for vernacular translations of the psalms. While Luther offered his masterly German translation of the Psalter together with some psalm-based hymns that moved away from a literal version of the psalm, Calvin, on the other hand, prompted by his desire for sung prayer, engendered a flood of vernacular psalmody poetically fashioned in various meters. Metrical psalmody quickly became the solid musical core of Calvinist worship internationally and endeared itself to other non-Calvinist Christians across the world.

---

53 Garside, *Origins of Calvin's Theology*, 18–19.

54 Garside, *Origins of Calvin's Theology*, 32. Calvin does not indicate a source for his reference to Augustine.

Finally, while Luther's view of music as creature by nature included a resistance to stylistic canonizations,[55] Calvin, perhaps inadvertently, greased the skids for views of assembly music that were bent on marginalizing certain genres.

Music and Emotion

Does Luther's grasp of music's use (*usus*) have any bearing on how people today think about music? If one is not willing to dismiss his views on these matters as a knee-jerk adoption of popular beliefs of his time—this chapter representing such unwillingness—then one can explore whether his thoughts resonate with subsequent theories regarding the relationship of music and emotion.

Luther moved directly from music to feeling, from creature to observable experienced use. Subsequent generations showed some hesitancy in making such moves. The story is complex but worth a rehearsal. In retrospect, the ebb and flow of the musical influencers, those who carved out deeply held opinions on the matter, helped to becloud what seemed to the Reformer to be obvious, observable, and, above all, theological.

Earlier we traced the landscape of medieval psychology with its elaborate schemes of humors and affects, eventually landing on the doorstep of the world in which Handel and Bach lived. There was no question in their minds that music was somehow or another "affective," that is, intimately bound to emotion. Music for the shepherds, coming from the hands of both composers, and so-called rage arias make the point. We further noted how Bach's contemporary Johann Mattheson began in the late 1730s to advocate a retreat from heady counterpoint and, in contrast, champion expressive melody. When seeking to create such melodies, Mattheson advises, "In every melody, we must make the movement of feeling (if not more than one) the main purpose."[56]

55 In his comprehensive evaluation of Calvin on music, Oskar Söhngen concludes, "Calvin therefore rejected a musical unity between spiritual and secular [*wetlichen*] styles and fostered instead a singular churchly, sacral style." "Theologische Grundlagen der Kirchenmusik," in *Die Musik des evangelischen Gottesdienstes*, ed. Karl Ferdinand Müller et al. (Stauda, 1961), 46. Translation by the author.

56 As quoted by Eduard Hanslick, *On the Musically Beautiful*, trans. from the German by Lee Rothfarb and Christoph Landerer (Oxford University Press, 2018), 11. Hanslick identifies the source as *Der Vollkomm. Capellmeister* [1739], 143.

That's a step away from Bach and Handel, who probably accomplished that goal but wouldn't have thought it to be framed in such a straightforward way.

But students of theirs did. One of Bach's last students, Johann Philipp Kirnberger (1721–1783), proposed toward the end of his life that "a melodic phrase (theme) is a comprehensible sentence in the language of sentiments, which allows a sensitive listener to feel the emotional state that evoked it."[57] A new factor here is elevated attention to the musical delivery system of an emotion.

Gottfried Weber, an early nineteenth-century writer on music, provided Kirnberger's conjectures with clearer definition: "Music is the art of expressing sentiments by means of tones."[58] Weber, intentionally or not, more intensely looked to the composer as key for the successful, and artful, transmission of emotions. Weber's view resonated with others. In 1853 opera composer Fermo Bellini wrote, "Music is the art that expresses sentiments and passions by the means of sounds."[59]

These four sources are but a sampling of other such citations that Austrian music critic Eduard Hanslick (1825–1904) garnered in a very influential book titled *On the Musically Beautiful* (1854, with multiple revised editions through the end of the century).[60] Hanslick set himself to resist the trend represented by these authors. He raised doubts about whether music was in the business of feelings. His misapprehensions were not innocent; on the contrary, he openly denigrated the ideas and music of Franz Liszt, Richard Wagner, and their many disciples. Hanslick's critique caused what one might describe as a culture war, with Wagner and his disciples on one side and Johannes Brahms and Hanslick on the other. The conflict was widespread.

While allowing for something like emotion or feelings in a musical experience, Hanslick took umbrage with the trappings that accompanied Wagner's project, his unprotested priestly status, and Wagner's belief that a composer who expertly issues forth emotion can thereby penetrate the essence of all things and inhabit the emotional universe. The music critic had no use for such grandiosity.

57 As qtd. in Hanslick, *On the Musically Beautiful*, 12. Hanslick identifies the source as *Die Kunst des reines Satzes* [1779], 2:152.

58 As qtd. in Hanslick, *On the Musically Beautiful*, 13. Hanslick identifies the source as *Theorie der Tonsetzkunst*, 2nd ed. [1821], 1:15.

59 As qtd. in Hanslick, *On the Musically Beautiful*, 13. Hanslick identifies the source as *Manuale di Musica* (Ricordi, 1853).

60 See n. 56.

Instead, Hanslick attempted to grasp the larger picture: "With considerable agreement, the entire spectrum of human feelings has been considered the content of music because people believed to have found in feelings the opposite of conceptual certainty."[61] By returning to the rational aspects of music, Hanslick gave notice of where he was headed. He understood that his project was an aesthetic one, the search for beauty in music. Exploring the nature of beauty in music, he wrote, "It is a specifically musical beauty. By that we understand beauty that is independent and not in need of an external content, something that resides solely in the tones and their artistic connection. The meaningful relationships among intrinsically appealing sounds, their mutual concord and discord, their fleeting and coalescing, their soaring and subsiding—that is what arises in free forms before our intellectual contemplation and pleases as beautiful."[62]

Hanslick's views met with both affirmation and resistance, indicative of the many alternative, if not conflicting, understandings of the relationship between music and emotion that fueled music-making well into the twentieth century. Voices emerged along the way that were equally as influential as Hanslick's. For instance, in his 1939–40 lectures at Harvard, Igor Stravinsky took a strong stand against the trends modeled by Wagner and fostered by his followers. In their place Stravinsky advocated for order and discipline in music: "Insubordination boasts of just the opposite and does away with constraint in the ever-disappointed hope of finding in freedom the principle of strength. Instead, it finds in freedom only the arbitrariness of whim and the disorders of fancy. Thus, it loses every vestige of control, loses its bearings, and ends by demanding of music things outside its scope and competence. Do we not, in truth, ask the impossible of music when we expect it to express feelings to translate dramatic situations, even to imitate nature?"[63]

On the one hand, we have here a portion of a manifesto announcing new directions for musical composition; on the other hand, Stravinsky questions embedded views as to what music is essentially about and for. His confident linguistic style bolstered his stance, of course. Others advocated for similar ways forward via less academically framed means. Paul Hindemith (1895–1963) championed order, discipline, and craft as goals in musical composition,

---

61 Hanslick, *On the Musically Beautiful*, 14–15.

62 Hanslick, *On the Musically Beautiful*, 40.

63 Igor Stravinsky, *Poetics of Music in the Form of Six Lessons* (Vintage Books, 1956), 79.

thereby sidelining whatever reactions might ensue. His textbook on the subject gained wide usage among an entire generation of composers born in the 1920s and 1930s.[64] Hindemith and Stravinsky, among many others, made it possible to think about music apart from its supposed vocation to communicate and arouse emotion.

Those involved in providing music for the Christian assembly during these years bobbed along on the ebb and flow of the music/emotion currents. In some circles a growing disdain for feeling as a factor in assembly music pushed some into being ardent campaigners for styles that reflected the primacy of craft, order, and discipline. Those would be adequate words to describe the German church musical revival and some post–World War II American ventures of the same nature. When pop styles found a more established foothold in the church's musical endeavors, some welcomed these newer trends as legitimizing the marriage of religious feeling and music. Still others feared that a firm embrace of unvarnished religious feeling would dangerously lead to the trance-like practices of music common among Pentecostals and other free-church groups.

The long arc of church musical history here reveals a grand mix of views on the relationship between emotion and music, not much different from the history of music as a whole. For various reasons, few looked to Luther for support despite the fact that on first blush it looks like he could be counted on to go to bat for feeling/emotion as the primary purpose of music.

A closer look suggests a more nuanced view. Luther fostered music's unique ability to restore psychological equilibrium (hence his examples) and thereby assist in God's ways of inhabiting the heart. The post-Bach crowd, on the other hand, gradually came to essentially bracket out divine initiatives in favor of noticing and adoring the skills of the music creator who maneuvered the emotional landscape. Such attitudinal tendencies were what irked both Hanslick and Stravinsky.

Questions surrounding emotion and music eventually evaporated due to an expanding interest in aesthetics, the quest for critiquing art and identifying beauty. Given that nearly everyone had their own views on musical feelings, it became way more fun, as it were, to spar over beauty. As such interests gained popularity during the mid-nineteenth century, fewer and fewer individuals asked how emotion and music worked or even what an emotion is. That is,

---

64 Paul Hindemith, *The Craft of Musical Composition*, trans. Arthur Mendel (Associated Music Publishers, 1942).

until recently. In the past several decades, social scientists, specifically psychologists of music, have systematically set themselves to address a panoply of issues regarding music and emotion. They begin by acknowledging the existence of divergent views: "It is probably true that most people experience music—somehow, somewhere—every day of their lives, often with an accompanying affective response of some sort; . . . music arouses strong emotions in people, and they want to know why. However, despite the ubiquity of emotional responses to music, it seems that, for a long time, such reactions have defied psychological explanation."[65]

Two spark plugs in the contemporary version of this project are Patrik Juslin (Uppsala University) and John A. Sloboda (University of Keele, UK). Together they have coedited several anthologies; perhaps the one of greatest value to the uninitiated reader is *Music and Emotion*.[66] It contains twenty chapters by twenty-one authors from a variety of disciplines. Multidisciplinary perspectives provide one with a sense of how complicated the endeavor is and how pervasive its implications in human lives.

Some might dismiss their efforts as pointless, useless research into what everyone knows to be true from the outset. The authors are not of that mind. They point out, instead, that three domains flourish today simply because they have accepted as true the deep connections between music and emotion. These domains are the treatment and diagnosis of performance anxiety, film music, and music therapy.

Wherever one puts oneself on the music/emotion spectrum, the findings of these researchers, individually and collectively, provide ways to articulate the relationship of music and emotion without resorting to opinion-peddling. Years of diffuse research have yielded what can now be regarded as reliable presumptions, some of which are quite realistic about where matters currently stand.

For instance, most recognize a lack of consensus with respect to what music is for,[67] a factor that reflects continuing differences regarding music and emotion. On a more positive note, self-reporting in a plethora of testing

---

65 Patrik N. Juslin and John A. Sloboda, "Music and Emotion: Introduction," in *Music and Emotion: Theory and Research*, ed. Patrik N. Juslin and John A. Sloboda (Oxford University Press, 2001). 3.

66 See n. 65.

67 Isabelle Peretz, "Listen to the Brain: A Biological Perspective on Musical Emotions," in *Music and Emotion: Theory and Research*, ed. Patrik N. Juslin and John A. Sloboda (Oxford University Press, 2001), 127.

situations indicates that most people experience emotional responses to music. These can range from a sense of stable mood, to a transient feeling, or to a feeling of pleasure.[68] Further, research has repeatedly verified that people are "deeply implicated"[69] as active enablers (partners) when they experience emotional responses to music, often approaching music new to them with the expectation of becoming emotionally involved.[70]

Finally, many of these writers hold it to be certain that the connection between music and emotion is not direct but rather the result of an interdependence of factors associated with the context.[71] Luther himself might be an example here, for his reflections on music's use were rooted in his experience of the monastic community, particularly its prayer life.

Results of this rather recent research help the contemporary listener make better sense of the musical encounter in general and of Luther's understanding of music's use in particular. The many perspectives brought to bear on this research invite new ways of thinking about all kinds of music. Within the scope of this book, there are several of these views that seem especially pertinent, offering tools for articulating the musical experiences that people of faith treasure.

Juslin and Sloboda propose that, like an umbrella, sources for emotional responses to musical happenings consist broadly of two kinds. *Intrinsic* sources "are those that are non-arbitrarily embedded in structural characteristics of the music."[72] *Extrinsic* sources "include both *iconic* sources, which come about through some formal resemblance between a musical structure and some event carrying emotional tone, and *associative* sources, which are premised on arbitrary and contingent relationships between the music being experienced and a range of non-musical factors, which also carry emotional

---

68 John A. Sloboda and Patrik N. Juslin, "Psychological Perspectives on Music and Emotion," in *Music and Emotion: Theory and Research*, ed. Patrik N. Juslin and John A. Sloboda (Oxford University Press, 2001), 84.

69 Sloboda and Juslin, "Psychological Perspectives," 98.

70 Tia DeNora, "Aesthetic Agency and Musical Practice: New Directions in the Sociology of Music and Emotion," in *Music and Emotion: Theory and Research*, ed. Patrik N. Juslin and John A. Sloboda (Oxford University Press, 2001), 169.

71 John A. Sloboda and Susan A. O'Neill, "Emotions in Everyday Listening to Music," in *Music and Emotion: Theory and Research*, ed. Patrik N. Juslin and John A. Sloboda (Oxford University Press, 2001), 415.

72 John A. Sloboda and Patrick N. Juslin, "Music and Emotion: Commentary," in *Music and Emotion: Theory and Research*, ed. Patrik N. Juslin and John A. Sloboda (Oxford University Press, 2001), 459.

messages of their own."[73] *Intrinsic sources* for emotional responses to music are difficult to delineate, much less explain. That is one of the reasons Hanslick's critique, though earnest and perhaps a timely counterpart to the likes of Liszt and Wagner, came across as a complaint from a grouchy critic. Leonard B. Meyer changed all of that.

With his 1956 book, *Emotion and Meaning in Music*,[74] Leonard B. Meyer managed to avoid opinionated generalizations and to steer a course less divisive. Anchored in psychological theory of the time, Meyer set out to draw thoughtful connections between emotion and innate characteristics of music. Nicholas Cook and Nicola Dibben summarized Meyer's work this way: "In essence, Meyer sees music as setting up expectations in the listener (or, to put it another way, implications in the music) which are in general fulfilled or realized, but often only after postponement or apparent diversion. It is here that Meyer's approach to emotion comes in. The basic principle, which Meyer also drew from contemporary psychology, is that emotion or affect is aroused when a tendency to respond is arrested or inhibited."[75] The expectations Meyer refers to can be structural or harmonic. A simple example of the former occurs, for instance, when the final strophe of a hymn is interrupted by an unexpected interlude whose purpose is not immediately clear. The experience intensifies if the accompanist then decides to change the key of the hymn at this juncture.

Harmonic expectations are more common. Beethoven adeptly developed moments of harmonic ambiguity, offering the possibilities of several differing destinations. Tendencies therefore were inhibited. The concluding chord of Bach's monumental St. Matthew Passion is not fully resolved on the downbeat but is arrested by an appoggiatura in some of the accompanying instruments, an unsettling moment for a first-time listener.

Extrinsic sources for emotional responses to music include performance style, iconic factors, and social overtones. With respect to performance style, Meyer observes, "In music and speech pure tone, true pitch, exact intonation, perfect harmony, right rhythm, even touch and precise time play a relatively small role. . . . The unlimited resources for vocal and instrumental expression

73 Sloboda and Juslin, "Music and Emotion: Commentary," 459.

74 Leonard B. Meyer, *Emotion and Meaning in Music* (University of Chicago Press, 1956).

75 Nicholas Cook and Nicola Dibben, "Musicological Approaches to Emotion," in *Music and Emotion: Theory and Research*, ed. Patrik N. Juslin and John A. Sloboda (Oxford University Press, 2001), 57.

lie in artistic deviation from the pure, the true, the exact, the perfect, the rigid, the even, and the precise. This deviation from the exact is on the whole, the medium for the creation of beauty—for the conveying of emotion."[76]

How a performer consistently uses "artistic deviation" is what provides a sense of personal style and what affords stature. The latter emerges from comparatively large-scale, positive responses to the emotion(s) activated. In pop styles that is assumed. When it comes to the music of the Christian assembly, musical leaders in deference to their vocation tend to step back from such deviations so that the purposes of the gathering are not subverted. Divergent circumstances make this a tricky matter, especially because the deviation mechanisms described here are central to musical practice.

Iconic sources are extrinsic sources that "come about through some formal resemblance between a musical structure and some event carrying emotional tone."[77] Singers of hymns have personal histories with certain hymns, with various sinews connecting a hymn to memorable spiritual experiences. The mature leader of the church's song recognizes that fact, knowing that perceived violations of such relationships can lead to bitter feelings. In a broader view, the issue worthy of attention here is that emotional responses to music often are generated by nonmusical factors—but very powerful ones, nonetheless. Such responses can be negative but are often positive and integrative because they release and render manageable deep-seated aspects of an individual's spirituality.

A third extrinsic source for emotional response to music resides in music's *social dimensions*. For over a half century, sociologists, including the larger-than-life figures of Max Weber and Theodor Adorno, have probed the ways by which music interacts with culture. Theories came and went, but recognition of strong ties endured. Tia DeNora thinks the focus has changed, in that there is now an "attempt to conceive of music as a potentially dynamic medium, to consider what music may 'do' in, to, and for the social relations in which it is embedded."[78] It is now possible, DeNora continues, "to conceptualize music as a device for the constitution of emotive action in and across a range of social settings."[79]

76 Meyer, *Emotion and Meaning in Music*, 202.
77 Sloboda and Juslin, "Music and Emotion: Commentary," 459.
78 DeNora, "Aesthetic Agency," 164.
79 DeNora, "Aesthetic Agency," 165.

No more noticeable is such a view than in the ways music works for adolescents. Massive music fests and concerts, in which the lines between performers and listeners blur, offer emotional release that gives vent to fears, hopes, confusions, and joys, which in turn are felt and experienced socially. The music serves as a symbolic boundary for a status group, in effect providing an identity that in some cases can last far beyond the completion of adolescence.

The takeaway of these observations is that musical events, also those within worship assemblies, are weighted with social dimensions and that these social dynamics are a source for emotive response. In some cases, communal interests may be the major factor driving an emotive response. Assembly music, too, interacts with assembly culture, even as it serves as a "device for the constitution of emotive action."[80] Sorting out all of this can be challenging but probably necessary. The South African protest songs (e.g., "Freedom Is Coming") originated as musical icons for the intertwining of politics, community, life, and faith. Whether they can offer the same kind of emotive response apart from the intertwined factors that prompted them is complicated by the social dynamics present in any musical event and especially prominent in these protest songs.

The renewed study of emotion and music has more to offer than has been summarized above. Some authors await further research on how the brain reacts to music, implying caution over some of the accounts made popular decades ago. Obviously, some aspects of this new research into music and emotion are less related to the issues Luther has placed before us. One exception deserves special notice and serves as a coda to the chapter.

Music as Therapy

If it's true that there is no agreement on how music and emotion are connected, it's just as true to observe that music therapists thrive on the conviction that music is a means for helping some people more effectively manage their emotional lives. Recognized as an academic discipline for over fifty years, music therapy (or musical therapy) has flourished internationally in the last few decades in Europe, North America, Australia, New Zealand, and South Africa.[81] Universities both large and small feature music therapy

80 DeNora, "Aesthetic Agency," 165.

81 Leslie Bunt and Mercédès Pavlicevic, "Music and Emotion: Perspectives from Music Therapy," in *Music and Emotion: Theory and Research*, ed. Patrik N. Juslin and John A. Sloboda (Oxford University Press, 2001), 181.

degree programs, forming graduates who work in specialized grade schools, hospitals, prisons, centers for the aging, and hospices.

Music therapy rests on the assumption that music can assist in restoring or improving mental and physical health because of its ability to elicit emotional response. But the strategy is more nuanced in that, contrary to other forms of therapy, music therapy seeks not recollections or hopes but rather relationships experienced in the present moment. The existential nature of a musical event is central. From that mindset, therapists select and rotate situations of listening, performing, or composing. The last has gained a strong place among the discipline's tools, employing exercises aimed at group musical improvisation or fashioning lyrics, all meant to welcome musical expression no matter the expertise.

Stories of healing and wholeness abound. For some drug users the reduction in anxiety via the musical experience proved to be enough to lessen addictive patterns. Music therapists have proven themselves effective in easing difficulties related to pediatric oncology and have offered alternative paths for working with autistic children.

When Luther wrote about the use of music, he noted its affect-ive power by citing the examples of Saul, David, and Elisha. To be sure, other authorities had referred to these biblical vignettes when trying to buoy the case for music. Luther, however, saw them as instances in which music brought about healing and integration of mind and spirit. His impulses regarding music, emotion, and integration are in our own time supported by the thriving discipline of music therapy.

Therein lies an opportunity for people of faith. For those committed to serving those who are needy in mind, body, and spirit, the governess of human hearts stands ready to assist in ways waiting to be conceived. Tools may already be available. Assembly music does more than provide tunes to accompany words. Its use for healing and integrating individuals and communities is in the process of being revealed.

CHAPTER FOUR

Sweet Melody Bonded to Words

The Way to Every Human Heart

Having explained what music is and of what its observable use consists, Luther comes one step closer to successfully ushering his readings into the collection of music that brought PSI into existence. In this chapter, we consider human speech as an element of the domain of sound, venture into Luther's understanding of the word of God, examine some of the dynamics of melody bonded to words, and conclude with some echoes of his construct in relationship to contemporary music practices.

But first, to grasp the full impact of what Luther proposes in the fourth section of PSI, it will be helpful to note a few nuances and cues residing in the Latin version of this short segment.

TEXT MATTERS: WORDS AND SWEET MELODY

Luther clearly has in mind two distinct residents of the domain of sound but found it difficult to find the right identifiers. In a paragraph of about 120 words, he employed three different terms to describe what we have chosen to call *melody* and another three terms to reference what we have chosen to call *words*. Each of these six words crisscrosses others in its group but also carries subtle nuances that offer clarity.

In 4.2 Luther uses two different words to designate the "melody" factor of the *bond of melody and words* he so intensely explicated in these lines. *Melody* is first expressed with *vox* (*voice, tone of speaking, sound of speaker or instrument, language, dialect*), while in the same few lines he chose *musica* (*music, series of tones*) to describe the bond. He used both terms again, but then in 4.3, as he came closer to completing his argument, Luther reached for *melodiae* (*melody*), adding—not incidentally, one can argue—the adjective *suavi* (*sweet*).

In 4.2 and 4.3 the "text" dimension is identified by *sermo* (*discourse, conversation, speech, spoken words, dialect*), while in 4.3 and 4.4 Luther uses *verbo* (*word, talk, expression*) for this factor. Then in 4.4, Luther reached for *loquelae* (*a speaking or a language*) to express the bond of melody and words.

The bond of words and melody, of melody and words, is the distinct and particular gift music brings to the human being. Humans alone praise God with both words *and* song. It is no little matter that the church primarily coupled music with the words of scripture, especially the psalms and biblical canticles. Luther takes it further, declaring that the wedding of God's word with "sweet music" delivers Christ into the human heart, drives home the good and saving news of the gospel by means of sounded proclamation. As he puts it, "The voice is the soul of the word."[1]

Editor's note: Here the author's manuscript ends. In his book proposal, the following additional topics are named for consideration in chapter 4:

Excursus on Luther's theology of the Word
God's word as *nos extra nos* (Word addresses us from outside of ourselves)
Speech and the universal domain of sound
Unity of intellect and heart

See chapter 7 of this volume for the author's additional writing on Luther's theology of God's word.

1 Latin: "*cum vox sit anima verbi,*" WA 5:379. Qtd. in Johannes Block, *Verstehen durch Musik: Das gesungene Wort in der Theologie: Ein hermeneutischer Beitrag zur Hymnologie am Beispiel Martin Luthers* (Francke, 2002), 83, n. 84.

CHAPTER FIVE

The Divine Dance

An Invitation to Become Created Cocreators

Editor's note: The annotated table of contents in the author's book proposal contains this description and list of topics for chapter 5, which deals with section 5 of PSI.

Finally, Luther gets around to part-music, which for him occurred frequently at table after dinner. He knew about the art of composition and the creative energies involved with such a practice. Consequently, he had definite notions about the musical works of others, elsewhere holding up the talent of Josquin des Prez, in whose music he found the freedom that mirrors the gospel. When a composer does well, the outcome is like a divine dance, and that cooperation of created gift and human skill brings music to its full intended capacity.

Tables are for tasting: food as well as the Wisdom of God
Role of human co-creators: *musica artificialis* in context
Law and gospel in musical composition
Music as event
Divine dance at table: music in its full capacity

CHAPTER SIX

What Does This Mean?

Editor's note: The annotated table of contents in the author's book proposal contains this description and list of topics for chapter 6.

This chapter means to forefront relevant outcomes and implications of Luther's arguments. I have listed some examples but expect that others will arise as I write or that these will be reframed. The examples may appear to be tame but are probably not. When Luther writes about music as created gift, he means all music. So *all* music is a gift of God, meaning that the making of categories, especially for liturgical purposes, skews his understanding. Of course, taking his radical view yields its own set of difficulties, which are not to be ignored, nor are they to be made palatable by other rules and guidelines. In a way, this study makes daily practice more difficult but also more faithful, and that's the point.

The author sketched out for chapter 6 this list of questions for church music practitioners to consider, titled "Tunings," growing out of the study of Luther's theological views on music:

TUNINGS

1. If all music is *creatura*, created gift of God, can all music be used in assembly? What other factors are at work?
2. Does reading Luther's views suggest that a distinction between "sacred" and "secular" music be jettisoned?

3. If God is present in the whole musical world, what does this mean for church musicians' engagement with that broader world?
4. In what ways might you be involved in the misuse of music?
5. Do specialized music-maker groups work contrary to assembly? How can their rightful place be framed and integrated?
6. If you are a keyboard leader, what are some possible temptations of making music by yourself?
7. What challenges does the prevalence of recorded music present to your ministry?
8. Do you comprehend laughter and weeping as part of your ministry?
9. How does the practice of music unveil notions of community in your setting? Are those notions compatible with what Christian assembly is?
10. In what ways does your musical ministry broadcast an assertion that God is at work with a new creation?
11. Do you join the musical event expecting to apprehend the divine dance?
12. If music itself is revelatory, if the musician is not merely enhancing or decorating the gospel but integrally participating in the sounded proclamation and helping others to do the same, what are the implications for your vocation?

PART II

Selected Writings on Martin Luther, Music, and the Arts

CHAPTER SEVEN

Pole-Vaulting the Word into the Heart

God, Luther, and Your Voice

Reformation Lectures 1

Popular lore has it that Martin Luther advocated for the use of tavern tunes for the emerging repertoire of Reformation hymnody. The suggestion is plausible, if only because there is widespread agreement that Luther loved music (all kinds of music), had some things to say about it, and was anxious to engage all people in his discovery of the gospel. Plausibility, however, runs the danger of promoting hearsay, like that adage about Luther using tavern tunes. It got its start from a misunderstanding of the term *bar form*, which is a musical template (AAB) in widespread use at the time, frequently showing up in Luther's own hymns.

Other shared knowledge about Luther's musical inclinations is more felicitous and has inspired Luther's followers in many ways, though sometimes confounding them at the same time. In a very short sketch from 1530, titled Περὶ τῆς μουσικῆς (Concerning music), Luther wrote, "After theology I give the first place to music."[1] He doesn't bother to elucidate the phrase because the pagelong piece is a sketch, maybe an outline for an intended longer essay.[2] Nevertheless, the phrase leaves us puzzled. Should we understand it as a simple outburst of enthusiasm from an amateur music lover? Or was he attempting to

---

1 WA 30/2:696. For a list of similar expressions from Luther's writings and conversations, see Robin A. Leaver, *Luther's Liturgical Music: Principles and Implications* (Fortress Press, 2017), 373, n. 1.

2 Leaver, *Luther's Liturgical Music*, 86.

rank the staples of medieval education by awarding music the place of honor among the arts of the *trivium* (grammar, logic, rhetoric) and the *quadrivium* (arithmetic, geometry, astronomy, music) after, of course, recognizing theology as the "queen of the sciences"? Or are we heirs to a rather profound insight here that opens up a way to theologically think about music, given the fact that Luther, by often employing "word" and "theology" to designate the gospel, may have meant to say, "After the *gospel* I give the first place to music"?[3] For the moment I suspect the right answer might contain some or all of those possibilities.

Luther's pithy observation continues to arrest our attention, gaining legs when it (sometimes) is introduced as evidence amid squabbles between pastors and church musicians. Thus, it is more than anniversary jubilation that draws us again to what the Wittenberg Reformer thought about music and worship. He offers a thought or two that can address some of our most pressing issues, such as questions surrounding musical style, the shrinking role of people's music in worship, or how and why the church supports music.

POLE-VAULTING THE WORD (*IM SCHWANG*)

However, to benefit from Luther's wisdom and theological insights regarding these matters, we have to tum away from his oft-quoted observations on music and probe the breadth of his emerging grasp of the gospel. Although well versed in medieval treatises on music, and in part shaped by the views of their authors, Luther hinges his valuation of music to his understanding of the gospel. It is there, then, that we necessarily turn first, not only because of the benefits it might have for embracing music's role in today's church but also because periodic reviews of what he had to say about the gospel can and should nudge the preachers of our time to rethink what and how they preach.

In 1524, toward the end of a year in which he crafted the majority of his hymns, Luther wrote a short preface for a grandiose (at the time) project titled *Geystlich gesangk Buchleyn* (Spiritual song booklet, sometimes called

3 See, for example, Luther's 1530 letter to the composer Ludwig Senfl: "The prophets did not make use of any art except music . . . so that they held theology and music most tightly connected." LW 49:428.

the "Walter Choirbook" or the "Wittenberg Hymnal"),[4] a collection of thirty-eight motets using vernacular hymns, some by Luther, together with five Latin motets, in multivoiced settings by Johann Walter. In it the Reformer reveals a fundamental building block of his understanding of gospel and music: "Therefore I, too, in order to make a start and to give an incentive to those who can do better, have with the help of others compiled several hymns, so that the holy gospel which now by the grace of God has risen anew may be noised and spread abroad."[5] The latter part of that translation has been smoothed over a little; more literally, it might read, "So that the holy gospel which now by the grace of God has risen anew may be noised and oscillated," or—if I may—"noised and *pole-vaulted*."[6] In any case, Luther's view of gospel always calls out its auditory essence—the gospel is a sounding; it is something in motion. It travels on the wings of sound waves, we might say today.

He fixates on this auditory, motile dimension not because music dominates his thinking process. Rather, theology leads the way. In the preface to his translation of the New Testament, Luther explains how *gospel*, or *euangelium*, is a Greek word that means *good message*, *good tidings* [*gute Geschrei*], or "a good report, which one sings and tells with gladness." So that readers are clear about what he means by *gospel*, he submits that "the gospel of God or New Testament is a good story and report, sounded forth into all the world by the apostles, telling of a true David who strove with sin, death, and the devil, and overcame them, and thereby rescued all those who were captive in sin, afflicted with death, and overpowered by the devil. Without any merit of their own he made them righteous, gave them life, and saved them, so that they were given peace and brought back to God. For this they sing, and thank and praise God, and are glad forever."[7]

His fascination with gospel content linked to outward expression comes close to a preoccupation. In a "simple" preface to a 1522 collection of Advent and Christmas sermons, Luther offers this shorter summary of *gospel*: "There you have it. The gospel is a story about Christ, God's and David's Son, who died and was raised and is established as Lord. This is the gospel in a nutshell."[8]

4 Facsimile of 1525 edition: Johann Walter, *Das geistliche Gesangbüchlein "Chorgesangbuch,"* ed. Walter Blankenburg (Bärenreiter, 1979).

5 LW 53:316.

6 German: "*zu treyben und nun schwanck zu bringen*."

7 LW 35:358. See the full text also in TAL 6:413–422.

8 A Brief Instruction on What to Look For and Expect in the Gospels, LW 35:118; TAL 2:29.

Perhaps trying to bring some perspective to a growing fascination with printed text, he went on to observe that "the gospel should really not be something written, but a spoken word. . . . This is why Christ himself did not write anything but only spoke."[9]

For people whose lives would be unimaginable without e-commerce and e-readers and for whom basic communication occurs through the tapping of screens, it may be difficult to imagine why anyone might still want to fuss over an antiquated style of information transmission. To be sure, Luther was much closer to a time when all reading was oral, even if that meant reading to oneself. Yet his instincts may also have a bearing on our time. His marvel at sounded word aligns with some contemporary studies of orality, meaning, and communication.[10] As cozy as Luther's insights may be with other subsequent study, he was driven to his embrace of event-ualized gospel by theological principle. The incarnation of Christ demanded that the gospel be received *im Schwang*. Miikka Anttila writes that for Luther, "The Word is not a theological category of revelation, but a living reality that comprehends our whole existence. In singing, liturgy, prayer, preaching, and reading aloud, the Word is 'in motion' (*im Schwang*)."[11]

SINGEN UND SAGEN—SINGING AND SPEAKING

Being auditory, by nature in motion (*im Schwang*), the gospel is an event. When the Reformer finds himself required to explain how that event comes into being, he frequently reaches out to a favorite expression: *singen und sagen*, that is, singing and speaking. Typical is this excerpt from his preface to the Babst Hymnal: "For God has cheered our hearts and minds through his dear Son, whom he gave for us to redeem us from sin, death, and the devil. He who believes this earnestly cannot be quiet about it. But he must gladly and willingly sing and speak about it so that others also may come and hear it. And whoever does not want to sing and speak about it shows that he does not

9 LW 35:123; TAL 2:36.

10 So, for instance, Walter Ong has proposed that cultures built around writing tend to foster inwardness and a focus on individuality; see *Orality and Literacy: The Technologizing of the World* (Routledge, 2002).

11 Miikka Anttila, *Luther's Theology of Music: Spiritual Beauty and Pleasure* (de Gruyter, 2013), 133.

IIII.

Ein Kinderlied/auff die Weihenachten/vom Kindlein Jheſu/Aus dem ij. Cap. des Euangelij S. Lucas gezogen ꝛc.

D. Mart. Luther.

von himel hoch da kom ich her, ich bringe euch gute newe mehr, Der guten mehr bring ich ſo viel, dauon ich ſingen vnd ſagen wil.

VOn Himel hoch da kom ich her/

Figure 7.1. "Von himel hoch" in Babst Gesangbuch, 1545

believe and that he does not belong under the new and joyful testament."[12] Were it not for the difficulties related to translation, contemporary singers of Luther's hymns would know *singen und sagen* better than they likely do. In its original German, the first stanza of "From heaven above" reads:

Von Himel hoch da kom ich her	From heaven high I come here
ich bring euch gute newe Mehr	I bring you good new tidings
der guten Mehr bring ich so viel	of good tidings I bring so much
davon ich singen und sagen wil.[13]	thereof I will sing and speak.

Singen und sagen—singing and speaking, and in that order. In every instance Luther reaches for the phrase, the order of the words remains the same. For him the unique combination of verbs served to image the very nature of the gospel both in form (as auditory event) and in content. At the heart of the gospel is the incarnation: human and divine natures in one being, flesh and spirit appealing to the hearts and minds of humans through singing and speaking. The couplet emerges as a way to describe how humans properly and authentically respond to the mystery called incarnation.

The phrase also resonates with the Reformer's views on the essence of music. In the preface he wrote for Georg Rhau's 1538 collection of fifty-two motets, titled *Symphoniae iucundae*, Luther comes closest to presenting a systematic treatise on what he believed music to be, paralleling in many ways the medieval manuals he apparently had studied.

Early in this relatively lengthy project, he proposes that "you will find that music was impressed on or created with every single creature, one and all,"[14] further noting that nothing is without sound or harmony. In support of that claim, he cites musical events of four different kinds. First, there are the sounds made in the air when something passes through it quickly; then there are the sounds of creatures, especially the songs of birds; then, third, there is the human voice as it speaks, laughs, and weeps; and finally, there is art music—composed or performed music, also called "artificial music" (*musica*

12 LW 53:332. The last sentence in German: "*Wer aber nicht davon singen und sagen wil / das ist ein zeichen / das ers nicht gleubet / und nicht ins new fröliche Testament.*" The name of Valentin Babst (or Bapst), the Leipzig printer of this hymnal (*Geystliche Lieder*, 1545), has long been associated with its numerous printings and editions.

13 WA 35:459. Literal translation by the author.

14 PSI 1:6. See p. 19 in this volume.

artificiales). Singing and speaking thus are linked by the world of sound, or as Anttila is bold to say, "Music is not derived from spoken language, but . . . *speech is a species of music*."[15]

Singen und sagen, singing and speaking: Wasn't that still happening in the sixteenth-century Western church? What was Luther's problem?

He was well aware that the word was being sounded, musically too, and knew that priests were preaching, even in the vernacular. The problem, as he saw it, was that the people were *not hearing the gospel*. There were at least two reasons for that. One had to do with the limited use of the vernacular. Even though some priests preached in German, their sermons occurred apart from the mass, so connections to the mass lectionary and to the table were blurred.

Second, an unbalanced focus on the saints, a complicated penitential system, and a plethora of liturgical accretions provided so many distractions that when the gospel had a chance to be heard, it was drowned out by diversions.

Simply sounding the word was not enough for Luther. Nor was it sufficient to garner intellectual assent to the content and relevance of the gospel. Under the rubric of *singen und sagen*, the mere sounding of jargon, a string of pleasantries, or assurances amid setbacks do not qualify as gospel, even though they may accomplish something of the *sagen* business. To achieve gospel event, more is needed, Luther would say.

The gospel must be heard. Something of the "true David who strove with sin, death and the devil" must be said in a way that reaches both the mind *and* the heart of a person. In the preface to his New Testament translation Luther makes this quite clear: "To know [Christ's] works and the things that happened to him is not yet to know the true gospel. . . . [There is] knowledge of the gospel . . . only when the voice comes that says, 'Christ is your own, with his life, teaching, works, death, resurrection, and all that he is, has, does, and can do.'"[16]

Full involvement in the gospel event occurs when the word is pole-vaulted into the heart of an individual. The voice does not address an audience in general. It addresses an individual, expecting not indifference but joyful embrace. Luther makes this clear by means of a rather colorful analogy in his commentary on First Peter: "The word is a divine and eternal power. For even though the voice or speaking quickly disappears, the kernel remains, that is, the meaning, the truth that the voice contained. It's like when I place into my

15 Anttila, *Luther's Theology of Music*, 91. Emphasis Anttila's.
16 LW 35:361; TAL 6:420.

mouth a glass that contains wine and then drink it. I can't very well push the glass down my throat with it. So also is the word that the voice brings. It goes down into the heart and remains lively while the voice continues outwardly but then fades away."[17]

THE WAY TO THE HEART

During the past several decades, Finnish Lutheran theologians have been exploring the notion of *heart* within the Reformer's writings. Representing the musical side of such scholarship, Miikka Anttila notes that for Luther, *heart* does not simply stand for feelings, as many would automatically assume. Luther rather uses the word to designate "the innermost being of a person as well as the source of thoughts, volitions, and feelings."[18] Thus, while feelings are surely included in his understanding of *heart*, the word is far more inclusive, even taking on some characteristics of *mind*.

A word equally important to Luther is *affect*, the Latin-derived term generally meaning *emotion* and serving him as a synonym for *heart*. In his *Lectures on Hebrews* (1518), Anttila reports, Luther makes a distinction between intellect and affect when contemplating the target and aim of the word of God: "For . . . 'mind' and 'heart' . . . mean intellect and affect. For to be in the mind means to be understood; to be in the heart means to be loved."[19]

Luther exhibits a noticeable consistency in his ever-expanding understanding of the gospel. It is first an auditory event, *im Schwang*. Second, for gospel *to* become good news, it must be heard; it must reach one's heart.

At this point we beneficially return to Περὶ τῆς μουσικῆς (Concerning music), his short sketch on music. There he wrote, "I love music / . . . For it creates joyful hearts / For it drives away the devil / . . . For it creates innocent delight."[20] The brevity of this document makes all the more remarkable the attention he directs to the *affects* music generates: joyful hearts, delight, and release from anything that sidetracks the gospel. Years later he amplified such amazement over music's affects by writing in the preface to *Symphoniae*

17 Epistel S. Petri gepredigt und ausgelegt (1523), WA 12:300. Cited in Johannes Block, *Verstehen durch Musik: Das gesungene Wort in der Theologie* (Francke, 2002), 108. Translation by the author.

18 Anttila, *Luther's Theology of Music*, 109–110.

19 Anttila, *Luther's Theology of Music*, 108. Citation is LW 29:198.

20 See n. 1, p. 105.

iucundae, "[Music] is a mistress and governess of those human emotions. . . . Who could number all these masters of the human heart, namely, the emotions, inclinations, and affections that impel men to evil or good?—what more effective means than music could you find? The Holy Ghost . . . honors her as an instrument for his proper work."[21]

Having come to recognize these powerful, salutary outcomes of music, Luther without hesitation concludes that it is not only a gift of God but the *best* gift of God, for it assists—no, that is probably too weak—it is the vehicle by which the gospel reaches the heart. Word (as in word of God) and music are equal partners, Anttila hears Luther say, for they both (1) are outward physical phenomena, (2) are aural and auditory, (3) move human emotions, and (4) serve as tools against evil desire.[22] If one takes Luther seriously, Anttila goes on to say, the partnership is not optional, nor can one introduce a substitute mate: "Music promotes theological understanding, and it can move the affect better than words alone. The Word needs and uses music in order to establish and nourish faith."[23]

Central to Luther's valuation of *singen und sagen* is his lifelong interaction with the Psalter. For over five years before he began his lectures on the psalms and for years thereafter, he actively engaged in the monastic prayer life. That meant weekly trips through the entire Psalter with the psalms sprinkled over the eight daily prayer times. While medieval habits of *reading* the psalms and lessons continued here and there, Luther, like his spiritual forebears, encountered the Psalter as musical entity. His manifest skill at and knowledge of the chant formulas were byproducts of this daily practice. Like many before him, Luther experienced the psalms as sung word of God.

He treasured the Psalter for other reasons. In the psalms he discovered a full palette of emotions that schooled one in living an unsuppressed yet faithful life while providing a vehicle for conveying the breadth and depth of divine mercy. For him the Psalter was not just a catalog of spiritual feelings but also home for the human heart. He pressed in his own time to have it replace the popular but exaggerated stories about the saints. Introducing the psalms, he wrote, "For here we find not only what one or two saints have done, but what has been done by the one who is the very head of all saints. We also find what all the saints still do—such as the attitude they take toward

21 LW 53:323.

22 Anttila, *Luther's Theology of Music*, 97.

23 Anttila, *Luther's Theology of Music*, 136.

God, toward friends and enemies, and the way they conduct themselves in all dangers and sufferings."[24]

His own intense experience with the psalms led Luther to see the Psalter as the place where the heart is given airtime, as it were; it *is* the book of all saints: "Everyone, in whatever situation that person may be, finds in the psalms words that fit [one's] case or situation—that suit [one] as if they were put there just for [that person's] sake, so that [one] could not put it better, or find better words or wish for better."[25] True to his interaction with the psalms in daily prayer and to the long interpretative tradition of the church, beginning already with the four evangelists, Luther viewed Christ as the "door to the psalms,"[26] claiming that the Psalter "promises Christ's death and resurrection."[27]

It is worth recalling that Luther's exuberance for the Psalter derives both from its panoply of affects and from its customary musical embodiment. Both of those characteristics qualify the psalms as a vehicle for God's most intimate reach into the heart. Commenting on Psalm 100, Luther wrote, "To sing is to confess and praise God with hilarity [*cum hylaritate*] and to find in God kindness and joy, because God is just in judgment, because God fights for us and is merciful, and because God administers good things."[28]

Singing the psalms, then, creates an opportunity for God's word to reach us from outside of ourselves, offering comprehension through text and providing an open door to our hearts through affect-laden phrase and music by which God nourishes God's unity with us and ours with God. Through music the word of God is pole-vaulted into the hearts of the faithful.

WHAT DOES THIS MEAN?

Everyone who has read or studied Luther's Small Catechism knows what comes next: "What does this mean?" I venture three broad observations:

---

24 Preface to the Psalter (1528/1545), TAL 6:207. See also LW 35:254.

25 TAL 6:210; LW 35:256.

26 Block, *Verstehen durch Musik*, 96.

27 TAL 6:207; LW 35:254.

28 Psalmvorlesung, WA 4:132. Translation by the author.

1. To quote Luther again, "The church is a mouth-house."[29] We will do well by taking more seriously the power of the sounded word in our liturgies. That would include among pastors a deeper respect for our callings to proclaim the gospel; among all of us a commitment to work at hearing the gospel in this noisy world of ours; and among church musicians an esteem for God's sung word as a "personal-life stage" (as Johannes Block describes it)[30] on which each individual through singing engages one's being, heart, and mind, relationally with God and with others. In other words, singing is of the essence of the church.
2. Luther's love for the Psalter should be received by us as a nudge and inducement to explore anew the riches of its sentiments. This means seizing every opportunity to utilize psalms in our services of holy communion, morning prayer, and evening prayer and in moments of meditation or prayer in other settings. Moreover, we will do well by ceasing to speak the psalms as if they were merely readings and learn how to sing them, whether that be publicly or privately. In a culture that reduces the life of the heart to screen taps that call forth emojis or channel anger via social media bullying, the Psalter offers a welcoming home where the faithful can deal with their emotions in God's presence.
3. Because singing vaults the word of God to the heart, music brings motion or movement to the gospel event, evidenced by the joy that God's word generates. Joy for Luther is not a psychological state or an intellectual awakening but is, in its own incarnational way, something that spreads quickly to limbs, eyes, and mouth. Singing, together with its twin, dancing, is the home of faith and its barometer. Let us then do all in our power to teach the young to sing, to challenge judgments made about any individual's vocal skills, and to sing and dance God's word into the hearts of God's beloved.

29 German: "*Darumb ist die kirch eyn mundhawß, nit eyn fedderhawß.*" Adventspostille (1522), WA 10/1, 2:48.

30 Block, *Verstehen durch Musik*, 212: "*lebenspersönlichen Bühne. Gesang und Person stehen in hermeneutischer Korrelation.*"

CHAPTER EIGHT

What Do You Do with the "Braying of Donkeys"?

Luther on Re-Forming Worship

Reformation Lectures 2

WITTENBERG WORSHIP WARS

We begin with a story of some rather tense days from the latter part of 1521 in the city of Wittenberg. One of the reasons Luther posted the Ninety-Five Theses on October 31, 1517, was to initiate debate over the issues he raised in that document. Such debates or public discussions were not unusual and served to disseminate ideas, gain clarity about issues, and perhaps bring about change of mind or practice.

Luther was successful. During the next months and years, he debated all over Germany. At Heidelberg in 1518, his fellow Augustinians gave him opportunity to publicly declare his theology of the cross. In Augsburg he faced off in 1518 with the papal legate, Cardinal Cajetan, while some months later, in 1519, he confronted the noted Catholic theologian Johann Eck in Leipzig. Each debate seemed to generate the need to up the ante in terms of his opponent or investigator. Patience grew thin in Rome, so in 1520 Pope Leo X served notice to Luther that he was banned from the church. His response, famously, was to throw the so-called Bull into a fire that was started to burn books of his opponents.

Ecclesiastical procedures to contain the audacious monk were failing. On April 17, 1521, he was summoned to appear before Emperor Charles V in

Worms. It was at this meeting that he was requested to recant his writings, to which he made his famous reply that sparked new levels of controversy, commitment, and perhaps audacity too. Debate is what he got, together with animosity from his anxious opponents and growing fear from his supporters concerning his safety.

Elector Frederick the Wise, sympathizer and friend of Luther since 1518, arranged after the conclusion of the inquisition at Worms to have Luther "abducted." He eventually ended up at the Wartburg castle outside of Eisenach on May 4, 1521. It is there that Luther completed the translation of the New Testament into German as well as an impressive number of other writings, representing a burst of energy that assisted him in coalescing his theological thinking around insights that would serve him for the rest of his career.

Meanwhile, back in Wittenberg, restlessness was brewing. Luther once commented that the city "was on the edge of civilization,"[1] its site perhaps encouraging behavior with low levels of civility. But the city did have a university, founded in 1502, and it was there that Luther began his teaching career in 1513. Among his colleagues there were Philipp Melanchthon, who began teaching there in 1518, and Andreas von Bodenstein von Karlstadt (ca. 1477–1541), who had joined the faculty in 1505.

All Saints Church, also called the Castle Church, where Luther posted the theses, served also as the university church and as the court chapel of the elector. Elector Frederick the Wise had an interest in showcasing worship in his chapel and therefore liberally supported the personnel who arranged for and delivered elaborate liturgical events. They were organized as the All Saints Foundation, together numbering more than eighty-five people, among them canons, vicars, and musicians including singers young and old.[2] Luther's colleague Karlstadt was an erstwhile member of that group, no doubt at a time when his views were more in line with the group's prevailing sympathies. Members were, after all, interested in perpetuating the rather comfortable life they had, and so as a foundation they maintained a strong adherence to Rome.

Luther's cause, however, was gaining support in Wittenberg. In August 1521, a few months after his sequestering at the Wartburg, Luther wrote to his friend Philipp Melanchthon, indicating that on returning to Wittenberg

1 Hans Schwarz, *True Faith in the True God: An Introduction to Luther's Life and Thought*, rev. ed. (Fortress Press, 2015), 15.

2 See Robin A. Leaver, *The Whole Church Sings: Congregational Singing in Luther's Wittenberg* (Eerdmans, 2017), 37.

he wanted to make changes in the liturgy that would more closely reflect the experience of the upper room. The press of all the debates and accompanying theological work had prevented him from giving much thought to what his theological breakthroughs would mean in terms of practice. Here he was not only out of sync with Karlstadt but also at odds with him because the latter had been itching for some time to get things moving. Melanchthon, in whom Luther had much trust, was hesitant to take sides and so tried to let matters unfold naturally, hoping for a common strategic way forward. Developing circumstances, however, eliminated any possibility of finding out what Luther might have done on his return.

In October 1521 Karlstadt took matters into his own hands and petitioned Elector Frederick to initiate reforms in the churches of Wittenberg. Word spread quickly among the populace, and members of the All Saints Foundation became increasingly agitated, fearing for their own futures. Karlstadt pressed on nevertheless and elicited support from the various Wittenberg clienteles. Beginning in December, liturgies were reportedly "disrupted," indicating that Karlstadt had somehow ignited a kind of mob behavior to advance his agenda.[3]

On Christmas Eve worship attendees disclosed that a priest had been intimidated and that in a scuffle some lamps had been knocked over. The next morning in a packed church, Karlstadt revealed the extent of the changes he had in mind. He presided at the mass dressed in street clothes, preached in German, omitted the required eucharistic prayer, and in its place shouted out the words of institution (otherwise normally whispered),[4] ignored the elevation of the consecrated elements, and distributed the sacrament in both kinds, placing the bread in the hands of the people.[5]

Word of Karlstadt's actions quickly reached Luther. He had been hoping that, after an incognito visit by Luther to Wittenberg earlier in the month, Melanchthon would steer a different course to worship reform. Instead, Melanchthon appealed to Elector Frederick to bring back Luther from the

3 Leaver, *The Whole Church Sings*, 38–39.

4 Since the late Middle Ages, possibly earlier, it was customary that the priest speak the eucharistic prayer, or canon, in a soft voice—both to underline the belief that the words were Christ's and to make acoustical space for the private prayers of the people. See Joseph Jungmann, *The Mass of the Roman Rite: Its Origins and Development*, trans. Francis Brunner (Benzinger, 1955), 2:204.

5 This was particularly egregious since prevailing piety dictated that human hands should not defile the consecrated bread. See Jungmann, *Mass of the Roman Rite*, 2:208–209.

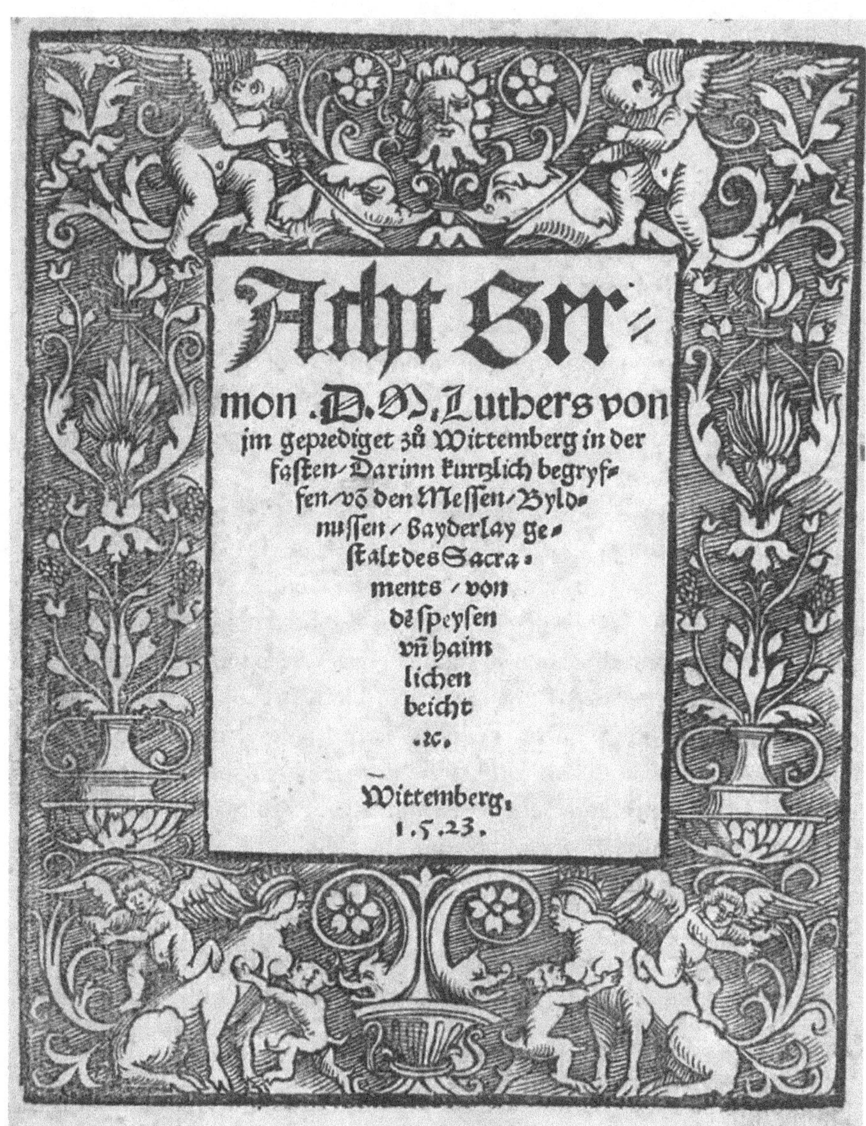
Acht Ser=
mon .D.M. Luthers von
jm geprediget zů Wittemberg in der
fasten/ Darinn kurtzlich begryf=
fen/ vō den Messen/ Byld=
nussen/ Bayderlay ge=
stalt des Sacra=
ments / von
dē speysen
vñ haim
lichen
beicht
.ꝛc.

Wittemberg.
1.5.23.

Figure 8.1. *Eight Sermons*, March 9–16, 1522, title page

Wartburg castle. The elector reluctantly agreed but only after waiting several weeks. In early March 1522, Luther returned and, beginning on March 9, the first Sunday of Lent, delivered his famous "Eight Sermons at Wittenberg," a series of sermons on eight consecutive days.[6]

Adding to the intensity of discord, the town council earlier in the year 1522 had approved the changes Karlstadt had proposed and then authorized the removal of images from the churches. From all indications the radical changes introduced by Karlstadt had little or no traction, but his actions hardened conflicting views of how to put theology into action. Feelings ran deep, exhibited by the drastic progression, in some instances, of the removal of images into the destruction of images.

THE BIGGER STORY

In truth, Luther was no pacifying agent when it came to worship reform. Over several decades, he employed a rhetoric that could easily have been understood by the impatient rabble-rousers as outright encouragement. In 1520 he wrote that we "must . . . put aside whatever has been added to [the sacrament's] original simple institution: such things as vestments, ornaments, chants, prayers, organs, candles, and the whole pageantry of outward things."[7] Years later he still complained about the "clamor of monks and nuns and priests . . . who do it like a donkey, only for the sake of the belly."[8]

Just before Karlstadt initiated his Christmas 1521 reforms in Wittenberg, Luther penned a document titled *The Misuse of the Mass*, by means of which he reflected a maturing comprehension of sacramental theology. Unaware of the drama unfolding in Wittenberg as he was writing this treatise, he unwittingly fanned the flames from miles away when he described worship there as so much "bawling and bellowing."[9] The words are *plürren* and *brullen*, each meaning approximately the same: *blabber, brawl, bray, howl, roar*—words often used to describe the sound of a donkey.

---

6 Abdel Ross Wentz, introduction to Receiving Both Kinds in the Sacrament (1522), LW 36:233–235. These sermons are also known as the Invocabit Sermons (Latin name for Lent 1) and are available at LW 51:67–97.

7 The Babylonian Captivity of the Church, LW 36:36; TAL 3:39.

8 On the Councils and the Church, LW 41:164.

9 LW 36:226.

Two years later, in a self-described conciliatory tone, Luther introduced his Latin Mass, an outline for a reformed order of mass, by taking aim at "vestments, vessels, candles, and palls, organs and all the music, and . . . images."[10] His rhetoric sounds mercilessly radical and has consequently been heard over the centuries as a call to dismantle things liturgical.

No wonder, then, that the populace in Wittenberg so easily marched with Karlstadt. Though most people were likely oblivious to his publishing ventures, Karlstadt did release a "Disputation on Gregorian Chant" just months before his Christmas experiments. Therein he claimed that chant put a distance between the mind and God and that "deacons roar throughout the churches."[11] Roaring was in the air, apparently.

In fact, it seems to have been a rather common critical assessment of singing from the time, even among loyalists to Rome. In 1543 Bishop Friderick Nausea Blancicampianus of Vienna sent his suggestions for discussion at the Council of Trent, noting that cathedral canons would rather roar than sing in the choir.[12] It makes one wonder what was going on. Based on the evidence that interpretation of chant notation mutated over the centuries, one theory points to a vocal effect produced by ostentatious separation of repeated pitches (like a late-medieval technique called *hocket*), perhaps tainted by personalities seeking recognition rather than service. In any event, numerous comments point to a strong element of theater in the delivery of the sacred repertoire, and many took exception.

Nevertheless, it's doubtful that with his persistent deprecations Luther was simply adding his voice to a growing consensus regarding musical delivery. For him, musical matters usually came up within a larger context encompassing the totality of sacramental practice. Indeed, one might suggest that for him the "braying of donkeys" and "roaring" are catchall phrases meant to identify things, practices, or people that impede, derail, or betray the purpose of the liturgical event. Karlstadt (let's be gracious here) may have been prompted by similar motivations. Yet the two Wittenbergers advocated two different courses of action.

Convinced that theological breakthroughs necessitated action, Karlstadt took his trimming knife to the mass order and then introduced changes that in

10 LW 53:22.

11 Charles Garside Jr., *Zwingli and the Arts* (Yale University Press, 1966), 29.

12 Robert F. Hayburn, *Papal Legislation on Sacred Music 95 A.D. to 1977 A.D.* (Liturgical Press, 1979), 26.

his mind rightfully responded to the liturgical practices impeding, derailing, and betraying true purposes of the mass. Addressing the problem required street clothes, shouted words of institution, curtailed music, offering the chalice to everyone, and placing the bread in the hands of the communicants.

Obviously perturbed by the reports of what happened under Karlstadt's direction, Luther responded not with angry outbursts (though he did indirectly refer to Karlstadt as the devil)[13] but with a pastoral sensitivity that suffuses several contemporaneous writings. In part three of *The Misuse of the Mass*, written before the uproar in Wittenberg, he called out the continuing failure of priests to honor the commandments of God, a sign, he noted, of a priesthood unworthy to preside at mass. He then explained that he was devastated not so much by their behavior but because "they were ravenous wolves instead of shepherds."[14] Consequently, "they mislead and ruin the people."[15]

Having been brought back from the Wartburg to help restore peace, Luther showed his pastoral heart more openly in the eight sermons he delivered in early Lent 1522: "Why will you not in this respect also serve those who are weak in faith and abstain from your liberty, particularly since it does not help you if you do it, nor harm you if you do not do it. Therefore no new practices should be introduced, unless the gospel has first been thoroughly preached and understood."[16]

Eager to stay on subject, he authored a small book on worship reform intended for a wider audience, titled *Receiving Both Kinds in the Sacrament*.[17] The topic reflects the breadth and depth of concern Karlstadt's method of communion distribution must have generated. After a short introduction, Luther lays out ten steps the churches in Wittenberg need to take on the way to translating theory into action. The very first step is "to let the old practice continue."[18] He goes on, "Let the mass be celebrated with consecrated vestments, with chants and all the usual ceremonies, in Latin, recognizing

13 "We must expect that some of those who are now the spearheads of our movement will fall, be it Luther or someone else. When we fight with Satan, it is no mere academic disputation." LW 51:238.

14 LW 36:209.

15 LW 36:209.

16 LW 51:90.

17 LW 36:237–267.

18 LW 36:254.

the fact that these are merely external matters which do not endanger the consciences of people."[19]

In subsequent steps he urges that the words of the sacrament be preached to the people, confident that once they have heard the gospel, they will learn also what to desire in the Lord's Supper. He is adamant that in all things the law of love must prevail. In matters potentially less disturbing to the people, such as monks marrying and leaving their orders or the cessation of private masses, Luther feels no need to slow down sudden changes. He does, however, advise punishment for those who have destroyed images, another sign of his pastoral concern, in this case for those who had deep attachment to iconic likenesses.

"Until the gospel is preached and understood," he proclaimed from the pulpit, let the old practices continue. Aware of his own slow process of reaching a gospel-centered grasp of the mass, Luther not only expected the same from his fellow priests, monks, and believers but also saw harm in moving too quickly or unwisely. Moreover, he remained convinced that even though many of the accretions to the mass did get in the way of returning to the heart of sacrament, he was committed to let them continue for the sake of the faithful, until they were able to hear and "understand" the gospel.

When might that be? Clearly, as if lifting a ban, Luther declares it was time a little more than a year later. Until then he set himself to maintain an outlook somewhere between patience with the people and advocating change, between care for those who were weak and disdain for derailing practices. In 1523, however, Luther attested that "since there is hope now that the hearts of many have been enlightened and strengthened by the grace of God, . . . we must dare something in the name of Christ."[20] What Luther dared now after more than a year is his design of an evangelical mass, *Formula missae et communionis pro ecclesia Wittembergensi* (An order of mass and communion for the church at Wittenberg). He wrote with hesitation, still fearing "for the weak in faith, who cannot suddenly exchange an old and accustomed order of worship for a new and unusual one."[21] He fervently wished to avoid being counted among worship reformers the likes of which are "fickle and fastidious spirits who rush in like unclean swine

19 LW 36:254.
20 LW 53:19.
21 LW 53:19.

without faith or reason, and who delight only in novelty and tire of it as quickly, when it has worn off."[22]

At this point Luther feared that he would unleash an epidemic of attempts to overhaul the Latin rite. One can sense a certain hesitancy behind every recommendation. Because his intent was to offer only an outline of the mass with commentary, he sought to head off idiosyncratic elaborations of his work by calling for common efforts in this regard. Then he counsels, "It is not now nor ever has been our intention to abolish the liturgical service of God completely, but rather to purify the one that is now in use from the wretched accretions which corrupt it and to point out an evangelical use."[23]

The donkey business of wretched accretions with its braying and roaring now has a countering voice. Even as Luther dared something in the name of Christ, we dare something as well—rejecting, first of all, any temptation to enshrine his suggestions and recommendations as if they had shelf life for all time. Responding to his wisdom in these matters, we can dare to find equally behind Luther's liturgical proposals and his reactions to Karlstadt's ill-conceived project in Wittenberg some fundamental inclinations that can guide our everyday decisions regarding assembly practice.

FUNDAMENTALS FOR RESPONDING TO CONTEMPORARY BRAYING

The Wittenberg disturbances caused Luther to react in two different ways: (1) He sought to restore order in the city's churches, and (2) he offered his advice on shaping a new evangelical mass. From his restoration efforts, we can derive three fundamentals:

1. Let the formation of liturgy serve all the faithful. Luther's pastoral personality carried the day as he constantly kept in mind those who were slower to grasp the gospel and discouraged new practices that were meant to please their creators rather than to assist all to receive the gospel.
2. Let the primary goal of the assembly be to preach the gospel and have it understood. It isn't enough to simply say the gospel, to

22 LW 53:19.
23 LW 53:20.

mouth words the mind knows to be such. The gospel needs to be heard, understood, and received in the heart by an individual. Both preaching and understanding receive equal emphasis here. Presence at mass is insufficient, even if the words are in the vernacular. People must be helped to grasp the redemption being given in word and sacrament; indeed, he writes that the communicants should be able to explain why it is that they come to the table. Achievements of this kind are to precede the reforming of liturgy.

3. As much as possible, strive for consensus. Luther desired in 1523 that whatever might come of liturgical reform should represent a common effort. He disdained those who made changes on their own and thereby gave rise to sects. Such behavior caused offense among the people and hindered their growth in the gospel.

From his proposals on reforming the mass, we can sense much about how he approached matters of worship, here (somewhat arbitrarily) settling on three recommendations that remain pertinent:

1. Restore to the people the language for expressing the feelings of faith. Use of the Psalter at mass had been reduced to selected verses contained in the introit and gradual texts, both sung by the choir. Luther prefers instead to have the entire psalm sung in place of the truncated introit and with that reveals his personal love of the psalms as well as his conviction that the psalms profoundly give voice to human feelings.
2. Trust the word of God and test the lectionary. Luther's understanding of the lively interplay of Word enfleshed / the written word / the preached word / the gospel permeates nearly all his theological adventures, but it is especially poignant when he takes up matters of preaching and scriptural texts. He considers lectionary revision to be necessary because the citations in use fail to serve the gospel. His prevailing crusade to get the gospel heard is always worth emulating, including care for the texts chosen to most clearly convey the gospel.
3. Less tedium and more *Te Deum*. When weighing the benefits of retaining gradual texts of more than two verses, the Reformer chose to eliminate them because, he writes, "they quench the spirit of the

> faithful with tedium."[24] Sing them at home, he advises those who hold them dear. Elsewhere he wishes with all his heart for more vernacular songs, worthy to be sung in the church of God. True and robust praise by all God's people is to be sought and encouraged.

Broadly speaking, contemporary braying in liturgical practice happens in a variety of ways. It might consist of a now meaningless local habit whose origin is unknown but whose place is firmly entrenched; it might be an accretion that skews the purposes of the liturgy; it might be neglect of an important element; it might be an underlying lack of insight about what's happening; it might be unresolved differences regarding desired outcomes of the assembly; it might be the failure to comprehend the mechanisms of the liturgy itself; it might be the neglect of music. It might be all those things.

In preparation for this address, I wrote a friend (who is a bishop) to express my intentions for this part of the paper and to ask if the bishop notices "brayings" while on ecclesial visits. The bishop's experience is more extensive than my own. Within an hour I received a lengthy list that included things like having to crawl under a screen to preside at holy communion; lack of preparation/rehearsal by worship leaders; neglect of psalmody; a tendency to ignore valid avenues for shortening liturgical structure; and theologically questionable, improvised eucharistic prayers. In a subsequent communication, I heard annoyance about worship environments that seduce people to look at a screen while said bishop is preaching from an ambo a few feet away.

If someone were to choose just one of these observations as an exemplary playing field on which to engage Luther, the tyranny of technology easily qualifies. Projecting lectors and preachers on screens in most venues dilutes the potency of the word proclaimed, and thereby enfleshed, by introducing a medium that interrupts body-to-body interaction. Even though Luther would support and explore the latest in communication technology, such as the printing press, he would, I believe, advocate for trusting proclaimed gospel in the gathered community without such aids. The choice to project as an answer to some perceived "braying" may be flawed in that the real braying may be a failure to train readers or the failure of preachers to understand their calling as one of getting the gospel heard.

24 Order of Mass, LW 53:24.

Despite complications, contemporary "brayings" need to be addressed, but to do so always draws us back to Luther's practice of pastoral care. Above all we do well to commit with Luther to purify our assembly routines, not recklessly to abolish practice, even though purification may in some instances require just that. To live in this charged space between being bound on the one hand and being free on the other is to live the baptized life. That is never easy, but it is our calling.

CHAPTER NINE

Hailing the New Creation

Singing as a Mark of the Church

Reformation Lectures 3

The title of this presentation is a quote from a well-loved hymn. Songwriter Robert Lowry penned the phrase within a stanza leading to these words: "How can I keep from singing?"[1] "My life flows on in endless song, above earth's lamentation," he began. "I catch the sweet, though far-off hymn that *hails a new creation*." He hears an echo from the future, if there is such a thing, an auditory trace from the end time when all peoples come to the Holy City, the New Jerusalem, where God is its light and the Lamb its lamp (Rev. 21). In a mysterious way, Lowry is trying to say, the church has already checked in there. So, churched by baptism, he asks himself, "How can I keep from singing?" His implied answer is the answer of all the baptized: "I can't."

The second lecture in this series and this one are in fact about singing—singing in church. In the first lecture, "Pole-Vaulting the Word," the goal was to probe Luther's profound valuation of music as partner with the gospel. Luther bids us to embrace singing as a theological act. Here we will continue to consider singing, specifically—and music, generally—from a theological perspective by briefly thinking about it as a mark of the church. Then, moving to a historical perspective, we will see how the sixteenth-century church

1 Robert Lowry, "My Life Flows On in Endless Song," in *Evangelical Lutheran Worship* (Augsburg Fortress, 2006), no. 763. Lowry was a nineteenth-century Baptist pastor and academic who reportedly wrote more than one thousand hymn texts and tunes.

My Life Flows On in Endless Song

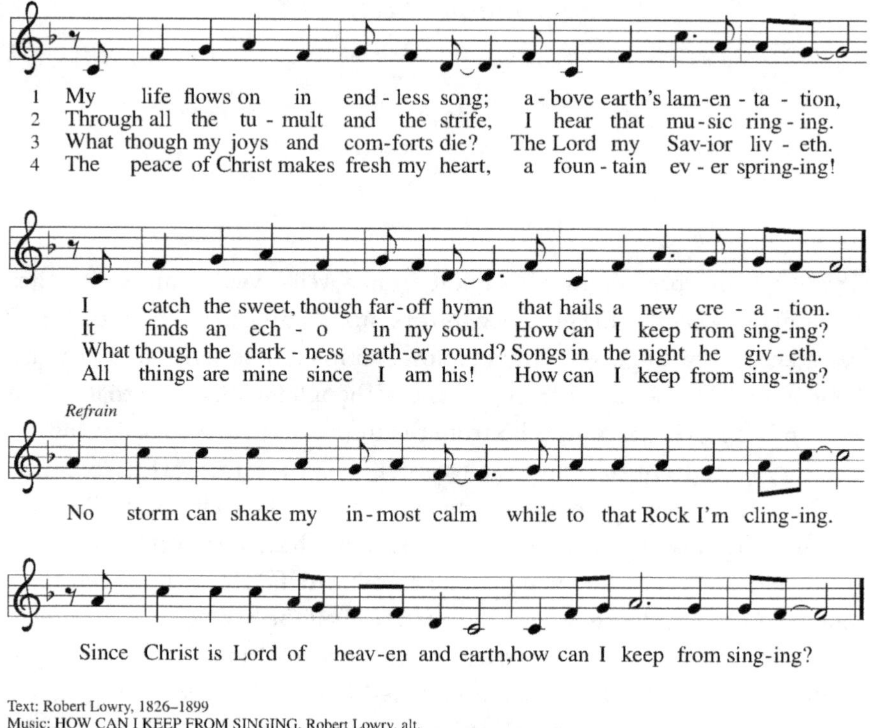

Figure 9.1. "My Life Flows On in Endless Song," Robert Lowry, 1869

of the Reformer came to manifest that marking, and finally we will consider singing from a sociological perspective.

INTERNET CHURCH SHOPPING VS. SIXTEENTH-CENTURY REALITY

When the urge arises, Millennials and their next of kin, Generation Z, often find church via social media. It may seem distasteful to relegate the Christian assembly to a level shared with carry-out pizza, but this trend is here to stay, particularly in urban areas. For enlightenment and fun, I recently googled "Christian church Pilsen" (Pilsen being a neighborhood adjacent to my own) and came up with a list of the "Best 10 Churches near Pilsen, Chicago, IL." The rating of "best" seemingly derives from the numbers and kinds of reviews supplied by the abovementioned cohort groups who have used the site. Factors that generated positive reviews included "holiness of space," a "priest who shook everyone's hand as they left," and the "added plus of a Zumba class after services." Not mentioned were the questions for which these factors served as answers. You can reconstruct those questions as well as I, and we would probably agree that our guesses come close to genuine concerns these cohort groups raise as they wrestle with finding the spiritual in their lives.

In this search process, the seekers and we take for granted the possibility of choice. Only two from my list of ten churches were of the same denomination. It is a veritable megamall of spiritualities out there. Five hundred years ago another scene existed, one that was dominated by what was to become the Roman Catholic Church. If you were Christian, if you were German, you were also Catholic with allegiance to Rome.

MARKS OF THE CHURCH

As it became clear five hundred years ago that the Lutheran movement had less and less of a chance to continue within the existing ecclesiastical confines, and as other Reformers began to attract followings with similar uncertain futures—all of whom, Lutherans and Reformed alike, finding it necessary to improvise organizational structures of various kinds—those confused by the array of new possibilities could not avoid the nagging question: "Where do I find the true church?"

We might find such a question fastidious and premodern, but for people in sixteenth-century pews, such a question loomed large. It hinged on severing connections with the only ecclesial organization they had ever known, and sometimes it meant facing division with family members who did not hold the same views. Luther recognized this anxiety as a pastoral problem needing to be addressed. His pastoral concern turned into a theological task, one that stood on the central pillars of his emerging grasp of grace, faith, and the gospel.[2]

Technically speaking, the theological task Luther undertook has been framed among systematic theologians as defining the "marks of the church" (*notae ecclesiae*). Luther, however, rarely uses such language, preferring to address the various components here and there as they came up for consideration, often in unrelated contexts. In retrospect, however, one can observe that while Luther was busy responding to new challenges, he concurrently was developing a cohesive understanding of what the marks of the true church might be.

His insights crystallized in a 1539 treatise titled *On the Councils and the Church*, written seven years before his death. In that work he consolidated his thinking on where the true church might be by listing the following seven identifiers:

(1) Preached Word of God
(2) Sacrament of Baptism
(3) Sacrament of the Altar
(4) The Forgiving of Sins
(5) Calling and Consecrating of Ministers
(6) Public Use of Thanksgiving and Prayer
(7) Possession of the Sacred Cross (misfortune and persecution).[3]

Concerning the sixth of these marks, Luther wrote, "Sixth, the holy Christian people are externally recognized by prayer, public praise, and thanksgiving to God. Where you see and hear the Lord's Prayer prayed and taught; or

2 Gordon W. Lathrop and Timothy J. Wengert, *Christian Assembly: Marks of the Church in a Pluralistic Age* (Fortress Press, 2004), 19.

3 LW 41:161–165; TAL 3:422–431.

psalms or other spiritual songs sung, in accordance with the word of God and the true faith, . . . you may rest assured that a holy Christian people of God are present. . . . However, we are now speaking of prayers and songs that are intelligible and from which we can learn and by means of which we can mend our ways."[4]

In broad strokes one could say that Lutheran churches over the years have exhibited this high view of song as a hallmark of the church, even though the stated theological foundations for the practice have sometimes been insufficient. More than ever before, today's pastors and church musicians need to know that when it comes to church and song, Lutherans sing not so much because we, like Luther, love music or love singing but because to sing is of the essence of the church. Finnish theologian Miikka Anttila writes, "Being a sign of the true church, song should not cease for a moment, because a response to the categorical giving of God is the categorical praise of the church."[5]

One cannot miss underlying similarities in these marks: Together they are interactive actions, relational and manifested in community, that is, in the Sunday assembly. This is true even of the cross, because the community by definition holds up its beleaguered members in prayer and charity. Luther, consistent in his crusade against identifying church by means of person or place, instead constructs his definition of church from the activities of the assembly, a point that causes Timothy Wengert to remark that for Luther, *church* is a verb, not a noun.[6]

Further, in his discussion of public praise, the sixth mark, Luther is quick to offer direction about how such praise is accomplished: Songs are to be employed that are "in accordance with the word of God and true faith" and are to be "intelligible . . . and from which we can learn and by means of which we can mend our ways." One might think that with so few songs available, he might withhold such limiting rubrics.

So far, the Reformer comes to the hallmarks of the church positively: Show me what you think is a Christian assembly, and it will be singing. Period. Most of us here belong to congregations in which this mark of the church is nominally operative, given appropriate lip service, and in some cases eagerly and adeptly promoted. Yet, as leaders, we are sometimes moved to wonder

---

4 TAL 3:430; LW 41:164.

5 Miikka Anttila, *Luther's Theology of Music: Spiritual Beauty and Pleasure* (de Gruyter, 2013), 101.

6 Lathrop and Wengert, *Christian Assembly*, 27.

Vorrhede D.
Mart. Luth.

DEr xcvj. Psalm
spricht/Singet dem
HERRN ein new-
es lied/Singet dem HERrn
alle welt. Es war im alten
Testament vnter dem Gesetz
Mose/der Gottes dienst fast
schwer vnd mühselig/da sie so
viel vnd mancherley Opffer
thun musten/von allem das
sie hatten/beide/zu hause vñ
zu felde/Welchs das volck/so
da faul vnd geitzig war/gar
vngerne thet/oder alles vmb

Figure 9.2. Preface to Babst Gesangbuch, 1545, page 1

about those who believe assembly time is sabbatical time for the voice. Luther faced the same kind of vocal reluctance and, in turn, couldn't refrain from rather harsh chastisement such as that in his preface to the Babst Hymnal: "Whoever does not want to sing and speak of [the gospel] shows that he does not believe and that he does not belong under the new and joyful testament, but under the old, lazy, and tedious testament."[7]

In my web search experiment, none of the online evaluators listed assembly singing as the chief attraction, though one person noted the musical prowess of the praise band as a swaying factor. To be honest, Luther's yardstick of hallmarks was absent among reviewers.

Yet, even after all these years, his defining list of marks is compelling precisely because it centers in word and sacrament. As such it is worth taking up on a regular basis to direct our own practical questions regarding congregational priorities, trajectories, budgets, and mission. When it comes to the sixth hallmark, a host of questions linger around the edges. Are we tempted to encourage singing because we want to prove to ourselves that we are church? That would be silly. Do we sing to earn glowing internet reviews? Dare we allow muffled song to become a cause of dismay?

Luther would have none of that, I'm sure. But he might urge us to more carefully attend to all seven marks so that people have something to sing about. It is possible that people prefer silence to singing because they have not heard the gospel, as the Reformer suggested. But then, too, those responsible for the church's song—pastors and musicians—must do all in their power to remove obstacles to singing and in every way possible to solicit and sustain the singing of each person in worship.

Just how this sixth mark of the church manifested itself among the first followers of Luther has been difficult to determine. Recent fresh looks at the evidence have yielded new projections, to which we now tum.

WHO SANG WHAT? DISMANTLING RECEIVED NARRATIVES

Might one assume that at 8 a.m. on November 1, 1517, followers of Luther began singing hymns? So much is improbable about that. We know it couldn't be, even though missing detail coaxes us to imagine quick changes on many

---

7 LW 53:333.

fronts. In truth the growth and extent of congregational singing among early Lutherans are difficult to accurately determine.

Reasons for this are manifold. Consider the following: (1) Singing of vernacular hymns was already common among church people, especially in situations apart from mass; (2) songs were learned by ear rather than by eye; (3) when songs were printed, they appeared as single-sheet issues (broadsides) rather than as pages in a hymn book; (4) extant examples of single songs or small collections are rare, suggesting that much has been lost; (5) attention to congregational singing varied from place to place, making generalities impossible; and (6) words of encouragement from Luther and others suggest that the singing train was not leaving the station quickly.

Indeed, it took six years after posting his theses for Luther to turn his attention to vernacular song. During the years 1523–1524, the Reformer engaged in a veritable outpouring of hymn-writing and became involved with the publication of several key song collections, suggesting that he himself did not attend to worship matters until other pressing needs were met.

These were productive years also for his musician colleague and friend Johann Walter. In 1524 Walter published a collection of hymns and motets titled *Geystlich gesangk Buchleyn* (Spiritual song booklet).[8] The volume contained thirty-eight settings of hymns in German and five Latin motets. It is one of the earliest known collections of hymns published in Wittenberg and garnered great interest because the collection seems to be designed for use by choirs, not by the congregants. Supporting this supposition is the fact that in most cases the tunes for the hymns appear in an internal (tenor) voice, following the compositional practices of the day but rendering assembly participation nearly impossible.

The scope, provenance, date, and contents of this collection have together generated a narrative about congregational singing in early sixteenth-century Wittenberg that has been, and still is, widely held. It goes something like this: Until later in the century, hymn-singing among Lutherans in Wittenberg, when it occurred, was chiefly the responsibility of the choir with possible scattered participation by congregants. This situation began to change after 1580 when simpler settings featuring the tune in the upper voice replaced the earlier, more complex compositions that cradled the tune in an inner voice.

8 See n. 4, p. 107.

At stake here is whether Luther's advocacy for vernacular hymnody ever caught on in his hometown during his lifetime. In a larger perspective, the received narrative meshes with a common perception of how slowly and sometimes agonizingly all significant liturgical change comes about. Some analysts even propose that the evidence points to a protracted conflict regarding the exercise of music within worship, whether it be the role of all the people or the responsibility of trained musicians.[9] It's a conflict still alive today, whenever some who worship approach communal song with the attitude "I'm behaving just like my forebears, so you are going to have to work really hard to get me to sound even one note."

A new narrative is unfolding, however. Over one hundred years ago, in 1895, the small collection of extant Reformation-era resources in hymnody grew with the discovery of a collection published in Wittenberg in 1526. Its title betrays the significance of the find: *Enchyridion geistlicher gesenge und psalmen fur die layen* (Handbook of spiritual songs and psalms for the laypeople).[10] Now located in Berlin, this volume is the only known copy of the collection. Oddly, scholars have largely neglected it—until recently.

In his book *The Whole Church Sings*,[11] Robin Leaver carefully traces the origins of this volume, compares it with other contemporary collections, and proposes that it was the congregational counterpart to the earlier booklet prepared by Johann Walter for choirs in 1524. If that's the case, then we must revise our thinking about congregational singing in Wittenberg during the early years of the Reformation. This discovery opens the likelihood that the Wittenberg faithful sang more in worship than what was previously thought. Moreover, the makings here of a new narrative support what we might have expected all along, namely that Luther's developing conviction about singing as a mark of the church reflected what in fact was occurring immediately around him, theory and practice linked together.

Yet one must be leery of oversized calculations when trying to make sense of this new information. The inclination of the Wittenberg people to sing

9 Joseph Herl, *Worship Wars in Early Lutheranism: Choir, Congregation, and Three Centuries of Conflict* (Oxford University Press, 2004), 68, passim.

10 The full title: *Enchyridion geistlicher gesenge und psalmen fur die layen / mit viel andern / denn zuvor / gebessert.* Detail on this book can be found in Robin A. Leaver, *The Whole Church Sings: Congregational Singing in Luther's Wittenberg* (Eerdmans, 2017), 102–108.

11 Leaver, *The Whole Church Sings*, 102–116.

vernacular songs had as its prompt not only theological musings about the hallmarks of the church but other factors as well, such as the prevalence and popularity of communal music-making.

THE POINT OF SINGING

Music touches our lives nearly every waking hour, but few ask about the significance or meaning of participating in a musical event, just to isolate a single aspect of music's pervasiveness. What *is* the point of singing? In contemporary culture, responses to that question tend to emerge from habitual experiences of certain individuals who exhibit recognizable talent and quality of presentation. Stepping back to observe where public attention is focused, or what is creating the buzz, or what arrests the aspirations of the young, one could surmise that prevailing understandings of music in the Western world revolve around the role of the soloist—the charismatic star who is bestowed with the right to perform for and therefore represent all the rest. This is largely true for both the popular and classic worlds of music. When it comes to music, the media fills time and space with reports of new ensembles, trending performers, the latest album releases, and measurements of accumulated wealth and fame. Garage bands get little press.

The commodification of music is so essential to our understanding of music that we are surprised even to hear it singled out. Music *is* big business. Music is thought of as a thing to be bartered; witness alone the magnitude of transactions on music streaming services.

There is an alternative way to respond to the question about music's meaning and significance. This second option has its roots in the twin disciplines of ethnomusicology (the study of music within the context of culture) and the sociology of music (the study of music as a social act). From scholars of these disciplines, we learn that across all cultures, at one time or another, people understood *music* to be a verb, not a noun or thing. We learn further that remnants of this appreciation of music remain even in a world of commodification. These disciplinary practitioners, convinced of the values behind this alternative, have begun to campaign for considering music as something done together with others and for realizing that its significance lies in the doing. Musicologist Christopher Small has invented a word to enlist personal interest again in the musical act: *musicking*—that is, "to take part, in any capacity, in a musical performance."[12]

GOING WITH THE FLOW

Participatory music-making is a social act and until the advent of recording was the only way music came into being. One of its characteristics is that it, like playing games or sports, tends to draw people into a state of heightened concentration, so much so that all other thoughts, concerns, and distractions disappear. Ethnomusicologist Thomas Turino calls this "flow,"[13] a condition that, he proposes, induces a sense of identification with the other participants and ultimately a feeling of an integrated self.[14]

Contrary to popular perceptions, flow is not a state achieved only by professionals or talented amateurs. Flow, according to Turino, results from any participatory musical event and therefore implies no hierarchical levels of engagement.

What, then, is a recording? Turino responds by providing a handy way of differentiating various kinds of musicking. According to his scheme, there are four "fields" of what we could identify as musicking. Each field is unique and should be valued according to its own purpose and goals:

> Participatory Performance (no audience/performer, no material gain; for all)
>
> Presentational Performance (one group for another, material gain possible)
>
> High Fidelity (connected to live performance in many ways, material gain)
>
> Studio Audio (not real time; creation and manipulation of sound, material gain)[15]

12 Christopher Small, *Musicking: The Meanings of Performing and Listening* (University Press of New England, 1998), 9.

13 Thomas Turino, *Music as Social Life: The Politics of Participation* (University of Chicago Press, 2008), 4.

14 Turino, *Music as Social Life*, 19–21.

15 Turino, *Music as Social Life*, 26–27.

In Turino's list of modes of generating music, we, as church people, can recognize some of the ways we experience music when we gather in our worship assemblies. Although he deliberately avoided the temptation to rank any one field over another, our goals and purposes as the people of God at worship instinctively lead us to prioritize participatory performance. Several reasons account for privileging participatory performance, such as its inclusive nature, its ability to induce a therapeutic sense of being totally immersed, and its capacity for surfacing a sense of identity—all of which are essential to being church.

To help his readers appreciate distinct salutary outcomes of participatory performance, Turino taps into theories about the use and importance of signs in social discourse and interaction. He especially promotes the work of Charles Sanders Pierce,[16] who has made semiotics, or the study of signs, central to his philosophical career. At this point a brief detour into some of Pierce's proposals reveals how rich with insight this consideration is for cultivating participatory performance and for our own pursuit of the meaning of singing in Christian assembly.

A sign is something that stands for something else, according to Pierce. In Western musical traditions, such signs are of two types. The first may be called "iconic," that is, a particular musical instrument, rhythm, or theme *suggests* some object or event to us; an example would be the orchestral music meant to evoke the descent into the Grand Canyon on the back of a donkey in Ferde Grofé's *Grand Canyon Suite*. The other type of sign Pierce and Turino label "indexical," that is, the music is so closely connected to a product, memory, or feeling that it elicits together with the music the event, object, or relationship to which it is bonded. Here examples would be a so-called jingle, endlessly repeated in commercials to create association with a unique brand, or a song that accompanied the moment when two people fell in love. Indexical signs of a musical kind thus also can serve as a medium of identity.

On a broader scale, individual songs, scorings, particular riffs, even an individual's voice all can and do serve as identity indexes and therefore become powerful triggers for surfacing the elemental bonds of a particular cohort group. Popular bands discover that certain songs serve as the index by which the fans identify themselves as a cohort. This is as true for the Grateful

16 See Turino, *Music as Social Life*, 5–10.

Dead as it is for a group of Lutherans who come together to sing "A Mighty Fortress Is Our God."

One of the most important meanings of singing together, if not the most important, is its agency as a social act. It is meant to enable everyone present to participate in an event that yields individual and corporate integration and enriches the group with a palpable experience of identity. Putting that into churchy jargon, we could say that assembly singing actively engages mind, body, and spirit to channel the Holy Spirit's work of building up the body of Christ individually and corporately and that such singing affords a powerful experience of divine presence as Christ reveals Christ's very self in the community's act.

Ecclesiastical versions of Turino's other three fields—presentational performance, high fidelity, and studio audio—enjoy a welcome home in some contemporary Christian assemblies. Economic engines offer their support and probably don't need help from those who care deeply about assembly singing.

But there are compelling reasons for mounting a campaign to arouse, cultivate, and sustain participatory performance in our congregations. Were that to happen, unexpected blessings will follow. And the "new creation," one that Robert Lowry heard as an echo, will be less distant and more the unamplified sound of the Holy City—our song from the future.

CHAPTER TEN

That Was Glorious

Another Look at Luther on Music as Gift of God

The 2007–2008 Chicago Symphony Orchestra (CSO) season began with subscription concerts led by the internationally acclaimed conductor Ricardo Muti. While he was engaged by the CSO as visiting conductor, the expectations for his short tenure were high, and all bets were on an electrifying partnership. By the end everyone felt uplifted. A review by John von Rhein, chief music critic for the *Chicago Tribune*, yielded this headline: "Maestro Muti, CSO Glorious."[1]

Is the use of the word *glorious* hyperbole, as if one were describing Ben and Jerry's ice cream on a warm afternoon? Or does it carry a deeper meaning, signifying something transcendentally impressive, a musical experience that feels like a visitation of the divine? Every so often, it seems, communities experience exceptionally gifted performers such as Franz Liszt, Vladimir Horowitz, Maria Callas, Frank Sinatra, Dave Brubeck, Prince—and these performers may be received with an awe that looks like a response to a holy visitation.

Martin Luther, though impressed by star musicians from his own day, went beyond isolating certain experiences or individuals as glorious. For him momentary epiphanies only pointed to the larger unqualified truth that *all* music is a gift of God. In his comprehensive study of Luther and music, Robin Leaver has cataloged Luther's variations on this claim. From these we learn

---

1 John von Rhein, "Maestro Muti, CSO Glorious," *Chicago Tribune*, September 27, 2007, sec.4, 1.

that music is an "excellent gift of God," "outstanding gift of God," "God's greatest gift," "an endowment and gift of God," and a "wonderful creation and gift of God."[2]

While some of these references are asides in nonmusical contexts, Luther's most sustained and coherent explorations of music as gift reside in two focused documents: the so-called *Encomion musices* (Musical companion), which exists in a shorter German version and a longer Latin version, and the second a sketch titled Περὶ τῆς μουσικῆς (Concerning music). The German version of the *Encomion,* long thought to be a truncated translation of the Latin,[3] is likely to have been the original version and appeared in a collection of sacred songs by Wolfgang Figulus, published in 1575.[4] The Latin version is consequently an amplification of the German and appeared as a preface to the 1538 *Symphoniae iucundae*[5] published by Georg Rhau from his Wittenberg printery. Περὶ τῆς μουσικῆς[6] is a sketch, partly in Greek, mostly in Latin, reportedly written in 1530.[7] Luther intended one day to expand it into a larger work, an indication that he gave more than passing thought to matters of music, its origins, and its use.

By boldly claiming music as a gift of God, Luther located music as a theological subject, a point to which we will return. Further, by insisting that music is a theological subject, he began to challenge conventional wisdom—which, according to the customary division of knowledge, lumped music together with mathematics, geometry, and astronomy—and charted a course against the currents of his time.

---

2 Robin A. Leaver, *Luther's Liturgical Music: Principles and Implications* (Fortress Press, 2017), 70.

3 Leaver, *Luther's Liturgical Music*, 11–12 and 313, presents a meticulous review of the stages of scholarship with respect to these versions, citing Walter Blankenburg as the first to unravel the evidence and propose this plausible solution to the puzzling evidence and suggested scenarios.

4 Wolfgang Figulus, *Cantionem sacrum . . . primi tomi decas prima* (1575). See Leaver, *Luther's Liturgical Music*, 11.

5 The full title is *Symphoniae iucundae arque adeo breves quatuor vocum* (Symphonies, delightful as well as short, in four voices); the volume contained fifty-two motets for the Sundays of the church year. A translation of the Latin preface appears in LW 53:321–324. (Editor's note: See also chapter 1 of the present volume for a translation by Leofranc Holford-Strevens.)

6 WA 30/2:696.

7 Leaver, *Luther's Liturgical Music*, 86.

Because Luther brings music into the playground of theology, church musicians, beginning with Georg Rhau himself, have made the most of his unbridled enthusiasm and theological endorsement. Luther's fame certainly enhanced the Wittenberg printer's collection of part songs with an aura of importance, but Luther's views also provided the collection with a legitimacy not only among the professional cantors but also among theologians and pastors. Over the long haul, this claim of Luther's has often infused new life into tired and beleaguered church musicians by providing comfort amid conflict, bestowing theological understanding for moments of musical ecstasy, bolstering a personal sense of call and purpose, and lending justification to results of musical experimentation. Advocates of new sounds especially take refuge in Luther's claim that *all* music is a gift of God.

In this respect Martin Luther is a kind of patron saint for the enterprise of worship music. In the introduction to a 1978 Lutheran publication meant to accompany emerging new service books, the authors wrote, "In emphasizing music as God's—not man's—creation and as God's gift to man to be used in his praise and proclamation, and in stressing particularly the royal priesthood of all believers, Luther laid the foundation for the involvement of every Christian—congregation, choir, composer, instrumentalist—in corporate praise at the highest level of ability."[8] Here an appeal to music as God's gift is meant to prepare the way for, among other things, identifying quality in musical experience as both a goal and a responsibility. But, to initiate a closer look at some of these deductions that claim Luther as justifier, one might ask: Who decides what might be at the "highest level of ability"? Can such an assumption really be supported by Luther, or do we have here a classical bias looking for authority?

Luther is claimed as a friend to church musicians beyond his Lutheran heirs. Don E. Saliers, in his thoughtful study of music and theology, observes that "'worship wars' make serious thinking about relations between music and theology especially urgent."[9] Trailblazers for this serious thought, Saliers notes, are Luther and Bach, since for both "the communication and the reception of the Christian Gospel were unthinkable apart from music."[10]

8 Carl Halter and Carl Schalk, eds., *A Handbook of Church Music* (Concordia, 1978), 15–16. Schalk uses the rhetoric of this paragraph in his *Luther on Music: Paradigms of Praise* (Concordia, 1988), 45.

9 Don E. Saliers, *Music and Theology* (Abingdon, 2007), ix.

10 Saliers, *Music and Theology*, 22.

Saliers is right to enlist Luther for serious talk about worship music. An appeal to music as gift of God pervades the guild and continues to inform current churchly projects among Lutherans. On the pages devoted to music from *Principles for Worship*, the map for the development of *Evangelical Lutheran Worship*, the very first thing one notices is the heading, "Music is from God."[11] Then the first principle announces, "God creates music as part of the whole creation and gives it to humankind to develop and shape."[12] Background for these statements heavily relies on Luther, though the second of the supports reads, "In the first chapter of the Bible we hear how God gives human beings the gift and responsibility of forming creation, which includes music."[13]

This author does not on the whole take exception to these observations; in fact, I helped to shape them and have used Luther in my own cheerleading of the church musical task.[14] Yet positing music as theological subject and attributing to it divine provenance, by the very weightiness of the claims, call for clearer understanding about what Luther may have had in mind with these assertions. Two observations will help move us along.

From the outset we should rule out Luther's interest here as an attempt to develop a justification for the use of music in worship.[15] To do so he would subvert his foundational insights into the gospel. In fact, he complained that too much music from his time was a product of the law and not of the gospel.

Second, by thinking of music as gift, he undoubtedly had something in mind. There is an "it" involved here—both with respect to "gift" and with respect to "music"—as well as an unknown question to which his assertion seemed to provide an answer. The question was something like the following: So, Brother Martin, what is music? Or what is the significance of music? Such a line of inquiry leads one into a thicket of ruminations about the origins of music. Into these brambles Luther had already gone. We can certainly follow.

---

11 Evangelical Lutheran Church in America, *Principles for Worship*, Renewing Worship, vol. 2 (Augsburg Fortress, 2002), 24.

12 Evangelical Lutheran Church in America, *Principles for Worship*, 24.

13 Evangelical Lutheran Church in America, *Principles for Worship*, 24.

14 Mark P. Bangert, "Dynamics of Liturgy and World Musics: A Methodology for Evaluation," in *Worship and Culture: Foreign Country or Homeland?*, ed. Gláucia Vasconceles Wilkey (Eerdmans, 2014), 107–123.

15 Christoph Krummacher, *Musik als praxis pietatis: Zum selbstverständnis evangelischer Kirchenmusik* (Vandenhoeck & Ruprecht, 1994), 51.

Before we begin explorations of the prickly thicket, one should ask why such ruminations are important. On the one hand, should Luther be right, their importance derives simply from a desire to be worthy gift receivers and gift givers, which then is to be at the heart of participating in God's act of redemption in this world. On the other hand, their importance connects to considerations about the use of music in general and its use in worship. Music, for instance, can subvert the purposes of worship, and we all desire to be worthy custodians of the mysteries of God. In other words, answers to the questions have practical implications.

When seeking wisdom on the origins and significance of music, the notion of music as gift of God opens a range of interpretations. How did Luther arrive at a definition with such magnanimous implications? Given his knowledge of and dependence on the scriptures, one might have expected him to search for origins in the Bible. If he was so moved by music, he might have begun a theology based on the exegesis of Genesis 4:21. In this passage the writer informs us that Jubal, descendant of Cain, was the father of all those who play the lyre and pipe. In his commentary on Genesis, however, Luther leaves behind an opportunity to rhapsodize about origins.[16] Instead, it seems, his thoughts about music came from other sources. So we turn to what those sources were, in all likelihood.

As was true of other disciplines, received knowledge on music in Luther's time came via several current and highly respected treatises, or textbooks, each of which consisted of a compilation of accepted wisdom from the revered teachers of the past. Authors from one generation passed on to the next what seemed most central and important. To add or subtract any element of central teaching about music amounted to inexcusable carelessness, if not arrogance. Everyone understood that new directions could be advanced only from established principles. Knowledge about music therefore grew slowly and came in complex batches. After the fifth century, this high regard for received knowledge took on ecclesial dimensions because many of the authors were also bishops and teachers of the church. Students learned the material by memorizing large sections, bringing about the preservation of concepts through the retention of literal phrases.

16 LW 1:318.

The entire history of music theory therefore presents itself as quite cohesive, interdependent, and generational.[17] Today, one could obtain a sense of it by going backward from Luther to what seem to be distant origins or, as the case will be here, by proceeding from the dim past forward.

According to Western accounts of origins, the mathematician and philosopher Pythagoras discovered music in the sixth century BCE. The story goes that Pythagoras was walking the streets one day with his entourage when he came upon a blacksmith hammering away on red-hot metal. Pythagoras noted that the four hammers, weighing in at twelve, nine, eight, and six pounds, respectively, produced sounds that in various combinations seemed very agreeable. He discovered that when the twelve- and six-pound hammers were sounded together, he heard an octave (how he knew that it was an octave is not part of the story). He calculated the ratio as 2:1. When the smith sounded the twelve- and eight-pound hammers, Pythagoras heard the interval of a fifth with a ratio of 3:2. The twelve- and nine-pound hammers yielded an interval of a fourth with a ratio of 4:3, and the nine- and eight-pound hammers provided a whole tone (or whole step) with a ratio of 9:8.[18]

There are several things to note about Pythagoras. First, the major intervals of much Western scalar music are accounted for in this tale of origins, leaving behind some important details for others to clarify. Second, since Pythagoras's favorite interval was the fifth, a perfect one at that, he set out, relying on the fifth, to construct a scale that would account for the pitches or intervals of familiar melodies. He was only partly successful, discovering that the maneuvering of fifths, and eventually also fourths, yielded in the end a slightly off-kilter octave. In terms of hammers, it meant that relying on his favorite perfect fifth gave him in the end hammers that weighed twelve pounds and six pounds, two ounces. Trying to solve that dilemma took hundreds of years; the problem itself suggested an imperfect system, a nagging thought for those who held to divine origins for music. Finally, linking together weight and sound set the stage for others to ruminate about further linkages, raising

17 For a comprehensive overview of the history of music theory, see *The Cambridge History of Western Music Theory*, ed. Thomas Christensen (Cambridge University Press, 2007).

18 Since Pythagoras is thought to have traveled in the ancient Near East, where the ratio theory was already known, it's probable that he chiefly elaborated on received knowledge; see Quentin Faulkner, *Wiser than Despair: The Evolution of Ideas in the Relationship of Music and the Christian Church* (Greenwood, 1996), 33.

the possibility that the whole universe might somehow be held together in perfect harmony by universal ratios.

About 150 years after the death of Pythagoras, thoughts about the origin and significance of music reached new levels. Plato, thoroughly familiar with a widespread and growing fascination with music, reckoned that harmony in this world exhibits itself in many ways and that music, along with other arts and activities, directly affects human beings either for the good of society or to its detriment. "More than anything else," he wrote in the *Republic*, "rhythm and harmony find their way to the inmost soul and take strongest hold upon it, bringing with them and imparting grace, if one is rightly trained."[19] In his mind, training and education were for the good of the ideal state and therefore essential. Hence, every aspect of pedagogy needed attention, even gymnastics. After an extended dialogue over these matters, he concludes (through the mouth of Socrates), "For these two, then, it seems there are two arts which I would say some god gave to mankind, music and gymnastics."[20]

The combination of "god" and "gave" in this quote from Socrates passed by Plato unchallenged. His contemporaries believed that artistic achievements in general were divinely inspired and bestowed by the muses. Of the nine acknowledged by them, the original two were Polyhymnia (poetry, music, and song) and Terpsichore (dance).[21] Music's divine origin was firmly entrenched in classical thinking.

For the next six to seven hundred years, serious thinkers about music held number (and ratio) to be the pervasive force that maintains the equilibrium of everything that is. From time to time, one aspect of this comprehensive view took precedence over another, as in the endless debates about the power or ethos of certain kinds of music. But behind these emphases and their variations remained the belief that in the beginning music came to humans as divine bestowal, and it held everything together. By the late fifth century CE, received knowledge turned into systematic formulation. Anicius Boethius (ca. 480–525/526), a Roman statesman (and Christian), gave shape to prevailing opinion in his *De institutione musica* (Concerning the principles of music). Music, he wrote, is of three kinds. First, "there is the music of the universe,

19 From the *Republic*, in *Source Readings in Music History: Antiquity and the Middle Ages*, ed. Oliver Strunk (Norton, 1965), 8.

20 Strunk, *Source Readings: Antiquity*, 12.

21 Daniel J. Schneck and Dorita S. Berger, *The Music Effect: Music Physiology and Clinical Applications* (Jessica Kingsley, 2006), 23.

. . . the elements and the variety of the seasons which are observed in the heavens."[22] Second, there is human music, that which blends "the body's elements or holds its parts together."[23] Finally, there is instrumental music, the "kind of music which is described as residing in certain instruments,"[24] of which the voice is one.

It is fair to say his summary records opinions older by several centuries. Educated Christians carried this knowledge with them as part of their view of the world, though for them, as Hermann Abert suggests, the potentially theological aspects of these matters elicited most interest.[25] The list of those Christian forebears who lived and breathed in the Pythagorean atmosphere is long, including Clement of Alexandria, Basil the Great, John Chrysostom, Jerome, and especially Augustine (354–430).[26] While Boethius achieves recognition for clearly passing on the Greek theoretical base for music untouched by his Christian beliefs, Augustine, who preceded Boethius by one hundred years, was the first who took the received knowledge and recast it into Christian categories. This he ventured despite his own personal fear of music's powers.[27]

Augustine was a teacher of rhetoric. Before his conversion, he began work on *De musica* (About music). The first five books or chapters of this sizable treatise deal with the intricacies and principles of prosody. Augustine wrote the sixth and final book after his conversion. In it he deals with *numerositas*, which for him means numbers as the foundation of all things, showing his Pythagorean pedigree. As the title for the second part of this last book, Augustine slips in the first line of a popular hymn at the time, *Deus Creator omnium* (God, Creator of all).[28] That's a clue to what's coming.

Staying close to Pythagoras, he nevertheless sets out to develop an interpretive framework. Augustine makes clear that the sounding order of the cosmos derives not from itself but is the work of the divine Creator. Behind this order

---

22 Strunk, *Source Readings: Antiquity*, 84.

23 Strunk, *Source Readings: Antiquity*, 85.

24 Strunk, *Source Readings: Antiquity*, 85.

25 Hermann Abert, *Die Musikanschauung des Mittelalters und ihre Grundlagen* (Niemeyer, 1905), 82–83.

26 See James McKinnon, *Music in Early Christian Literature* (Cambridge University Press, 1987), 28–36, 64–71, 78–90, 138–146; and Abert, *Die Musikanschauung*, passim.

27 "When it happens that I am moved more by the song than by what is sung, I confess to sinning grievously, and I would prefer not to hear the singer at such times." From the *Confessions*, in *Strunk's Source Readings in Music History*, rev. ed., ed. Leo Treitler (Norton, 1998), 133.

28 Erik Routley, *The Church and Music*, rev. ed. (Gerald Duckworth, 1967), 60.

is God's love waiting to be acknowledged. He writes, "The soul through the principle of number and order—something it loves—in all things, is called to the love of God."[29] Augustine's synthesis of music theory and theology was thorough. When writing about the origin of the soul, he asserts, "Music, that is, an empathetic knowledge of shaping things well, has been given to the mortal, spirit-bestowed human in order to point the human to lofty things."[30]

Abert observes that while Augustine and others provided a theological path to a merger of Greek musical theory and Christianity, the music that prompted the quest after origins in the first place was largely ignored. Nevertheless, Augustine's Christianizing efforts inspired the next generations of music theorists, including Cassiodorus, Isidore of Seville, Rhabanus Maurus, and John of Murs, to name a few. Cassiodorus (ca. 490–ca. 585), who followed Augustine by almost a century and whose work *Instructiones* was probably the most influential textbook throughout the Middle Ages, summarized his discussion of modes this way: "And to embrace all in a few words, nothing in things celestial or terrestrial which fittingly conducted according to the Creator's own plan is found to be exempt from this discipline [of numbers]."[31] Rhabanus (or Hrabanus) Maurus (ca. 780–856), archbishop of Mainz and abbot at Fulda, declared that "the heavens themselves move by virtue of the harmony of modulation."[32]

The preservers of the traditions tenaciously held to the ancient principles. Parisian theorist John of Murs (ca. 1290–ca. 1347) posited numerical relationships, those both of sound and of rhythm, as the foundation of all music and favored the interval of the fifth as the key to the entire mystery.

Augustine's project of bringing together Christian theology with received musical theory lost ground to other concerns over time, but well into the seventeenth century, theorists faithfully acknowledged the divine origin of

---

29 Latin: "*Ad Dei amorem provocatur anima ex numerorum et ordinis ratione quam in rebus diligit*" (*De musica*, VI:2), as qtd. by Winfried Kurzschenkel, *Die theologische Bestimmung der Musik* (Paulinus, 1971), 146.

30 Latin: "*Musica, id est scientia sensusve bene modulandi ad admonitionem magnae rei, etiam mortalibus rationales habentibus animas Dei largitate concessa est*" (*De origine animae hominis*, V:13), as qtd. in Kurzschenkel, *Die theologische Bestimmung*, 146.

31 From the *Institutiones*, in Strunk, *Source Readings: Antiquity*, 92.

32 Latin: "*Et coelum ipsum sub harmoniae modulatione revolvitur*" (*De universo libri XXII*), as qtd. in Oskar Söhngen, "Theologische Grundlagen der Kirchenmusik," in *Die Musik des evangelischen Gottesdienstes*, vol. 4 of *Leiturgia: Handbuch des evangelischen Gottesdienstes*, ed. Karl Ferdinand Müller et al. (Stauda, 1961), 93.

music as a pro forma matter.[33] The legacy of Pythagoras therefore continued beyond the Reformation, though for present purposes we can end its journey with John of Murs.

John's influence in central Europe was vast. Candidates for the master's degree at Leipzig University, according to the 1410 statutes, were required to read his *Musica*.[34] The same held for master's candidates at Wittenberg University beginning in 1501 and at Erfurt University beginning in 1412, meaning that Luther probably read and studied that treatise, as specified by the regulations, for at least a month.[35] The tradition associated with Rhabanus Maurus at Fulda lived on in musician and theorist Adam, who, coincidentally, taught at Wittenberg University in 1502.[36]

As an Augustinian monk, Luther had no doubt breathed the spirit of Augustine. He had either read *De musica* or at least knew of its major points through the writings of Adam of Fulda or John of Murs. Surely he knew of Pythagoras; in his lectures on Genesis he complains that the creation of Adam and Eve seems so utterly miraculous to us when things like propagation don't. He ventures an explanation: "We do not," he writes, "marvel at the countless other gifts of creation, for we have become deaf toward what Pythagoras aptly terms this wonderful and most lovely music coming from the harmony of the motions that are in the celestial spheres."[37] In his *Encomion musices*, Luther lauds music because it is a gift of God while at the same time noting that "nothing on earth is without its sound and harmony."[38] It must have been in the air; Calvin, too, identified music as a blessing of God (*benediction Dei*),[39] and Melanchthon observed that "the soul is a sort of harmony and by its very nature it perceives and loves numbers."[40] In the background one can hear Boethius uttering prompts.

---

33 For example, Wolfgang Caspar Printz: "Accordingly, now is it certain that the highest God therefore soon after the creation of all things bestowed upon humans the discovery of the singing art; so we infer that long before Jubal vocal music or the singing art would have been discovered." *Historische Beschreibung der edelen Sing- und Kling-Kunst* (Mieth, 1690), facsimile ed., ed. Othmar Wessely (Akademische Druck- und Verlagsanstalt, 1964), 2.

34 Probably *Musica speculativa* (1323).

35 Leaver, *Luther's Liturgical Music*, 27.

36 Söhngen, "Theologische Grundlagen," 304, n. 244.

37 Lectures on Genesis, LW 1:126.

38 Leaver, *Luther's Liturgical Music*, 314.

39 Söhngen, "Theologische Grundlagen," 46.

40 As qtd. by Marion Lars Hendrickson, *Musica Christi: A Lutheran Aesthetic* (Peter Lang, 2005), 40.

So far, we have discovered that, for Luther, music is a complex that presumes its divine origin, assumes a division of the octave shaped by the intervals of the fifth and the fourth, includes nearly all aspects of life, has unexplained influence over human behavior, and finds its significance by way of its nature as divine gift. Of all these persuasions, the last one takes prominent place today, though it should be clear that on this point he is less inventive than he is faithful to the tradition in which he lived.

That tradition gave him permission, or even nudged him, to think theologically about music. Since I count myself in the same tradition, I attempt below to outline another way to think theologically about music, even to think of it as gracious gift, without having to subscribe to Pythagorean hammers or to spirits and souls that are subject to ratios.

To do that I propose to intersect Luther's complex of opinion with current thinking about music's origins and significance. Of course, that is unfair. Were Luther alive today he would have already sought dialogue with contemporary voices exploring music. But he is not, and we benefit from standing at the intersection to grapple with new information and new insights.

Example 1: In the last half century, influential scholars have begun to seek the origins of music in evolutionary biology. *Biomusicologists* is the inventive name they have given themselves, and they assert from the outset that "music has its primary base in the human's biological inheritance, not in any cultural heritage."[41] One function of music, claims Nils Wallin, one of the pioneers in this specialized research, is "the contribution to retaining, restoring, and adjusting an individual's vital character, as well as enabling him to recognize and manipulate emotions as mental forms under social constraints."[42] Musical functions, biomusicologists propose, reside in the limbic part of the brain, recognized as the very old structure of the brain that encircles the central parts of the brain stem.

Despite the esoteric, if not eerie, explorations offered here, descriptions of music that flow from this young discipline touch on many aspects of music that we perceive as true—emotions as mental forms, music as a language of emotion, and music as basic to humanity. Wallin even allows for music's relationship to the larger structures of life: "Silence, therefore, to be broken and transformed into sound gestures or music, is a kind of analogue to the

41 Nils L. Wallin, *Biomusicology: Neurophysiological, Neuropsychological, and Evolutionary Perspectives on the Origins and Purposes of Music* (Pendragon, 1991), xx.

42 Wallin, *Biomusicology*, 329.

quantic vacuum that is postulated in some modern cosmological models for the creation of the universe."[43]

All this sounds like Augustine and Luther—translated into contemporary terms. Yes and no. Although biomusicologists acknowledge relationships between music and characteristics of the universe—indeed, they posit reciprocal interactions between the performance of music and the behavior of the performers (so much so that, in a sense, biomusicology serves as the theoretical base for music therapy)—they nevertheless hold to the evolution of music as a byproduct of the evolution of the human being. Should we want to maintain our claim on music as gift of God, we will have to revise notions about a music drop from a flyby deity who happens to like us.

Example 2: The study of music from cultures that are non-Western yields musical systems that are radically different from what's familiar to us and would have been to Luther too. In the Pythagorean scheme of things worked out to its logical ends, the octave is divided into twelve steps, each measuring one hundred cents.[44] What does one then do with a Thai scale that divides the octave into seven equidistant parts?[45] What does one do with xylophone tunings from Central Africa that are non-equidistant pentatonic or, more exotically, equidistant pentatonic?[46] Then there is the very complicated classical music of India, in which the interval size has been measured at twenty-two cents, sixty-six cents, or ninety cents.

These examples not only cause wonderment for the music lovers of the Western world but also raise some questions that are ultimately theological. If one assumes that music performed in these interval patterns represents a stage on the way to a more agreeable sound, like that we know in the West, then a hierarchical rating system has taken over the notion of gift, bestowing on Pythagorean harmonies, and therefore all traditional Western music, the honor of being the standard. This kind of Western hubris infects our behavior

43 Wallin, *Biomusicology*, xix. See in this respect the creative linkings of music and cosmology in Arthur Peacocke and Ann Pederson, *The Music of Creation* (Fortress Press, 2006).

44 A cent is, mathematically, a logarithmic measurement introduced by A. J. Ellis (1814–1890) for measuring musical intervals.

45 Terry E. Miller, "Thailand," in *Southeast Asia*, ed. Terry E. Miller and Sean Williams, vol. 4 of *The Garland Encyclopedia of World Music* (Garland,1998), 263.

46 Simha Arom and Frédéric Voisin, "Theory and Technology in African Music," in *Africa*, ed. Ruth Stone, vol. 1 of *The Garland Encyclopedia of World Music* (Garland, 1998), 266–267.

more than we might think. To be blunt, the kind of African music that many enjoy in twenty-first-century worship, for example, emerged from the blending of some original African melodies and some made-to-sound-original African melodies, the blending then made to sound more agreeable by the addition of conventional hymn harmony introduced by the missionaries. This kind of blending has a name, *kwaya*,[47] which gives away its origins, and is looked on by African musicologists such as Kofi Agawu as a result of "colonizing."[48] Obviously annoyed by the way things are in Africa today, he observes, "The hierarchic SATB arrangement that churchgoers encounter on Sundays and that boys and girls are forced to endure as members of community and school choirs does not occur in traditional African music."[49]

The colonialism Agawu describes also shows up these days in a slightly different manner. Behind the mask of so-called world music, genuine musics of "the other" are disappearing into bland hybrids that are designed to appeal to broad spectrums of people. In this scheme of things, recordings are taking the place of real encounters with musicians, removing from the musical experience any trace of engaging with "the other." The result, laments Laurent Aubert, is that the musicians of other cultures, and therefore the cultures themselves, are forced to give up "anything too specific that exists in their own musical tradition, in the meantime systematically searching for convergence points and developing all possible potential for spectacle."[50]

Luther, obviously, need not be blamed for neglecting a kind of musical green zone in which people honor the music of the other. The point is rather that ethnomusicologists, those who study the musics of other cultures, by their own concerns move us to ask: What about music *is* gift? Is it the raw material, such as "physical vibrations, the proportions and relationships of different

47 The word *kwaya* obviously sounds like *choir* and refers to the kind of music that emerged from European hymnody and African style put together via the evangelical encounters in the nineteenth century. Gregory Melchor-Barz has researched contemporary manifestations of the style. In Tanzania it is linked with the production and sale of *kandas* (cassettes) by church groups heavily influenced by trends in Western popular music. See Barz's page at https://www.bu.edu/africa/profile/gregory-melchor-barz/.

48 Kofi Agawu, *Representing African Music: Postcolonial Notes, Queries, Positions* (Routledge, 2003), 8.

49 Agawu, *Representing African Music*, 10.

50 Laurent Aubert, *The Music of the Other: New Challenges for Ethnomusicology in a Global Age*, trans. Carla Ribeiro (Ashgate, 2007), 55–56.

pitches," as Leaver reads in Luther?[51] Is it the notes, as Luther writes?[52] Or is it an elusive unifying theory that holds the entire universe together?

It is my opinion that the traditional way of evaluating music as a gift of God is no longer helpful, especially when used to justify a particular practice of worship music. Here is another way. From gratitude that wells up from the bottom of their being, Christians regularly confess, "We believe in one God, . . . maker of heaven and earth, of all that is, seen and unseen."[53] There is something precious about deliberately considering music as part of the seen and unseen. But if looking *to see* is the point here, then perhaps we should look elsewhere than at unifying theories of ratio and hammers. Luther himself may provide us with a more productive alternative. In the Latin version of his *Encomion musices*, Luther wrote, "Thus it was not without reason that the fathers and prophets wanted nothing else to be associated as closely with the Word of God as music. . . . After all, the gift of language combined with the gift of song was only given to [humans] to let them know that they should praise God with both word and music."[54]

For interpreters of Luther, this linkage of music and the word of God is ground equally fertile as Luther's claim on music as gift of God. His focus on the word of God throughout his theological career makes a focus on this combination even more attractive. Further, this change of perspective leads the current discussion away from the first article of the creed to the second article of the creed, where God's definitive gesture toward the world is incarnation in the *Logos*, the Word of God.

To sharpen this connection, it is useful to hear once again what Luther meant by *word of God*, more specifically what he meant by *gospel*. In his introduction to the Gospels he wrote, "And gospel should really not be something written, but spoken word which brought forth the Scriptures, as Christ and the apostles have done. This is why Christ himself did not write anything but only spoke. He called his teaching not Scripture but gospel, meaning good news or a proclamation that is spread not by pen but by word of mouth."[55]

---

51 Leaver, *Luther's Liturgical Music*, 70.

52 On the Last Words of David, LW 15:274, cited by Leaver, *Luther's Liturgical Music*, 70.

53 First article of the Nicene Creed in the translation of the English Language Liturgical Commission, in *Evangelical Lutheran Worship* (Augsburg Fortress, 2006), 104.

54 LW 53:323, as qtd. by Leaver, *Luther's Liturgical Music*, 317.

55 A Brief Instruction on What to Look For and Expect in the Gospels, LW 35:123.

Sounded word of God and music go together, they participate together, Oskar Söhngen reminds us, in that "sphere" we call *sound*. That shared commonality always generated in Luther a large dose of amazement, even as it led him once more to recognize the heavenly source for both God's word and music.[56]

His amazement, however, is far more than a naive and sentimental way of expressing giddiness over the joy of music. Luther, in fact, takes this another step. In his commentary on Romans 10:17 he identifies the human ear as *the* organ of a Christian person (*organa Christiani hominis*) because it is through the ear that one hears the gospel and comes to faith.[57] Through the preaching of the gospel, the Holy Spirit "first leads us into his holy community, placing us in the church's lap, where he preaches to us and brings us to Christ."[58] With that, of course, we have been led into the third article of the creed, giving one cause to join Luther in saying that the very Holy Spirit of God honors music as an instrument for the Spirit's proper work.[59]

It is not unfair, I believe, to describe Luther as one who holds music and God's word (gospel) together via the sphere of sound; for him it is impossible to distinguish between the two, that is, the gospel will always have musical aspects to it. Music thus is analogue to the word, and yet it is even more than that; it is the vehicle for apprehending and realizing the community the gospel creates.

Luther may have had this in mind when, in his commentary on Genesis, he wrote that the "miracles one sees are of less importance than those of which we hear."[60] To be sure, his point in its context is to call attention to miracles at hand rather than those reported from the past. "The fact that Christ fed four thousand people with seven loaves was a great and wonderful work," he noted, "but every day he feeds the whole world."[61] The enactment of God's grace in the present moment is where the action is, he might have said, so

---

56 "*Daß die Musik aus dem selben Bereich der auricularia stammt wie das Evangelium, . . . das allein ist schon ein Moment, das Luther immer wieder zum Staunen bringt*" (That music stems from the same sphere of acoustics as the gospel, . . . that alone is already a realization that always amazes Luther), Söhngen, "Theologische Grundlagen," 65. Translation by the author.

57 The comment comes from Luther's Lectures on Hebrews, WA 57:222; see Söhngen, "Theologische Grundlagen," 64–65.

58 Large Catechism, BC 435–436.

59 Preface to Georg Rhau's *Symphoniae iucundae*, LW 53:323.

60 LW 7:70–71.

61 LW 7:70–71.

give attention to the power of spoken word, to its inherent musical nature, and to the community it forms.

To declare that music is a vehicle for apprehending and realizing the community that gospel creates is to attribute significance to music. Will such an assertion stand up to current thought about the meaning and significance of music? Will there be sympathetic vibrations from the musical community—will it resound there?

Consonances show up at three junctures, at least, and these consonances constitute the ingredients by which one might begin to understand music as gift of God in another way:

1. As part of a growing trend to downplay music as manuscript, musicologist Christopher Small has coined a new word to get at what he thinks music is really about; the word is *musicking*.[62] With this neologism he means to emphasize the act and context of making music rather than the text (score, music manuscript) that sometimes precedes, sometimes follows the act itself. Hence, in his mind there is no such thing as a piece (text) of music that bears in itself an ideal performance, which musicians aspire to achieve. Rather the text is a general map that enables every ensemble to experience a momentary musical event that has its meaning and significance in the event itself.[63] By way of this line of thinking, a recording of an event is just that, a record of something that happened once and can't happen again. It is a dim memory and mostly unrewarding approximation of the musical act devoid of most possibilities for *musicking*—not unlike videos of Christian assembly around the communion table. Musicking by its very nature provides the vehicle for the freedom of the Spirit to inspire and shape assembly and in this way takes on the nature of being gift. It is here, it seems to me, that an outline of talking about music in worship can begin.
2. While the playing field identified as the sociology of music is an expanse contested by all sorts of interested players, the majority of

62 Christopher Small, *Musicking: The Meanings of Performing and Listening* (University Press of New England, 1998).

63 "*To music is to take part, in any capacity, in a musical performance, whether by performing, by listening, by rehearsing or practicing, by providing material for performance (what is called composing), or by dancing.*" Small, *Musicking*, 9. Emphasis in original.

those on the field dearly hold the notion that the musical experience possesses sociological dynamics.[64] Small observes, for instance, that the "act of musicking establishes a set of relationships in the place where it is happening, and it is in those relationships that the meaning of the act lies."[65] Music gives us a way of being in the world, a way of making sense out of it.[66] Because of the nature of music, we do it with others, and we do it in such a way that we can apprehend and enact the social transactions that are or should be important to us.[67] In some instances, these transactions are easy to observe: The group dynamics of jazz improvisation incarnate cohesiveness and trust among individuals. In others the transactions are subtler, such as negotiated (or nonnegotiated) relationships between musicians and Christian assembly. Failure to take account of these sociological transactions leads to fruitless battles over repertoire in the realm of worship music and blurs one's appreciation for music as gift. When taken seriously, the blessings of enacting Christian assembly through music far outweigh occasional slip-ups. The gift is that we possess a way, a profound way, to apprehend *gospel* as well as *church* with all their complex and edifying dynamics. Gospel and assembly are set free from idea to become palpable, living entities.

3. If music is sonic assembly with its complex social transactions, then it comes with ethical dimensions. Musicking, to return to Small's verbal invention, reveals the ways people live in this world, and that's true of the music in the Christian assembly as well. Honesty, care, and honor, among other Christian virtues, are the stuff of music, too, especially with respect to peoples and civilizations whose music we share. Just because we have paid the copyright fees to use a song from Taiwan does not excuse us from learning to understand and care for the peoples and assemblies whose song this is. The world's musics as well as its varied Christian assemblies are not for plundering, nor are they for sale. Musicking the liturgy is

64 For examples, see Peter J. Martin, *Sounds and Society* (Manchester University Press, 1995); and John Shepherd, *Music as Social Text* (Polity Press, 1991).

65 Small, *Musicking*, 13.

66 Simon Frith, *Performing Rites: On the Value of Popular Music* (Harvard University Press, 1996), 272.

67 Nicholas Cook, *Music: A Very Short Introduction* (Oxford University Press, 1998), 78.

> the beginning of accountability toward God and the other. Musical events, at times and unfortunately, can mold us in ways that give way to the patterns of consumer culture. But, more importantly and positively, they can realize for us new, alternative patterns whose melodies permeate our collective behavior for the sake of the world. That is a gift rooted in the dynamics of sound.

The same Ricardo Muti who helped us begin this discussion founded an ensemble in Piacenza and Ravenna called the Luigi Cherubini Youth Orchestra. Of that orchestra he says, "The orchestra exists to give young musicians the possibility of becoming good professional musicians. I try to prepare them to have an ethical approach to music. I want to give them not only the possibility of knowing the fantastic world of the great composers but how to live in society. That is the ultimate lesson."[68]

Considering music as gift of God has taken us through the first article of the creed by way of the second and third. Chances for a fruitful intersection of current musical thinking and Christian assembly increase if one positions oneself squarely in the second article, acknowledging the Logos, the second person of the Trinity, as the real gift who makes possible the sphere of sound, sonic relationships, and Christian assembly.[69] By definition, music in all its manifestations is integral to those dynamics. To affirm that with joy is to sit at Luther's table after dinner and music (*musick*) your way through the evening.[70] That is its glory.

---

68 von Rhein, "Maestro Muti, CSO Glorious," sec. 4, 1, 14.

69 Krummacher, *Musik als praxis pietatis*, 25, in contrast to Söhngen, believes that Luther's theology of music derives initially from the second article without minimizing the first. Because of justification through grace, the child of God is set free to use music as creature and gift of God.

70 Leaver, *Luther's Liturgical Music*, 43–47, describes the lively music scene at Luther's dinner table, which often included people like Melanchthon and the publisher Georg Rhau. In January 1535 he wrote to an unknown composer, "We sing as well as we can here at table and afterward. If we make a few blunders, it is really not your fault but our ability, which is still very slight even if we have sung over [the piece] two or three times. . . . Therefore you composers must pardon us if we make blunders in your songs, for we would much rather do them well than badly." Leaver, who provided this translation, cites WA BR 7:154.

Figure 10.1. Josquin motet from discantus partbook, *Symphoniae iucundae*, 1538

CHAPTER ELEVEN

Johann Sebastian Bach and Martin Luther

Born some two hundred years apart, Luther (1483–1546) and Bach (1685–1750) led lives that converged in sundry and remarkable ways. At the age of fifteen, Luther came to Eisenach for about four years to study at the community Latin school of St. George, singing in the choir there. Born in Eisenach and baptized at St. George, Bach attended the same school, learning the hymns of Luther and singing in the choir. Up a large hill outside of Eisenach the Wartburg castle, seen almost daily by the boy Bach, served as Luther's home for several months in 1521, where he translated the New Testament. Luther often visited Weimar, his home away from home, whose court Bach served in 1703 and again from 1708 to 1717. The composer's last place of employment at St. Thomas in Leipzig professed Reformation foundations because Luther had preached there in 1539, twenty years after his appearance at the famous Leipzig Disputation.

LOYALISTS TO THE CHRISTIAN FAITH—REFORMED

Bach was born into a Lutheran family. His father was director of the city musicians and as such took on extensive responsibilities for music at the Eisenach churches. After his parents died, Bach lived with his older brother in Ohrdruf, where he learned the rudiments of Luther's Small Catechism. From 1700 to 1702 he attended St. Michael's School in Lüneburg, where he was led through more amply formulated Lutheran teaching as contained in the *Compendium* (1610) of Leonard Hutter, later known as "Luther born again." To obtain the Leipzig cantorate in 1723, Bach successfully underwent two theological examinations focused on the *Formula of Concord*, signifying his grasp of the issues Lutherans entertained over the years.

After his death, the inventory of Bach's theological library discloses that he had amassed fifty-two titles in eighty-one volumes, including two sets of Luther's writings (Jena and Altenburg editions); three volumes of his *Haus=Postill* (Sermons for home); assorted volumes from current orthodox Lutheran authors; devotional literature; and the (now) famous Calov Bible, a three-volume biblical commentary by Abraham Calov (1612–1686), who expanded Luther's translation with other of his writings and Calov's own observations. Bach's copy of the work shows underlining. marginal notations, and corrections, all suggesting that he had extensive knowledge of the Bible. Contemporary authors, facing pockets of resistance, have factored in such evidence to establish a plausible view of Bach's hearty spirituality. Two favorite themes of Luther—the crib and the cross (incarnation and death)— frequently appear in the librettos Bach chose for his cantatas, as in the oratorios and passions.

STUDENTS OF THE BIBLE

When Luther set himself to translate the Bible from its original languages into German, he determined to bring the texts to the people and therefore chose words and thought patterns that common folk would understand. With that he coincidentally converged with a growing, partially humanist-inspired interest in rhetoric, that liberal art so central to the traditional educational process, including his own. This newfound interest in rhetoric should not be construed as Luther's way of wearing a humanist badge. His understanding of gospel as a "speaking act" prompted him to mate rhetorical processes and with his goal of bringing the biblical text to the people. "Rhetoric moves and excites (*Rhetorica moviret vnd beweget*)," he commented at the table,[1] eager to employ this tool for the proclamation of the gospel.

Reverence for Luther's translation of the Bible continued into the eighteenth century. In the choral works of Bach, biblical text serves as a major ingredient. The composer therefore interacted daily with Luther's translation, as,

1 WA TR No. 2199A.

for example, in the librettos of the cantatas; in the narrative that propels the Christmas Oratorio; and in the passions, for which, contrary to a growing practice among his peers, Bach used Luther's translation rather than versified replacements. In Bach's own copy of the St. Matthew Passion, the biblical narrative is entered with red ink.

Bach's interaction with the Luther translation occurred both at the office, as it were, and at home, insofar as one can assume the Bible was central to the Bach family spirituality. At the professional level, the composer had tools at hand such as a multivolume biblical exposition by Johann Olearius (1678–1681), now believed by some scholars to have significantly influenced Bach's understanding of scriptural texts used in his more than two hundred cantatas.

How might Bach have accomplished a smooth move from a mature, Lutheran-tinged biblical understanding to a musical event? First, he worked in an ecclesiastical culture that embraced the word of God as something sounded, both narration and sermon. Second, he was heir to a cantor/composer tradition that, rooted in the sixteenth century, drew its energy from text.

Classic rhetoric proposed that words achieve results when individually or together they teach *(docere)*, move (*movere*), and delight (*delectare*). About the same time that Luther sought to find the right words and structures for his translation, composers, also under the influence of humanism, angled for musical ways to draw attention to words and their meaning. Soon they developed a kind of musical rhetoric built on practices much older and inspired by older linguistic devices. Musical theorists in the 1500s were the first to codify the artifice in published manuals. By using these tools, generations of composers found a way to pay attention to biblical text as a "speaking act," transforming it into musical event, the intricacies of which are seen most clearly in Bach's predecessors such as Johann Hermann Schein (cantor at St. Thomas in Leipzig from 1616 to 1630), Heinrich Schütz (1585–1672), and the works of Bach himself.

Nearly every movement of Bach's choral works contains a figure (musical image) that helps to convey the meaning of a word, just as one will witness signs of the more expansive musical affect spreading across larger segments of text—a typically baroque aspiration. Bach was, after all, a baroque composer, by definition intent on creating those affects that would teach, move, and delight his partners in the musical speech act. By additionally employing the opera-derived, declamatory recitative style for biblical text, he was able to bring Luther's theology of proclamation to a level that has captured the attention of subsequent generations.

EXPONENTS OF RECEIVED MUSICAL TRADITION

Apart from being beneficiaries of experienced instruction in voice and instrument, both Luther's and Bach's understandings about the origins and purposes of music were shaped by growing into a tradition of singular roots that powered their individual experiences of music. From his required reading of treatises like that of John of Murs (ca. 1290–ca. 1347), Luther highly regarded music as an integral part of creation and therefore a divine gift, as possessing power to alter moods, and as a natural companion to the word of God. While not a person who wrote much about himself, Bach devoted himself to the companionship of music and word, explored the rainbow of affects or passions that baroque aesthetics offered, recognized his art as gift—ending many of his compositions with "S.D.G." (To God alone be glory), and in his own way embraced music as creature while shaping the raw material into imaginative new embodiments. For him, as for Luther, *all* music is gift of God, even though for both men, music's possible misuse is an ongoing threat.

CHAMPIONS OF PEOPLE'S MUSIC

Luther never lost his love for the art music of his time, evidenced by the singing of motets around the dinner table and his admiration for contemporary musical luminaries such as Ludwig Senfl and Josquin des Prez. His occasional acerbic outbursts against chant and organ music had more to do with text and circumstance than with principle. His grasp of music as sounded event led him to privilege the individuals in such a moment, a perfect manifestation of how he understood the gospel as address to every unique person. For this reason he advocated for music in schools and couldn't abide any church leader without the muse.

The Reformer's thirty-six hymns flow easily out of this scenario but also serve a greater goal. By metricizing the gospel, he found a way to everyone's heart and mind so that each individual was uniquely involved, while together their song embodied the community. The Lutheran chorale therefore served as a mark of the church, its widespread flowering a sign of its experienced usefulness.

Bach also grasped music as sounded event—his vocation as cantor assumed such, and like most composers, he wrote music for specific ensembles and occasions. Toward the end of his life, of course, he did spend time with "abstract" music (e.g., "The Art of the Fugue"), but even then his weekly duties continued, as he struggled with obstinate superiors to achieve the highest kind of musical education in the St. Thomas School. His leadership of local musicians at the city coffee shop ought to be evaluated as an embrace of music for everyone, but the clearest bonds with Luther emerge from his commitment to the chorale. Utilizing hymns old (many from Luther) and new, the composer drew on this resource to personalize the messages of cantatas, passions, and oratorios, sometimes by means of tune alone. If there is a single link between Luther and Bach, the chorale is the most likely candidate.[2]

---

2 Editor's note: Chapter 11 is from *Encyclopedia of Martin Luther and the Reformation*, ed. Mark A. Lamport. Copyright © 2017 Rowman and Littlefield. Reprinted by permission.

CHAPTER TWELVE

With Countless Gifts of Love

Arts and the Liturgy

"With countless gifts of love"[1]—like a mantra these words flow through our lives. At some point we begin to realize that the countless "gifts of love" are primarily people, and one such person, Herbert Lindemann, we are all privileged to acknowledge these days.

In this context it is obvious that "countless gifts" also designate those many creations we call works of art. We come by that appellation easily because, for most of us, our own inventories of favorite works of art are derived from personal love affairs with them and because, theologically, we have been taught by Martin Luther to embrace music, at least, but surely all the artistic media as *dona Dei*, gifts of God, bestowed, we confess, out of love.

At that point our happy consensus may begin to break apart, for when we begin to press questions about which arts or what genres go together with liturgy or about what percentage of the church budget should be allotted to investment in the arts, others may seek refuge from our disagreements and our press for decision. Persisting entanglements regarding the arts in the church have led to this rather frank analytical observation from two American writers: "Art is not really necessary to Christian salvation at all. The church

1 Editor's note: The theme of the 1989 Institute of Liturgical Studies at Valparaiso University, where this lecture was delivered, was "With Hearts and Hands and Voices," echoing the second line of the hymn, "Now thank we all our God," which also contains the penultimate line, "with countless gifts of love." See *Evangelical Lutheran Worship* (Augsburg Fortress, 2006), nos. 839 and 840. Herbert Lindemann, liturgical scholar and pastor, was acknowledged at this institute.

can get along without art."[2] We all know Christian brothers and sisters who subscribe to that operating credo.

The situation is complicated by the nearly unlimited accessibility to the arts in our culture. Aesthetic experiences, whatever they are, are so plentiful that one needs to work at the guilt that arises from apathy toward the panoply of opportunities. My neighbor confessed this artistic sin a few days back by admitting to greater joy over the sound of his new CD player than over the Mozart it played. Our technology and wealth infect us with a practiced avoidance of artistic depth, or with what Edward Robinson has called "Acquired Immunity to Mystery Syndrome."[3]

How do we who love the arts respond? With restlessness, to be sure. We watch helplessly as fiscal engineers at various institutions—long ago trained to categorize the arts as alternatives to tennis and volleyball or as tolerable tokens of culture irrelevant to the workplace—trim off the fat of mystery from society's life and from the church's life. Artists fear for their lives, as well as for the world of art they believe essential to the welfare of us all. No wonder they band together, as church musicians have recently done, admirably to explore together the sinews of their profession, though often being forced to look more and more like trade unions.

Years ago, I set out to find or develop that single linkage between music and liturgy that would compel both musician and pastor, artist and theologian, to subscribe to their inextricable partnership. Permit me to give you a progress report: I'm still looking—not that there aren't some warm contenders.

Were it not for my recent African experience, I would have urged on you a reconsideration of music and art as *creaturae Dei* (creatures of God)—part of the creation, as Luther said—whose conservation should be guarded by the church with the same vigor it employs to campaign against nonrecyclable cups, to conserve the atmosphere.

Or I would commend to you the insights that derive from viewing liturgy, music, and all the arts from the posture of the cultural anthropologist, specifically through the lens of structuralists, those who press us to discover meaning in the interrelationship of parts and in how things happen.

Or I would make a case for the inseparable bonds between the components of ritual and the arts, bonds that have been observed, supported, and fostered

---

2 Frank and Dorothy Getlein, as qtd. in Edward Robinson, *The Language of Mystery* (SCM Press, 1985), 59.

3 Robinson, *The Language of Mystery*, 81.

by the anthropological and philosophical studies of people like Suzanne Langer and Carl Kerenyi.[4]

Or I might have urged us to examine the relationships between some current church art and the ancient practice of rhetoric. We might discover that we are "being had" by artists who are interested only in propaganda. Some church artists are intent on persuasion these days, be it through moralistic anthem texts or banners with slogans. Such works depart from efforts at lifting the arts as doorways through which we are pushed to mystery, which is one of the things liturgy is about.

Finally, it would be tempting to explore with theologians and artists a possible mutual ground for discussion. Something like that appears to be evolving from a convergence of fresh mappings of the artistic spirit and life. Writing from within the Matthew Fox school of spirituality, Cynthia Serjak has recently argued for a new recognition of the bondings between music and cosmology. Serjak invites Christians into new discoveries of the spiritual dimensions of the cosmos through music.[5] Another book, *Harmonies of Heaven and Earth*, by Joscelyn Godwin, professor of music at Colgate University, challenges us to discover and rethink the interrelatedness of all things through music, a tenet held at least as early as Boethius (sixth century CE) and at the core of treatises on music through the Reformation.[6] Set that into the context of the popularity of Stephen Hawking's book *A Brief History of Time*, in which the author concludes that it is only a matter of time before we will be presented with a unified theory of the universe: "Then we shall all, philosophers, scientists, and just ordinary people, be able to take part in the discussion of why it is that we and the universe exist."[7] It's intriguing to ask whether Boethius and Hawking and Serjak have something in common and whether the key is music.

But then came Africa, that is, my own twelve-week visit, during which I sought to discover the uniqueness of traditional African music and art. The project surfaced two insights concerning African art that I offer today as two more linkages between art in general and the liturgy. The first might be titled "Gifts Without Strings," by which I mean that works of art are essentially

4 Some of this work has been done by Edward Foley, *Music in Ritual: A Pre-theological Investigation* (Pastoral Press, 1984).

5 Cynthia Serjak, *Music and the Cosmic Dance* (Pastoral Press, 1987), 147–169.

6 Joscelyn Godwin, *Harmonies of Heaven and Earth* (Inner Traditions, 1987).

7 Stephen W. Hawking, *A Brief History of Time* (Bantam, 1988), 175.

self-contained body-and-soul entities set for engagement. The second bears the heading “Now Thank We All . . . with Hearts, Hands, and Voices,” by which I mean to examine the significance of the process of creating art. Following that you will hear how one might particularize these linkages born from a Global South experience.

GIFTS WITHOUT STRINGS

Tanzania in East Africa became home for my spouse, Kristi, and me for a quarter of a year. We were embraced by the faculty, staff, and students at Lutheran Theological College, Makumira, a magnet seminary for the Evangelical Lutheran Church in Tanzania. Excursions into nearby and distant villages and to other of the church’s educational facilities broadened our experience. One such safari took us to Ruhija Evangelical Academy, set on the bluffs overlooking the western shore of Lake Victoria near the city of Bukoba. Ruhija is a mini university, combining a school for evangelists with a school for traditional African art and a school for church music. The entire surrounding area is home for Tanzanians from the Haya kingdom, which in precolonial days extended into modern-day Uganda and Zaire.

It was at Ruhija that we were introduced to the drum and one people’s inextricable involvement with it. Knowing that true African hospitality means engagement at every level, we were not surprised to be directed on our second day there to participate in a class drum lesson for the church musicians. Thirty drums and drummers—both of all sizes. Inside each drum was what appeared to be a loose piece of wood. Could this be a deficient instrument for the visitor, I asked myself, madly trying to follow the rhythms of our master drummer? Afterward it became clear: Like other drums across Africa, my drum contained a small knot tied from cowhide string, the identifying trademark of its maker, who later explained further to me that the knot is the soul of the drum. For the Haya, it truly is.

Later that same day, as we walked through the lush, nearby *shambas* (family gardens), Wilson Niwagila, the principal of the school, unraveled for us some of the deep bonds between the Haya people and their drums. There was a time, Wilson explained, when only the king had drums; they were sounded before and while he spoke as chief warrior and spiritual leader. Years later only certain drums, or drums of a particular size, were assigned that special task. In the minds of the people, these sacred drums became identified with the king himself. Soon the ritual custodian and musician stored them in a special hut where they, like the king, would be protected and accorded special honor. Even when these drums weren't played, the people reckoned them to be soul-and-body entities worthy of care, for they were thought to be equivalent to the king.

This kind of orientation is in the bones and sinews of the Haya people. In 1971 ethnomusicologist Klaus Wachsmann observed similar attachments to the drum among Roman Catholics at the Cathedral in Nnameremba in modern Uganda. One church drum announced its opening in 1892; by 1908 there were six drums for that purpose; and by 1971 all of them were housed in a special hut.[8] Among Haya Lutherans in Bukoba, drums announce the beginning of all festival services at the Cathedral in Bukoba. In the sanctuary itself hang altar and lectern paraments embroidered with cross *and* drum, inviting these Haya people to hear Christ in the drums. Who knows whether the Haya also honor the Spirit of Christ encased in the body of the drum?

Is the drum art? Or is it a membranophone whose art issues in sound? Africans are much more inclined to welcome the drum itself as art; they in fact build them at Ruhija's school of traditional African art. To ask the question another way, do soul and body come together here? Is the drum form and its sound the real substance? Does the work of art refer to something external to the work? Is that "something" best and ultimately presented through cognitive and verbal means?

According to John Cook, some theologians have tended to respond to queries such as these by assigning the arts a penultimate role on the way to comprehension. For instance, Cook faults Jacques Maritain because he thought artworks are tools for revelation, pointing beyond themselves, thus providing another way of looking at the real world. According to this view, art serves simply as means to some other end. Paul Tillich, despite his high view of art, also held that art assists us by offering clues about a predetermined view of the world and God.[9] It can be thought of as dispensable once insight is gained. Many Africans would find this to be incomprehensible.

---

8 Klaus P. Wachsmann, "Musical Instruments in Kigandu Tradition and Their Place in the East African Scene," in *Essays on Music and History in Africa*, ed. Klaus P. Wachsmann (Northwestern University Press, 1971), 101.

9 John Cook, "The Arts in Theological Education for the Church," *Theological Education* 25, no. 1 (Autumn 1988): 23–24.

In Africa, meanwhile, the souls of the drums kept rattling. Their seeming independent, self-contained life served as a kind of artistic parallel to other examples of African art, we discovered later. For instance, in West Africa this personalized attention to art surrounds the *Ibeji* twins, not-quite-identical wooden carvings valued by the Yoruba people. The twins take on a life of their own, being housed, dressed, and in certain instances provided with nourishment.

Is this general African understanding of art unique? My own reflections during warm Tanzanian afternoons without telephone and meetings may coincide with your own. I have always been tempted to approach works of art as living entities. My experiences with instrumental music nudge me to such enthusiasm. There is a kind of soul/body unity presented in Bach's Prelude and Fugue in G Major, for instance, which for me points nowhere; it simply *is*. Same composer for a vocal example: The Bach St. John Passion *presents* an experience of the passion that is possible no other way. It appears to be a living soul/body entity that covets interaction, *my* interaction. If it is a means to anything or anybody, it participates in the mystery we know as our Lord Jesus Christ, who, Paul tells us in Colossians, is mysteriously central to the work of art in another way—for Jesus is "before all things and in him all things hold together" (1:17). If this sounds like an elevation of the arts to things sacramental, I don't apologize, for Lutherans have always been a bit reckless about such matters.[10] Nevertheless, it is probably wise to keep the sacramental issue at bay, even though it's edifying to allow oneself to be teased by it on occasion.

Whether or not the Bach prelude and fugue shares something in common with the Haya drum, on the other hand, is a question given considerable clarity through an interpretative approach to African art proposed by Robert Plant Armstrong. He has sought to understand Yoruba art in its cultural setting and offers a way to apprehend all art in a manner that is tantalizingly resonant with experience.

He begins with the observation that a work of art is a thing in itself, without extrinsic meaning.[11] In this respect works of art are to be distinguished from

10 One discussion of this together with some citations from Luther is offered by Oskar Söhngen, "Theologische Grundlagen der Kirchenmusik," in *Die Musik des evangelischen Gottesdienstes*, vol. 4 of *Leiturgia: Handbuch des evangelischen Gottesdienstes*, ed. Karl Ferdinand Müller et al. (Stauda, 1961), 184ff. and 258.

11 What follows is a summary of some of the theories proposed by Robert Plant Armstrong, *The Affecting Presence* (University of Illinois Press, 1971), 1–100.

symbols; the latter are, strictly speaking, vehicles of meaning whose physical natures are somewhat arbitrary and whose significant meaning is external. For example, water triggers in us notions of washing, baptism, and possibly our own baptism. Few of those referents are immediately apparent or present; in fact, a major characteristic of symbols is their ability to transport and convey an accumulation of histories and meanings. Hence, their significance and value grow as the external referents multiply and are assimilated.

A work of art, on the other hand, is physically identical to its meaning, claims Armstrong, and via the means of metaphor, that work of art is identical to the emotion transacted. Works of art, he maintains, are actual presentations of the life of feeling; through metaphor (i.e., the movement from what is well known to the less well known), works of art incarnate the nonverbal, affective life of human beings. That life incorporates potency, emotion, values, and states of being. Because works of art present the life of feeling, they are themselves presences. Because they are themselves incarnations of being, they are affecting; that is, most come into our sphere of consciousness with the intent to cause effect. Presentation, asserts Armstrong, not representation, is the goal of art. Hence, he prefers to speak of works of art as works of affecting presence. They are self-contained, self-perpetuating, and even demonstrate a kind of immortality. So it is that one experiences the unmistakable presence of an artifact recently exhumed by archaeologists.

A work of affecting presence is like an actor; it has its own autonomy. In this way the presence is subject. However, in engagement a work of art also becomes object, receiving the attention of an auditor or perceptor. In certain highly charged instances, such a work of affecting presence receives extraordinary attention as if it were royalty or a demigod. Once created, it doesn't need its creator anymore—it is free from extrinsic meaning; it is its own meaning. Yet that meaning is derived from the initial impulses of its creator. Summarizing his own work, Armstrong writes:

> In [the] universe of feeling the affecting presence is a special thing, for whereas all objects and events in the realm of the sensibilities *are* by virtue of metaphor *what they convey,* the affecting presence is more than simply this. It is always, in one respect at least, the recipient of special treatment; unlike the decorative element . . . the affecting presence is a special kind of entity, an end in itself. It is a self-contained, self-sufficient, whole act of being. The affecting presence, then, is a

> very particular cultural reality, an entity, like the creator from whom it sprang and whom it perpetuates.[12]

If the soul/body entity, or what Armstrong calls *affecting presence*, has an existence independent of extrinsic meaning, then works of art confront us with reality otherwise inaccessible. We can relate to them as if to another person. One theologian, at least, comes close to such a lofty regard for the art encounter. Langdon Gilkey challenges us to make place for the arts because they provide a unique entrance to reality and then push us through that entrance. In a word, they disclose reality.[13] Such a high sense of purpose warms the hearts of those who love God because of and through "countless gifts of love," and it gives us courage to proclaim and live out assertions about the essential necessity for the arts in the church. Precisely because the arts cannot be translated entirely into other modalities, their disclosures must have implications for theological work, as theologian Karl Rahner has suggested.[14]

And how about the artists? Do they imagine themselves as creators of "beings" that have such effects? Some are rather forthright about their artistic intent. Aaron Copland, to be sure before his flirtations with serialism, commented, "What, after all, do I put down when I put down notes? I put down a reflection of emotional states. . . . Art particularizes and makes actual these fluent emotional states."[15] Chagall spoke of his painting as "a tissue of flesh, made up of all my thoughts, dreams, and experiences."[16] As flesh, it has taken on its own life, a presence intended to affect.

To obtain the full impact of Armstrong's observation, it is necessary to present a little fuller account. The feeling, potency, or value in a work of affecting presence is culturally determined. That explains matters of style and persisting forms and themes in a given group. Moreover, reflection on the arts in general suggests that affecting presences fall into categories fixed around one of three axes: spatial (sculpture, painting), temporal (music, poetry, and narrative), and spatial/temporal (drama and dance). Those three categories rest on another foundation, which Armstrong identifies as the cultural

12 Armstrong, *The Affecting Presence*, 194–195.

13 As qtd. in John Dillenberger, *A Theology of Artistic Sensibilities* (Crossroad, 1986), 221.

14 As qtd. in Dillenberger, *A Theology of Artistic Sensibilities*, 228.

15 Cited in Janet R. Walton, *Art and Worship* (Michael Glazier, 1988), 74.

16 Cited in Walton, *Art and Worship*, 80.

metaphoric base, or that which gives to a wide range of things their cultural identity (such as German Romanticism or American Neoclassicism). At bedrock is the universal metaphoric base, which makes it possible for people of all cultures to become engaged in some way by a work of affecting presence.

The axes in turn are culturally refined to accommodate the particular cultural base that is to be modulated. To better understand how that happens, Armstrong proposes a simple matrix consisting of two sets of opposites. An affecting presence tends to be modulated by either *intension* (tightly compacted and narrow-scoped detail) or *extension* (loosely arranged components). That's one set.

Another set moves between *continuity* (an attempt to demonstrate connections to the past or present) and *discontinuity* (no attempt at connections, a deliberate attempt at individuality). From these two sets, Armstrong derives four possible modulation patterns: intensive continuity, intensive discontinuity, extensive continuity, and extensive discontinuity.

Examples might deliver all of this from impractical erudition or clinical pigeonholing. Applied to music, intensive continuity shows up in a narrow tonal spectrum and in deliberate ties to tradition, intensive discontinuity shows up in a narrow tonal spectrum with varieties of junctures and segments, extensive continuity is evident in broad tonal spectrum and deliberate relatedness, and extensive discontinuity is noticeable in broad tonal spectrum with no genetic development.

How this can be of assistance becomes clear when you put these patterns to work. Armstrong has helped me understand the uncomplicated chordal vocabulary so typical to East African church music. Chordal structure and progressions are relatively new in the African experience, having been chiefly introduced by nineteenth-century missionaries. Those missionaries were and are highly regarded, however. Hence, uncomplicated chordal development is clearly a manifestation of intensive continuity. That same kind of modulation shows up in the ebony wood carvings of the Makonde people of East Africa. They display their creativity in variation upon variation of single artistic ideas: for example, in the narrow vertical human totem or in the corpus of Christ detached from the cross. All in all, East Africans develop art that reflects a culture that is intensive and highly desirous of continuity.

We experience affecting presence through cultural modes. Many of the characteristics of these modes, as we will point out later, resonate with Christian liturgy and suggest how well art and liturgy can get along. Gifts without strings, these soul/body entities that Armstrong calls *affecting presences* demand from us a certain seriousness. Any other alternative suggests casual behavior that prejudges the worth of the presence. Sometimes, however, some art-like entities only appear to be presences. Advertising jingles, department store dummies, some posters, and many church banners have as their sole purpose to persuade you and me to offer loyalty to a particular product. They solicit confidence in their integrity as affecting presences, may even display certain valid characteristics, but in the end, it is clear their sole purpose is profit rather than an enlargement of our apprehension of reality.

Other problems persist. Our availability to affecting presence is diminished by the bulk of stimuli that address our senses. It is nearly impossible to seriously hear any performance of Handel's *Messiah* during the Christmas season. We tend to protect ourselves from affecting presence overkill by filtering out most of the sound, hearing the music as pleasant background music. What's left, then, in our art-filled society, is to substitute economic motivations for a serious engagement. To buy and sell affecting presence is then championed as the primary way of dealing with works of art. We have become unwilling victims of that process, and we are the weaker for it.

But soul/body entities remain undaunted and tireless and stand as powerful witnesses that we can't go on pretending that the whole world of art out there is simply a billboard or merely for sale. Sooner or later, we will have to be engaged, even if it means saying no to affecting presence as if one were on a diet (as I did once for two years with *Messiah*). When such engagement seems appropriate again, it will bring us to new dimensions of mystery and possibly to new experiences of community. For affecting presences are diametrically opposed to individualism; they make it possible to apprehend the height and breadth of the whole human mystery and put us in touch with others. And, as will become apparent in the next section, engagements such as that are the means for discovering one's true identity in the cradle of community.

In sum, Haya drums and other like works of art confront us as self-contained soul/body entities set for engagement. Understood as affecting presence, they metaphorically present feelings, emotions, potency, and values through the work of their creators. Though filtered through cultural structures and various modes, they nevertheless address us with a seriousness that demands engagement, which in turn leads to the disclosure of reality. Because of the self-sufficiency of affecting presence, works of art provide entrance to life's mystery not otherwise possible.

NOW THANK WE ALL . . . WITH HEARTS, HANDS, AND VOICES

All works of affecting presence, Armstrong has instructed us, beg for some sort of engagement, which can range from saying no to having a substantial mental or emotional alteration in ourselves. Those arts that fall into the temporary/spatial axis—that is, drama, dance, and, to some extent, music—intensify the expectations for response of a physical sort. In our culture, that kind of response is often not encouraged because we have "civilized" such engagements to the extent that even a cough during a symphony concert is considered rude. Contrast that with a typical Italian opera audience, where overt participation is almost expected, especially if the performance doesn't meet up to audience anticipations.

Most of the cultural clichés about Africa are just that these days. Traditional folk dances are frequently done by specialized groups and then only for entertainment. But certain behavioral patterns that we might expect do persist. Participation in a musical event is assumed, for instance, even if that means a gentle swaying of heads or arms.

Parish liturgies in Africa include some performer/listener situations, but the established pattern is the singing of hymns and liturgy by everyone. Participation is a condition of attendance—it's the reason for coming in the first place. Hymn and liturgical accompaniment is unnecessary, for the parishioners simply move from one segment to the next, all having the pitch somehow embedded in their bones. Perhaps communal pitch memory is a sign of deeply shared musical experience, not unlike the kind of pitch memory John Blacking has observed among some children of Africa when they band together to perform their songs, on each occasion using the pitch in which they originally learned them.[17]

This desire to participate in communal music shows itself in other ways. During our stay at Ruhijà, the church music students, together with the rest of the student body, presented us with a concert. We arrived early into what can only be described as a spontaneous jam session. A few church music students had begun to play on the xylophones; others joined in on drums; more found

17 John Blacking, "Music and the Historical Process in Vendaland," in *Essays on Music and History in Africa*, ed. Klaus P. Wachsmann (Northwestern University Press, 1971), 197.

rattles, kayambas, and finally anything that sounded, until everyone was in on an improvisation that had every bit the characteristics of affecting presence.

A similar unfolding of community through music occurred at a Roman Catholic seminary near Arusha, in Tanzania. At the close of the mass, the whole congregation broke into a trope based on the response "Thanks be to God" (*Asante*), sung after the presider had said, "Go in peace, the mass is ended." From every corner of the rectangular space came the sounds of voices; then, one by one, the voices were embellished by a tambourine here, claves there, one drum here, another there until there was an expansive outburst of improvisatory praise. No one missed the moment.

This compulsion to participate most clearly manifests itself in the African understanding of rhythm. Common perception holds that Africans and their descendants in this country have rhythm, as is often said, and we have come to expect rhythmic prominence from African and African American music. To become a master drummer in Africa requires many years of apprenticeship and a series of initiation rites, presumably so that the novice can deal with the affecting presences embodied in the drums. Europeans and Americans understand the uniqueness of African rhythm when it is explained as layers of differing rhythms much like layers of melody lines that comprise polyphonic music. That's the structure; the meaning is another matter.

For many Africans, according to master drummer Robert Chernoff,[18] rhythm occurs when there are at least two different but simultaneous patterns. A single pattern is always incomplete; it is merely an ingredient. Further, two rhythmic patterns are normally given to two people, three patterns to three, and so on. Although it might be true that a talented drummer in Africa or in North America could simultaneously negotiate two or three patterns, in Africa these patterns are shared with others. Without participation, rhythmic patterns have no meaning. Hence, silences here and there in the rhythmic presentation are invitations for another to enter with a unique personal contribution. Even if there is no formal pattern to be offered, says Chernoff, Africans expect those physically present to offer some addition to the whole, if only a gentle movement of the head, indicating a unique comprehension of all the elements. Everyone expects to be engaged. In this context, improvisation was born and is nurtured. The master drummer skillfully holds it all

18 What follows derives from John Miller Chernoff, *African Rhythm and African Sensibility* (University of Chicago Press, 1979), passim.

together and like a good host arranges for "space" so that always one more person might find a place in the group.

An African rhythmic presentation is a social happening, which is why most social events successfully evolve through music. Where there is music, something is happening. Because of such intricate social and communal understructure, musical presentations, especially rhythmic epiphanies, pulsate with ethical sensitivity and care. From this base the musical event draws meaning, according to Chernoff: "In music, random improvisation and imprecision spoil the delicate structure of the rhythms, and in society random expressions spoil the delicate structure of communication."[19]

Because music is a mode of being in society, Africans understand music as a "species-specific trait of humans."[20] They are puzzled with the typically North American approach to music as a tool for competition, the best, the loudest, or the richest receiving reward. For the African, music is simply shared experience. The African way is attractive. With all our hearts we wish for once that we didn't have to beg, cajole, threaten, or seduce people into opening their service books and mouths for the hymnody of the parish. We grow weary of devising ever-new ways for garnering support for the arts in and for the liturgy. It is enough to make artists give up.

Fortunately, most don't. They are a stubborn lot, to be sure, but there may be another reason they are determined to assist the church in its liturgy. All artists from time to time reflect on the process of creating—what it is, how it happens, and its significance for their lives. Some say that the creative process brings them closer than anything else to the being of God.

Like God, the creative process is profoundly complex. One study has focused on a single aspect. Performance, Ellen Basso has discovered, is integral to the Kalapalo people of Central America and to their interaction with communal myth. Performance is undertaken as a way to embrace culture and to integrate one's own experience with it.[21] Basso's study in fact changes our notions of performance from something done under the scrutiny of others to an event of cultural or cultic significance in which individuals, artists and nonartists alike, creatively participate. There is help here for those interested in the nature of ritual.

---

19 Chernoff, *African Rhythm and African Sensibility*, 167.

20 John Blacking, *How Musical Is Man?* (University of Washington Press, 1973), 44.

21 Ellen B. Basso, *A Musical View of the Universe* (University of Pennsylvania Press, 1985).

Basso maintains that performances assist one's development by integrating changing roles, ideas, and ideals into the received tradition. What is held true by the group is explored and developed through action. Performed events are the place where creative experimentation is both appropriate and expected, and through it new understandings emerge, and they in turn find expression and new forms. In an attempt to distinguish Kalapalo experience from our own, Basso reflects that we tend to place emphasis on the finished work of art as something to perceive or hear, while people from the Kalapalo tradition invest in performance as the art of creating, for through it one is given opportunity to rearrange the factors of tradition and present experience. The creative process in performance constitutes a "clarification of reality,"[22] and at least within the Kalapalo tradition these performances arc chiefly musical.[23] We are here led to an understanding of the function described as improvising on a well-known hymn tune. According to Basso, performance of this kind provides personal growth for the participant. But there are other benefits as well.

From this perspective, cultural forms created within a performative frame can be regarded as strikingly imaginative sources of variation and adaptation to changing conditions—reservoirs for models of new social relationships, attitude, and moral-evaluative systems, the materials for new cultural inventions.[24]

Shared experiences resulting from common engagement with works of art—that is, works of affecting presence—activate levels and tracks of bonding that deepen our sense of community. That is why we like to visit art museums *with* somebody. In performance this process is heightened because there is a chance to reconstruct or rearrange our worlds of value through the interplay of tradition and actual experience, of self and other selves.

PERPLEXED WITH COUNTLESS GIFTS OF LOVE

Try as it might sometimes, the church cannot remove itself from the influence of the arts. Within or alongside the liturgy, the arts challenge the church to be

22 Basso, *Musical View*, 4.

23 Basso, *Musical View*, 8, cites a comment from Claude Lévi-Strauss that "an understanding of music might be the key to understanding myth."

24 Basso, *Musical View*, 5.

itself precisely in, with, and under the arts. Additional understandings about the inner workings of art suggest that we explore some redesigned linkages between the arts and liturgy, with the frank admission that what follows is only the beginning of such a process.

It would of course be foolish to assume that each of us knows what the other means by *liturgy*. To get at the task quickly, permit me to ruminate about arts and the liturgy under three commonly accepted functions of liturgy: (1) liturgy as epiphany of the church, (2) liturgy for the life of the world, and (3) liturgy as the work of the people.

Jean-Jacques von Allmen's insightful observation concerning liturgy as the epiphany of the church[25] serves to lift the liturgical assembly from the category of mundane gathering to a timeless, boundless particularization in the monarchy of God. You can say that all you want, perhaps know it, but never experience it unless assisted by the arts. If the arts are works of affecting presence, Christian examples carry the exciting potential of embodying an epiphany of the Holy Spirit, for they were sparked into existence by creators musing in, with, and under the Spirit. This, it seems to me, is the truth behind iconography, as articulated by St. John Chrysostom: "After [the saints'] death . . . the grace of the Holy Spirit inexhaustibly dwells . . . in their holy images."[26] In a comprehensive way, the whole of Christian art is a manifestation of the workings of the Holy Spirit and presents us with a specialized epiphany of church that is parallel and complementary to the liturgy, at least if the observations about affecting presence are accurate. Works of affecting presence support liturgical epiphany and in their own way ensure the tradition of the church. In this way, "the record of history lives in the arts," as Martha Graham has said.[27]

Further, that tradition perpetuated by works of art, besides being living and therefore changing, is a tradition apart from the verbal and cognitive, centered rather in the feelings, emotions, and values of the saints before, for better or worse. Works of art are a record of how the church *felt* in the power of the Spirit, a scary thought to theologians trapped in their own left brains.

---

25 Jean-Jacques von Allmen, *Worship: Its Theology and Practice* (Oxford, 1965), 42–56.

26 Cited in Léonide Ouspensky and Vladimir Lossky, *The Meaning of Icons* (St. Vladimir's Seminary Press, 1983), 44.

27 Cited in Mircea Eliade, *Symbolism, the Sacred, and the Arts*, ed. Diane Apostolos-Cappadona (Crossroad, 1986), xvi.

Like the verbal tradition, works of art need periodic critique and reevaluation. Some no longer engage positively, as, for example, presences that beg surrender to death for the cause of virginity. Some presences, if they are to have *affect*, require profound engagement, hard work, if not special invocation of the Spirit (organ works of Messiaen?). Yet complication carries no special blessing. In the relationship between liturgy and the arts, less is probably more. Bombardment leads to total disengagement and eventual boredom with affecting presence or the liturgy itself.

Continuity is important to the church, for its liturgy exists in the company of saints, as one holy catholic and apostolic church. Works of affecting presence, then, will have their greatest impact when they fall within the continuity mode of the matrix proposed by Armstrong. Sometimes intensive continuity assists (nineteen-stanza chorales for a German parish); sometimes extensive continuity serves (such as Corbusier's pilgrim chapel at Ronchamp).

We like to speak as well about the church at liturgy for the life of the world. In spite of the in-house nature of Christian eucharistic liturgy—an event primarily meant for those initiated—Christians purport to gather in liturgy in order to ritualize God's actions on them and their own actions in the world as the body of Christ. Resurrected life is the sole energy for the entire liturgical action. However, the cultic activity of the church at worship grows in clarity and authenticity as the church feels the pulse of the world, its emotions, its values, and its sense of being. Precisely because of that attention to the world, the church will discover those ways to filter the gospel energy into the bloodstreams of life.

Ultimately this is one complex process requiring delicate (should we say *artistic*?) balance in the liturgy. But the arts supply assists at crucial junctures in the liturgy to contextualize Christian ritual. The *pulse* of the world, or, more modestly, of our culture, best reveals itself in the arts. Attention to the arts, to contemporary art (and artists), will yield not only innumerable fields of evangelism and service but also places where the reality of this world is being disclosed for affirmation and blessing.

Another face of liturgy is its never-ending task of empowering the assembly to be the body of Christ for a hungry world. There is abundant talk among theologians these days regarding the imaging of the faith. *Imaging* is a buzzword. By it church folks hope to provide fresh ways of comprehending world and faith. It takes stamina, sometimes, to hear out theologians on this matter, for their much talk leads to boredom. Images are what artists are about. Hymnists and poets, as always, have moved more who worship these days than many a prosaic preacher struggling to provide new images by telling us a story. Unless, of course, the preacher is artist too. But ordination does not bestow the muse. The very task prescribed by theologians is the task meant for the artists. Artists are the ones who can embrace the feelings, values, and hopes of those who are battered, those with AIDS, and oppressed minorities, and artists are the ones who can *present* them to the rest of us, inducing empathetic response from us and from those whose hope, yet unknown, is in Christ.

Losing faith in this fundamental gift of the arts has impoverished liturgy and thus the church. Reinvestment promises integrity of the liturgy, integrity of the people who do liturgy, and integrity of the whole church as it worships for the life of the world.

Liturgy (from *leiturgia*), most of us now know, means *the work of the people*: all the people. Each person's tongue is important to the chorus of saints. Offering one's own tongue to the chorus of tradition was a way Christian scholars understood their contributions to the church's teaching. Glossing, as it is called, dates from at least the time of Christ. In a way this modest method of participation, practiced by writers and composers alike, is central to the notion of performance discussed earlier. Performative glossing is what we do when we sing hymns, march in procession, or even share the greeting of peace. In each one of these events, we expand our own accumulated experience of a particular liturgical event and are surprised by ever-new realizations from the experience itself. Performative arts in or as liturgy yield a tradition always being challenged and altered. People are given permission to blend their lives with tradition, and people have a chance to build integrity into their lives through participation. The significance of live performance understood this way accentuates the prominence of music and drama in liturgy and should mobilize liturgists and musicians alike against any kind of prepackaging of liturgy that bypasses participation.

How can one escape the conclusion that every possible way must be explored to encourage and facilitate performative or participatory events in the liturgy? In a time often bereft of linkages between arts and liturgy, the vision of a fully participating community dare never be lost to artists and theologians alike. Otherwise, we will be cursed to a cult of virtuosos and to a cadre of pseudo-professionals who think arts in the church have to do with interior decorating.

"Now thank *we all* our God with hearts *and* hands *and* voices" is more than an old song; it is a persistent invitation to live and play as whole people in the presence of God for the world and to receive those countless gifts the Spirit of God patiently waits to give us.

Bibliography

Works frequently cited are identified by the following abbreviations:

BC *The Book of Concord: The Confessions of the Evangelical Lutheran Church*, edited by Robert Kolb and Timothy J. Wengert. Fortress Press, 2000.

LW *Luther's Works: American Edition*, 82 vols. Concordia and Fortress, 1955–.

PSI Luther, Martin. "Martinus Luther musicae studiosis." Preface to *Symphoniae iucundae arque adeo breves quatuor vocum*. Georg Rhau, 1538. Translated by Leofranc Holford-Strevens in J. Andreas Loewe, "'Musica est optimum': Martin Luther's Theory of Music." *Music and Letters* 94, no. 4 (2013): 573–605.

TAL *The Annotated Luther*, 6 vols. Fortress Press, 2015–2017.

WA *Luthers Werke: Kritische Gesamtausgabe* [*Schriften*], 73 vols. Böhlau, 1883–2009.

WA BR *Luthers Werke: Kritische Gesamtausgabe, Breifwechsel*, 18 vols. Böhlau, 1930–1985.

WA TR *Luthers Werke: Kritische Gesamtausgabe, Tischreden*, 6 vols. Böhlau, 1912–1921.

Abert, Hermann. *Die Musikanschauung des Mittelalters und ihre Grundlagen*. Niemeyer, 1905. Reprinted, Schneider, 1964.

Abrams, Meyer H. *The Mirror and the Lamp*. Oxford University Press, 1953.

Adam of Fulda. "Musica, pars prima." *De musica*. In *Scriptores ecclesiastici de musica sacra potissimum*, edited by Martin Gerbert. Typis San-Blasianis, 1784; facsimile edition: Olms, 1963. Online at Thesaurus Musicarum Latinarum, siglum FULMUS1.

Agawu, Kofi. *Representing African Music: Postcolonial Notes, Queries, Positions*. Routledge, 2003.

Anttila, Miikka. *Luther's Theology of Music: Spiritual Beauty and Pleasure*. de Gruyter, 2013.

Armstrong, Robert Plant. *The Affecting Presence*. University of Illinois Press, 1971.

Arom, Simha, and Frédéric Voisin. "Theory and Technology in African Music." In *Africa*, edited by Ruth Stone, vol. 1 of *The Garland Encyclopedia of World Music*. Garland, 1998.

Attali, Jacques. *Noise: The Political Economy of Music*. Translated by Brian Massumi. University of Minnesota Press, 1985.

Aubert, Laurent. *The Music of the Other: New Challenges for Ethnomusicology in a Global Age*. Translated by Carla Ribeiro. Ashgate, 2007.

Bangert, Mark P. "Dynamics of World Musics: A Methodology for Evaluation." In *Worship and Culture: Foreign Country or Homeland?*, edited by Glaucia Vasconcelos Wilkey. Eerdmans, 2014.

——— "Listen to the Birds: Luther on Music." *TEAR Online* [journal of the Centre de Recursos Litúrgicos de Faculdadas EST no Igreja Evangélica de Confissão Luterana no Brasil] 4, no. 1 (Summer 2015): 114–137. http://periodicos.est.edu.br/index.php/tear.
———. "Rehabilitating the Vocation of the Cantor with the Help of the Early Church and Johannes Bugenhagen." In *Subject to None, Servant of All: Essays in Christian Scholarship in Honor of Kurt Karl Hendel*, edited by Peter Vethanayagamony and Kenneth Sawyer. Lutheran University Press, 2016.
Basso, Ellen B. *A Musical View of the Universe*. University of Pennsylvania Press, 1985.
Bayer, Oswald. *Martin Luther's Theology*. Translated by Thomas H. Trapp. Eerdmans, 2008.
Begbie, Jeremy S., and Steven R. Guthrie, eds. *Resonant Witness: Conversations Between Music and Theology*. Eerdmans, 2011.
Blacking, John. *How Musical Is Man?* University of Washington Press, 1973.
———. "Music and the Historical Process in Vendaland." In *Essays on Music and History in Africa*, edited by Klaus P. Wachsmann. Northwestern University Press, 1971.
Blankenburg, Walter. "Luther und die Musik." In *Kirche und Musik: Gesammelte Aufsätze zur Geschichte der gottesdienstlichen Musik*, edited by Erich Hübner and Renate Steiger. Vandenhoeck & Ruprecht,1979.
Block, Johannes. *Verstehen durch Musik: Das gesungene Wort in der Theologie: Ein hermeneutischer Beitrag zur Hymnologie am Beispiel Martin Luthers*. Francke, 2002.
Blume, Friedrich, ed. *Protestant Church Music: A History*. Norton, 1974. Translation of a major portion of *Geschichte der evangelischen Kirchenmusik*, 2nd edition, edited by Friedrich Blume. Bärenreiter, 1964.
Bowman, Wayne D. *Philosophical Perspectives on Music*. Oxford University Press, 1998.
Brown, Steven, Björn Merker, and Nils L. Wallin. "An Introduction to Evolutionary Musicology." In *The Origins of Music*, edited by Nils L. Wallin, Björn Merker, and Steven Brown. MIT Press, 2001.
Brown, Steven. "The 'Musilanguage' Model of Music Evolution." In *The Origins of Music*, edited by Nils L. Wallin, Björn Merker, and Steven Brown. MIT Press, 2001.
Bunt, Leslie, and Mercédès Pavlicevic. "Music and Emotion: Perspectives from Music Therapy." In *Music and Emotion: Theory and Research*, edited by Patrik N. Juslin and John A. Sloboda. Oxford University Press, 2001.
Buszin, Walter E. *Luther on Music*. North Central Publishing, 1958.
Chernoff, John Miller. *African Rhythm and African Sensibility*. University of Chicago Press, 1979.
Christensen, Thomas, ed. *The Cambridge History of Western Music Theory*. Cambridge University Press, 2002.
Cohen, David E. "Notes, Scales, and Modes in the Earlier Middle Ages." In *The Cambridge History of Western Music Theory*, edited by Thomas Christensen. Cambridge University Press, 2002.
Cook, John. "The Arts in Theological Education for the Church." *Theological Education* 25, no. 1 (Autumn 1988): 23–24.
Cook, Nicholas. *Music: A Very Short Introduction*. Oxford University Press, 1998.
———, and Nicola Dibben. "Musicological Approaches to Emotion." In *Music and Emotion: Theory and Research*, edited by Patrik N. Juslin and John A. Sloboda. Oxford University Press, 2001.
Cope, David. *New Directions in Music*. 7th ed. Waveland, 2001.

Deflem, Mathieu. "Popular Music and Social Control: The Moral Panic on Music Labeling." *American Journal of Criminal Justice* 45 (2020): 2–24.

DeNora, Tia. "Aesthetic Agency and Musical Practice: New Directions in the Sociology of Music and Emotion." In *Music and Emotion: Theory and Research*, edited by Patrik N. Juslin and John A. Sloboda. Oxford University Press, 2001.

Dillenberger, John. *A Theology of Artistic Sensibilities*. Crossroad, 1986.

Duffy, Kathryn Ann Pohlmann. "The Jena Choirbooks: Music and Liturgy at the Castle Church in Wittenberg Under Frederick the Wise, Elector of Saxony." PhD diss., University of Chicago, 1995.

Elert, Werner. *The Structure of Lutheranism*. Translated by Walter A. Hansen. Concordia, 1962.

Eliade, Mircea. *Symbolism, the Sacred, and the Arts*, edited by Diane Apostolos-Cappadona. Crossroad, 1986.

Evangelical Lutheran Church in America. *Principles for Worship*. Renewing Worship, vol. 2. Augsburg Fortress, 2002.

Evangelical Lutheran Worship. Commended for use in the Evangelical Lutheran Church in America and the Evangelical Lutheran Church in Canada. Augsburg Fortress, 2006.

Falkenroth, Christoph. *Die Musica speculativa des Johannes de Muris*. Steiner, 1992.

Faulkner, Quentin. *Wiser than Despair: The Evolution of Ideas in the Relationship of Music and the Christian Church*. Greenwood, 1996.

Feld, Steven. *Sound and Sentiment: Birds, Weeping, Poetics, and Song in Kaluli Expression*. University of Pennsylvania Press, 1982.

Finscher, Ludwig, Andreas Jaschinski, and Ilka Sühring, eds. *Die Musik in Geschichte und Gegenwart: Allgemeine Enzyklopädie der Musik*, 29 vols. Bärenreiter, 1994–2008.

Foley, Edward. *Music in Ritual: A Pre-theological Investigation*. Pastoral Press, 1984.

Frith, Simon. *Performing Rites: On the Value of Popular Music*. Harvard University Press, 1996.

Garside, Charles, Jr. *The Origins of Calvin's Theology of Music*. American Philosophical Society, 1979.

———. *Zwingli and the Arts*. Yale University Press, 1966.

Godwin, Joscelyn. *Harmonies of Heaven and Earth*. Inner Traditions, 1987.

Gouk, Penelope. "The Role of Harmonics in the Scientific Revolution." In *The Cambridge History of Western Music Theory*, edited by Thomas Christensen. Cambridge University Press, 2002.

Geystliche Lieder. / Mit einer newen vorrhede / D. Mart. Luth. Babst, 1545. Facsimile edition, *Das Babst'sche Gesangbuch 1545*, edited by Konrad Ameln. Bärenreiter, 1929.

Halter, Carl, and Carl Schalk, eds. *A Handbook of Church Music*. Concordia, 1978.

Hanslick, Eduard. *On the Musically Beautiful*. Translated by Lee Rothfarb and Christoph Landerer. Oxford University Press, 2018.

Hawking, Stephen W. *A Brief History of Time*. Bantam, 1988.

Hayburn, Robert F., ed. *Papal Legislation on Sacred Music 95 A.D. to 1977 A.D.* Liturgical Press, 1979.

Helmer, Christine, ed. *The Global Luther: A Theologian for Modern Times*. Fortress Press, 2009.

Hendrickson, Marion Lars. *Musica Christi: A Lutheran Aesthetic*. Peter Lang, 2005.

Herl, Joseph. *Worship Wars in Early Lutheranism: Choir, Congregation, and Three Centuries of Conflict*. Oxford University Press, 2004.

Hill, Peter, and Nigel Simeone. *Messiaen*. Yale University Press, 2005.
Hindemith, Paul. *The Craft of Musical Composition*. Translated by Arthur Mendel. Associated Music Publishers, 1942.
Johnson, Bruce, and Martin Cloonan. *Dark Side of the Tune: Popular Music and Violence*. Ashgate, 2008.
Judd, Cristle Collins. "Renaissance Modal Theory: Theoretical, Compositional, and Editorial Perspectives." In *The Cambridge History of Western Music Theory*, edited by Thomas Christensen. Cambridge University Press, 2002.
Jungmann, Joseph. *The Mass of the Roman Rite: Its Origins and Development*. Translated by Francis Brunner. Benzinger, 1955.
Juslin, Patrik N., and John A. Sloboda, eds. *Music and Emotion: Theory and Research*. Oxford University Press, 2001.
Kalb, Friedrich. *Theology of Worship in 17th-Century Lutheranism*. Translated by Henry P. A. Hamann. Concordia, 1963.
Krentz, Christopher. *Writing Deafness: The Hearing Line in Nineteenth-Century American Literature*. University of North Carolina Press, 2007.
Krummacher, Christoph. *Musik als praxis pietatis: Zum Selbstverständnis evangelischer Kirchenmusik*. Vandenhoeck & Ruprecht, 1994.
Kurzschenkel, Winfried. *Die theologische Bestimmung der Musik*. Paulinus, 1971.
Lathrop, Gordon W., and Timothy J. Wengert. *Christian Assembly: Marks of the Church in a Pluralistic Age*. Fortress Press, 2004.
Leach, Elizabeth Eva. *Sung Birds: Music, Nature, and Poetry in the Later Middle Ages*. Cornell University Press, 2007.
Leaver, Robin A. *Luther's Liturgical Music: Principles and Implications*. Eerdmans, 2007. Reprinted: Fortress Press, 2017.
———, ed. *A New Song We Now Begin: Celebrating the Half Millennium of Lutheran Hymnals 1524–2024*. Fortress Press, 2024.
———. *The Whole Church Sings: Congregational Singing in Luther's Wittenberg*. Eerdmans, 2017.
Loewe, J. Andreas. "'Musica est optimum': Martin Luther's Theory of Music." *Music and Letters* 94, no. 4 (2013): 573–605.
Loewe, J. Andreas, and Katherine Firth. *Martin Luther and the Arts: Music, Images, and Drama to Promote the Reformation*. Brill, 2023.
Lundberg, Mattias, Maria Schildt, and Jonas Lundblad, eds. *Lutheran Music Culture: Ideals and Practices*. de Gruyter, 2021.
Marler, Peter. "Origins of Music and Speech: Insights from Animals." In *The Origins of Music*, edited by Nils L. Wallin, Björn Merker, and Steven Brown. MIT Press, 2001.
Martin, Peter J. *Sounds and Society*. Manchester University Press, 1995.
Mattfeld, Victor H. *Georg Rhaw's Publications for Vespers*. Institute of Mediaeval Music, 1966.
Mattheson, Johann. *Der vollkommene Capellmeister* (Hamburg: Herold, 1739), edited by Frederike Ramm with a new typeset of text and notes. Bärenreiter, 1999.
McCreless, Patrick. "Music and Rhetoric." In *The Cambridge History of Western Music Theory*, edited by Thomas Christensen. Cambridge University Press, 2002.
McKinnon, James, ed. *Music in Early Christian Literature*. Cambridge University Press, 1987.
Meyer, Leonard B. *Emotion and Meaning in Music*. University of Chicago Press, 1956.

Miller, Terry E. "Thailand." In *Southeast Asia*, edited by Terry E. Miller and Sean Williams, vol. 4 of *The Garland Encyclopedia of World Music*. Garland,1998.

Müller, Alfred Dedo. *Musik als Problem lutherischer Gottesdienstgestaltung*. Evangelische Verlagsanstalt, 1947.

Müller, Karl Ferdinand, and Walter Blankenburg, eds. *Die Musik des evangelischen Gottesdienst*, vol. 4 of *Leiturgia: Handbuch des evangelischen Gottesdienstes*. Stauda, 1961.

Nettl, Paul. *Luther and Music*. Translated by Frida Best and Ralph Wood. Muhlenberg Press, 1948.

Oettinger, Rebecca Wagner. *Music as Propaganda in the German Reformation*. Ashgate, 2001.

Ong, Walter. *Orality and Literacy: The Technologizing of the World*. Routledge, 2002.

Ouspensky, Léonide, and Vladimir Lossky. *The Meaning of Icons*. St. Vladimir's Seminary Press, 1983.

Palisca, Claude V. *Baroque Music*. Prentice-Hall, 1968.

Peacocke, Arthur, and Ann Pederson. *The Music of Creation*. Fortress Press, 2006.

Peretz, Isabelle. "Listen to the Brain: A Biological Perspective on Musical Emotions." In *Music and Emotion: Theory and Research*, edited by Patrik N. Juslin and John A. Sloboda. Oxford University Press, 2001.

Pettegree, Andrew. *Brand Luther*. Penguin, 2015.

Pike, Alfred. *A Theology of Music*. Gregorian Institute of America, 1953.

Plessner, Helmuth. *Laughing and Crying: A Study of the Limits of Human Behavior*. Translated by J. S. Churchill and Marjorie Grene, with an introduction by J. M. Bernstein. Northwestern University Press, 1970. Originally published as *Lachen und Weinen: Eine Untersuchung nach den Grenzen menschlichen Verhaltens*. Van Loghum Slaterus, 1941.

Pratt, Waldo Selden. *The Music of the French Psalter of 1562*. AMS Press, 1966. Reprint of the 1939 edition.

Printz, Wolfgang Caspar. *Historische Beschreibung der edelen Sing- und Kling-Kunst*. Mieth, 1690. Facsimile edition by Othmar Wessely. Akademische Druck- und Verlagsanstalt, 1964.

Robinson, Edward. *The Language of Mystery*. SCM Press, 1985.

Ross, Alex. "The Sound of Hate." *New Yorker*, July 4, 2016, 65–69.

Routley, Erik. *The Church and Music*. Rev. ed. Gerald Duckworth, 1967.

Saliers, Don E. *Music and Theology*. Abingdon, 2007.

Schalk, Carl. "Georg Rhau." In *The Canterbury Dictionary of Hymnology*, edited by J. R. Watson and Emma Hornby. Canterbury Press. http://www.hymnology.co.uk/g/georg-rhau.

———. *Luther on Music: Paradigms of Praise*. Concordia, 1988.

Schneck, Daniel J., and Dorita S. Berger. *The Music Effect: Music Physiology and Clinical Applications*. Jessica Kingsley, 2006.

Schrade, Leo. "The Editorial Practice of Georg Rhau." In *The Musical Heritage of the Church*, vol. 4, edited by Theodore Hoelty-Nickel. Concordia, 1954.

Schwanke, Johannes. "Martin Luther's Theology of Creation." *International Journal of Systematic Theology* 18, no. 4 (October 2016): 399–413.

Schwarz, Hans. *True Faith in the True God: An Introduction to Luther's Life and Thought*. Revised and expanded edition. Fortress Press, 2015.

Serjak, Cynthia. *Music and the Cosmic Dance*. Pastoral Press, 1987.

Shepherd, John. *Music as Social Text*. Polity Press, 1991.

Slater, Peter J. B. "Birdsong Repertoires: Their Origins and Use." In *The Origins of Music*, edited by Nils L. Wallin, Björn Merker, and Steven Brown. MIT Press, 2001.

Sloboda, John A., and Patrik N. Juslin. "Music and Emotion: Commentary." In *Music and Emotion: Theory and Research*, edited by Patrik N. Juslin and John A. Sloboda. Oxford University Press, 2001.

———, ———. "Psychological Perspectives on Music and Emotion." In *Music and Emotion: Theory and Research*, edited by Patrik N. Juslin and John A. Sloboda. Oxford University Press, 2001.

Sloboda, John A., and Susan A. O'Neill. "Emotions in Everyday Listening to Music." In *Music and Emotion: Theory and Research*, edited by Patrik N. Juslin and John A. Sloboda. Oxford University Press, 2001.

Small, Christopher. *Musicking: The Meanings of Performing and Listening*. University Press of New England, 1998.

Söhngen, Oskar. "Theologische Grundlagen der Kirchenmusik." In *Die Musik des evangelischen Gottesdienst*, vol. 4 of *Leiturgia: Handbuch des evangelischen Gottesdienstes*, edited by Karl Ferdinand Müller and Walter Blankenburg. Stauda, 1961.

Stauffer, S. Anita, ed. *Worship and Culture in Dialogue: Report of International Consultations, Cartigny, Switzerland, 1993, Hong Kong, 1994*. Lutheran World Federation, 1994.

Stravinsky, Igor. *Poetics of Music in the Form of Six Lessons*. Vintage Books, 1956.

Strunk, Oliver, ed. *Source Readings in Music History: Antiquity and the Middle Ages*. Norton, 1965.

———. *Source Readings in Music History: The Romantic Era*. Norton, 1965.

Treitler, Leo, ed. *Strunk's Source Readings in Music History*. Rev. ed. Norton, 1998.

Turino, Thomas. *Music as Social Life: The Politics of Participation*. University of Chicago Press, 2008.

Vasconceles Wilkey, Gláucia, ed. *Worship and Culture: Foreign Country or Homeland?* Eerdmans, 2014.

von Allmen, Jean-Jacques. *Worship: Its Theology and Practice*. Oxford University Press, 1965.

Wachsmann, Klaus P., ed. *Essays on Music and History in Africa*. Northwestern University Press, 1971.

Wallin, Nils L. *Biomusicology: Neurophysiological, Neuropsychological, and Evolutionary Perspectives on the Origins and Purposes of Music*. Pendragon, 1991.

———, Björn Merker, and Steven Brown, eds. *The Origins of Music*. MIT Press, 2001.

Walter, Johann. *Das geistliche Gesangbuchlein "Chorgesangbuch."* Facsimile of 1525 edition, edited by Walter Blankenburg. Bärenreiter, 1979.

Walton, Janet R. *Art and Worship*. Michael Glazier, 1988.

Watson, J. R., and Emma Hornby, eds. *The Canterbury Dictionary of Hymnology*. Canterbury Press. https://hymnology.hymnsam.co.uk/.

Wienandt, Elwyn A., ed. *Opinions on Church Music*. Baylor University Press, 1974.

Bibliography of Mark P. Bangert

BOOKS AUTHORED

That Divine and Most Excellent Gift: Martin Luther, Music, and the Arts. Fortress Press, 2025.

Getting Ready for Worship in the Twenty-First Century. Evangelical Lutheran Church in America Division for Congregational Ministries, 1996.

Symbols and Terms of the Church. Augsburg, 1990.

BOOKS EDITED

Worship Music: A Concise Dictionary, edited by Edward Foley. Liturgical Press, 2000. Lutheran editor/consultant and author of 25 entries.

Occasional Services: A Companion to Lutheran Book of Worship. Board of Publication of the Lutheran Church in America / Augsburg, 1982. Chairperson of the Inter-Lutheran Task Force on Occasional Services, which included representatives of The American Lutheran Church, the Association of Evangelical Lutheran Churches, the Evangelical Lutheran Church of Canada, and the Lutheran Church in America.

BOOK CHAPTERS AND ENTRIES

"Bach, Johann Sebastian and Luther," "Hymns in the Works of J. S. Bach, Luther's." In *Encyclopedia of Martin Luther and the Reformation*, edited by Mark Lamport. Rowman & Littlefield, 2017.

"Rehabilitating the Vocation of the Cantor with the Help of the Early Church and Johannes Bugenhagen." In *Subject to None, Servant of All: Essays in Christian Scholarship in Honor of Kurt Karl Hendel*, edited by Peter Vethanayagamony and Kenneth Sawyer. Lutheran University Press, 2016, 78–88.

"Dynamics of World Musics: A Methodology for Evaluation." In *Worship and Culture: Foreign Country or Homeland?*, edited by Glaucia Vasconcelos Wilkey. Eerdmans, 2014, 107–123. Revision of entry by the same title published in *Worship and Culture in Dialogue: Report of International Consultations, Cartigny, Switzerland, 1993, Hong Kong, 1994*, edited by S. Anita Stauffer. Lutheran World Federation, 1994.

"The Last Word? Dynamics of World Musics Twenty Years Later." In *Worship and Culture: Foreign Country or Homeland?*, edited by Gláucia Vasconcelos Wilkey. Eerdmans, 2014, 124–133.

"African Song." In *Musicians Guide to Evangelical Lutheran Worship*, edited by Jennifer Baker-Trinity, Scott Weidler, and Robert Buckley Farlee. Augsburg Fortress, 2007, 71–75. Revision of entry "Africa" published in *Leading the Church's Song*, edited by Robert Buckley Farlee. Augsburg Fortress, 1998, 110–125.

"The Meaning of the Great Three Days as Context for the Passions of Bach." In *Passion, Affekt und Leidenschaft in der Frühen Neuzeit*, edited by Johann A. Steiger. Harrassowitz, 2005, 2:591–606.

"The Nunc Dimittis in Cantatas of J. S. Bach: A Note of Death or a Note of Life? A Chapter in the History of Cantata Reception in the U.S.A." In *Johann Sebastian Bachs Kantaten zum Thema Tod und Sterben und ihr literarisches Umfeld*, edited by Renate Steiger. Harrassowitz, 2000, 223–235.

"A Brook Runs Through It: Fresh Water from the *Bach* for Today's Thirsty Church" (2000). In *Liturgy in a New Millennium: 2000–2003*, Occasional Papers #11, edited by Rhoda Schuler. Institute of Liturgical Studies, 2006, 19–31.

"Holy Communion: Taste and See." In *Inside Out: Worship in an Age of Mission*, edited by Thomas Schattauer. Fortress Press, 1999, 59–86.

"The Changing Fortunes of *Festum Visitationis* Among Lutherans and Cantatas BWV 147 and BWV 10." In *Die Quellen Johann Sebastian Bachs: Bachs Musik im Gottesdienst*, edited by Renate Steiger. Manutius, 1998, 401–416.

"Liturgical Music, Culturally Tuned." In *Liturgy and Music: Lifetime Learning*, edited by Robin A. Leaver and Joyce Ann Zimmermann. Liturgical Press, 1998, 360–383.

"The Prayers of the Community." In *Encountering God: The Legacy of Lutheran Book of Worship for the 21st Century*, edited by Ralph R. Van Loon. Kirk House, 1998, 83–97.

"Liturgical Traffic in Culture: Gridlock, Beginning Drivers, Detours, and DUI" (1997). In *Worship, Culture, and Catholicity: 1997–1999*, Occasional Papers #10, edited by Rhoda Schuler. Institute of Liturgical Studies, 2005, 18–32.

"How Does One Go About Multicultural Worship?" In *What Does "Multicultural" Worship Look Like?* Open Questions in Worship, vol. 7, edited by Thomas Schattauer. Augsburg Fortress, 1996.

"This Is My Blood of the New Testament: The Institution of the Lord's Supper in Bach's Matthew Passion." In *Das Blut Jesu und die Lehre von der Versöhnung im Werk Johann Sebastian Bachs*, edited by Albert Clement. Royal Netherlands Academy of Arts and Sciences, 1995, 215–232.

"Canonical Hours," "Church Music History: Medieval," "Church Music History: Classic and Romantic," "Mass," "Theology of Church Music: Pietism and Rationalism," "Theology of Church Music: 19th Century." In *Key Words in Church Music*, edited by Carl Schalk. Concordia, 1978.

"Franz Liszt's Essay on Church Music (1834) in the Light of Felicite Lamennais's System of Religious and Political Thought." In *Student Musicologists at Minnesota*, vol. 5, edited by Johannes Riedel. University of Minnesota: College of Arts and Sciences, 1973.

ARTICLES

"On Discovering the Affect of Kyrie 1 from the B-Minor Mass of Johann Sebastian Bach." *Worship* 91 (November 2017): 540–560.

"Listen to the Birds: Luther on Music." *TEAR Online* [journal of the Centre de Recursos Litúrgicos de Faculdadas EST no Igreja Evangélica de Confissão Luterana no Brasil] 4, no. 1 (Summer 2015): 114–137. http://periodicos.est.edu.br/index.php/tear.

"How My Mind Has Changed." *Currents in Theology and Mission* 38, no. 2 (April 2011): 90–92.

"Johann Sebastian Bach and the Christian Life." *Journal of Lutheran Ethics* 10, no. 5 (May 2010). Published by the Theological Discernment Team of the Evangelical Lutheran Church in America. https://learn.elca.org/jle.

"Liturgy and Stewardship." *Currents in Theology and Mission* 36, no. 5 (October 2009): 341–349.

"Bach and His Secular Cantatas: A Case Study." *Currents in Theology and Mission* 35, no. 5 (October 2008): 330–339.

"For Richer, for Poorer: Sebastian Bach through the Eyes of His Second Wife." *Lutheran Women Today*, published by Women of the Evangelical Lutheran Church in America (2006).

"The Gospel About Gospel: The Power of the Ring." *Currents in Theology and Mission* 31, no. 4 (August 2004): 246–259.

"Like Wheat Arising Green: The Legacy of the *Lutheran Book of Worship* for the Future." *Cross Accent: Journal of the Association of Lutheran Church Musicians* 11, no. 3 (Fall 2003): 4–10.

"Pruning at the Threshold." *Cross Accent: Journal of the Association of Lutheran Church Musicians* 7A (January 1999): 4–11.

"A School of Te Deums." *Currents in Theology and Mission* 24, no. 3 (June 1997): 185–193.

"Welcoming the Ethnic into Our Church Musical Diet." *Cross Accent: Journal of the Association of Lutheran Church Musicians* 5 (January 1995): 4–7.

"A Thousand Tongues: Babel or Pentecost." *Currents in Theology and Mission* 21, no. 2 (April 1994): 85–112.

"Gospel Motet: Theme and Variations." *Currents in Theology and Mission* 15, no. 1 (February 1988): 56–61.

"The Heart of Worship: A Contemporary Narrative Eucharist." *Currents in Theology and Mission* 13, no. 4 (August 1986): 228–231.

"Martin Luther: Magnet of Musicians." *Pastoral Music* 8, no. 3 (June–July 1984): 24–26.

"Music and the Occasional Services." *Church Music Memo* Issue 33 (1983): 2–11.

"Daily Prayer of the Church." *Currents in Theology and Mission* 4, no. 3 (June 1977): 176–181.

"Another Look at the Traditional Liturgy." *Church Music* 72, no. 2 (1972): 12–20.

MAJOR BOOK REVIEWS

Miikka E. Anttila, *Luther's Theology of Music: Spiritual Beauty and Pleasure*. In *Cross Accent: Journal of the Association of Lutheran Church Musicians* 25, no. 2 (Summer 2017): 28–30.

Jeremy S. Begbie and Steven R. Guthrie, eds., *Resonant Witness: Conversations Between Music and Theology*. In *Cross Accent: Journal of the Association of Lutheran Church Musicians* 20, no. 2 (Summer 2012): 36–39.

Tim Dowley, ed., *Christian Music: A Global History*. In *Currents in Theology and Mission* 40, no. 2 (April 2013): 139–140.

Renate Steiger, *Gnadengegenwart: Johann Sebastian Bach im Kontext lutherischer Orthodoxie und Frömmigkeit*. In *Bach: Journal of the Riemenschneider Bach Institute* 35, no. 2 (March 2004): 60–68.

Unpublished Works

Edward Rechlin: Organist and Musician of the Church. PhD diss., University of Minnesota, 1984.

A Lutheran Evaluation of Arguments Against the Use of Musical Instruments in Public Worship. Master of Sacred Theology thesis, Concordia Seminary. St. Louis, 1969.

UNPUBLISHED PUBLIC ADDRESSES

"Singin' in the Wind: Luther on Gospel and Music." Address at Association of Lutheran Church Musicians Region 3 Conference, July 2016.

"Leipzig 1730: Bach and a Midlife Crisis? Re-Imagining Bach." Address at Lenoir-Rhyne College, October 2013.

"Presiding at Holy Mess." Address at Lutheran School of Theology at Chicago Professional Leadership Conference, February 2008.

"Music as Path Through the Great Three Days." Event and date unknown, ca. 2000.

"Music and Images of the Resurrection." Address at Festival of the Resurrection, Evangelical Lutheran Church of St. Luke, Chicago, date unknown, late 1990s.

"With One Voice: Shaping Worship for the Sake of the World." Address at Southwestern Washington Synod, Tacoma, WA, 1995.

"Music and Worship in a Diverse Church." Event unknown, 1994.

"Cause All Useful Arts to Flourish." Address at Worship and Music Conference, Seguin, TX, July 1990.

"Ministers of the Merger." Address at Founding Meeting of the Lutheran Professional Church Musicians (Association of Lutheran Church Musicians), Columbia, SC, October 1985. Abridged form published in *Church Music Memo* Issue 43 (Augsburg, 1986): 2–7.

"Musical Criteria for Sound Worship." Address at Chicago Theological Seminary, 1984.

"Liturgy as Comfort." Address at Lutheran School of Theology at Chicago Professional Leadership Conference, May 1984.

"The Funeral Liturgy: Ritualizing Death in the Contemporary Christian Community, the Role of Music." Address at Institute of Liturgical Studies, Valparaiso, IN, February 1982.

"Pastoring Through Church Music." Event unknown, 1980s.

Program notes for works of J. S. Bach: 107 cantatas, Christmas Oratorio, Easter Oratorio, Magnificat, and St. Mark Passion. Prepared primarily for performances by the St. Luke Bach Choir, Evangelical Lutheran Church of St. Luke, Chicago.

Index of Works by Martin Luther and Others

Works by Martin Luther

Other Works

Index of Names and Subjects